The Complete Guide to Referencing and Avoiding Plagiarism

The Complete Guide to Referencing and Avoiding Plagiarism

Third Edition

Colin Neville

 Open University Press

Open University Press
McGraw-Hill Education
8th Floor
338 Euston Road
London
NW1 3BT

email: enquiries@openup.co.uk
world wide web: www.openup.co.uk

and Two Penn Plaza, New York, NY 10121-2289, USA

First published 2007
Second edition published 2010
First published in this third edition 2016

A catalogue record of this book is available from the British Library

ISBN-13: 978-0-33-526202-1
ISBN-10: 0-33-526202-3
eISBN: 978-0-33-526203-8

Library of Congress Cataloging-in-Publication Data
CIP data applied for

Typeset by SPi-Global

Praise for this book

"This is the definitive resource for students and staff at higher educational institutions. Colin Neville's extensive research into students' challenges with referencing and plagiarism has enabled him to produce a comprehensive coverage of not only how to reference, but also why and when to do so.

The third edition's sections around paraphrasing, summarising and 'taking ownership' in particular help students to understand how skilful referencing is an integral element of effective academic writing. They are shown how to turn a frustrating puzzle into a well-crafted piece of work."

Dr Martin Sedgley SFHEA, Head of Effective Learning,
Bradford University School of Management, UK

"Colin Neville's The Complete Guide to Referencing and Avoiding Plagiarism *is an elegant, approachable and fundamentally useful book that explores the what, why and when of referencing in the UK higher education context.*

The book is informed by research with real students about their thoughts, feelings and experiences of referencing. This is not a remote, dry academic text aimed at malingerers or those with low academic integrity – but a friendly guide that explores the issues and the feelings involved in the practice of referencing. It speaks with and for students who feel punished by a system that expects fluency in a practice that is often not taught – but is punished when misunderstood.

Every student should have a copy of this book – for it will help them understand not just referencing – but the shape and nature of the UK HE system. They will understand referencing as one of the 'rules of engagement' of a system of which they are a part – but in which they often feel powerless and voiceless. And indeed that is one of Neville's strengths: he approaches referencing in a way that reveals its part in academic practice – and in a way that enables students to operate more powerfully in the academic systems and institutions in which they want and need to succeed.

The Complete Guide to Referencing and Avoiding Plagiarism *should also be an essential text for time-poor and frustrated academics as well. It is salutary to hear those student voices – and to really see why for them referencing feels like a random and unnecessary chore. Once we can see through our students' eyes our practice – in the way that we teach students to read, write and argue – must change. If this practice is fundamental to academic practice – and it is – we must play our part in scaffolding student understanding of the what, why and when of referencing. This book will help all university professionals understand that task more deeply – it will help us to help our students."*

Sandra Sinfield, University Teaching Fellow and
Senior Lecturer in Education and Learning Development, Centre for the
Enhancement of Learning and Teaching, London Metropolitan University, UK

Summary of contents

Contents

List of tables and figures

Acknowledgements

I am grateful to the following for allowing me to use extracts from their work and publications.

- Mr Jonas Juenger, postgraduate student at the London School of Economics, for his winning entry in the 2009 *Learnhigher* Referencing Learning Area essay-writing competition, which is shown, with his permission, in Chapter 6.
- Mr Christopher Jackson, chemical pathology student at the University of Bradford, for his permission to use an extract from his third-year dissertation in Chapter 6.
- Dan Pullinger and Michelle Schneider of the Learning Services Team, University of Leeds, for their support, and for their permission to use and quote from their work that led to the introduction of a Rationalising Referencing Policy at that institution.

I would like to express my appreciation to the following for their help.

- Jude Carroll, a leading writer and commentator on plagiarism, for her advice, support and encouragement during the writing of the plagiarism chapter (Chapter 5).
- Mr Chew Chee Khiang, an Open University student in Malaysia, for his advice on referencing foreign names, which can be found in Chapter 12.
- Professor Lin Norton, Research Director, Dr Katherine Harrington, Director, and Dr Peter O'Neill, in the Write Now Centre of Excellence in Teaching and Learning (CETL), for supporting and approving the award of two mini-research grants to undertake my 2008–10 research surveys, and for allowing and assisting me to lead a referencing workshop at the London Metropolitan University Writing Centre.
- Finally, my appreciation and thanks go to all the students who have contributed their views to my research; without them it would not have happened.

*

Ego meum optimum

Introduction

What's new in this third edition?

- More examples of good practice in academic writing and referencing
- A new chapter on referencing in a digital age
- Up-to-date examples of internet and electronic source referencing
- A new chapter on avoiding plagiarism
- More 'test your knowledge' quizzes
- Comparison of UK home students' and international students' attitudes to referencing and avoiding plagiarism
- An updated 'Frequently asked questions' chapter

Target readership

The book is aimed at all students on undergraduate and postgraduate degree courses, or pre-degree courses, in Britain and elsewhere. It will be useful for all new students, including international students studying in Britain or in their home countries on courses linked or affiliated to UK universities.

I hope that it will also be useful for students studying already on degree-level courses who feel as this student does:

> I hate referencing because I am not very good at it and find I get marks deducted for bad referencing. The thing is, I have never been taught to write an essay, let alone how to reference.
>
> (Philosophy undergraduate, quoted in Neville, 2009, p.11)

Referencing and writing

Comments like that motivated me to write the first edition of this book in 2007. By that time I had worked in higher education for nearly 20 years, as a lecturer, course organiser and student learning support adviser, so I was experienced in helping students understand the reasons for referencing, as well as teaching them how to cite and reference sources. I found that, for many students, writing assignments was a constant struggle to deliver what was expected of them – and referencing an unwelcome chore added to an already onerous task.

Referencing was often perceived by students as a technical needle in a haystack, rather than an integral part of the haystack itself – something that was tagged on at the end of the process to avoid losing marks, or to prevent being accused of plagiarism. A fear of being accused of plagiarism often led them to write essays characterised by their disjointed procession of sources and citations, rather than as a coherent narrative. It was clear to me that the referencing difficulties of students, and particularly international students, were inseparable from other academic writing difficulties they were experiencing. These difficulties included paraphrasing, summarising and struggling to find their own writing style and 'voice'.

I realised, though, that many students ostensibly wanted information about how to format sources in a particular style, so in the first edition I attempted to strike a balance between the 'why' and 'when', and the technical 'how' of referencing; the second edition took this strategy a stage further.

The first two books were, then, a mix of comment, participative exercises, illustrative examples of referencing and writing, and examples of how to reference a wide range of sources. In the second edition I introduced the results of a survey I had carried out in 2008/9 to identify how students perceive the roles of referencing in academic writing; to identify the main referencing problems for students; and to consider the implications of the findings for higher education institutions, and in particular for staff development.

Third edition

This third edition introduces the results of my second survey (2009/10) of students, with its focus on international students, and their previous experiences in their home countries of referencing and plagiarism awareness. So this new edition combines both my surveys and represents the views in total of 632 students at 17 UK institutions of higher education – 359 undergraduate (57%), 273 postgraduate (43%) – studying across a broad range of subjects. International students represented more than two-thirds of all students (72%) in the combined surveys, and student 'voices' from these surveys are quoted extensively in this new edition.

The surveys have also been used again in this edition for the practical purpose of specifically addressing the writing and related referencing issues that trouble students. To this end there is a new chapter on referencing and writing, which includes the writing and citing issues that students find difficult, including paraphrasing, summarising and how to present evidence in a way that exerts one's own writing identity. This is done by illustrating good writing and referencing practice, in the form of academic writing examples, including a full-length essay. The quizzes and participative exercises in the earlier editions proved popular, so they have been retained and extended in the Part 1 chapters.

This edition also includes more examples of citing internet and electronic sources, as well as a new chapter on referencing in a digital age. This new chapter includes advice on discriminating between web-based sources and how referencing can easily be managed by the use of referencing software. It also includes a section on text matching software and how this is used, not just to detect plagiarism, but to help students develop referencing awareness in their written assignments.

Three parts

This book is divided into three parts, as follows.

Part 1

The seven chapters in this section are concerned with student perceptions of referencing (Chapter 1), the why, what and when of referencing (Chapters 2–4), and why plagiarism occurs and how to avoid it (Chapter 5).

Chapter 6 illustrates practical 'how to cite' issues of referencing, but also covers the relationship between critical thinking, selection of sources and effective writing. As mentioned earlier, there is a new chapter (Chapter 7) on referencing in a digital age, and this summarises the impact of the internet on referencing practice, including how referencing management software can take the drudgery out of citing and formatting sources. This chapter also looks at how to evaluate internet sources, and the way text matching software is used in institutions to deter plagiarism and help students develop their knowledge and skills in referencing.

Part 2

The three chapters in Part 2 present the range of referencing styles students are likely to encounter on UK courses and the often subtle formatting differences between them. Chapter 8 introduces and categorises 14 referencing styles applied within UK higher education institutions into three main groups, and presents illustrative examples of how sources are cited and referenced in these styles, including the name–date Harvard and APA styles, and footnote-related MHRA and Chicago styles.

Chapters 9 and 10, respectively, explain the differences between name–date and footnote-related styles, and offer comparative examples of the differences between them.

Part 3

In Part 3, Chapter 11 presents 33 categories of referencing examples categorised alphabetically by subject. Electronic sources are shown alongside printed or other resources, and each example is presented comparatively in two referencing styles: the British Standard (BS) versions of the name–date Harvard style, and the footnote-linked (BS) numerical style.

The book closes with a 'Frequently asked questions' chapter (Chapter 12) featuring 19 common questions asked by students about referencing principles and practice, and with answers to these.

Different levels

The book operates at a number of different levels. It offers a practical 'how to reference' guide for students and their tutors. This is important, as clarity and understanding of referencing practice can lead to increased confidence in academic writing.

More importantly, though, it offers advice, reinforced with practical examples of academic writing to demonstrate how referencing can be used to student advantage – to write more effective assignments.

Is this book redundant in a digital age?

But, surely, a book on referencing is an anachronism when students today can use referencing management software to find sources and organise their bibliographies?

In Chapter 7, I make a strong case in favour of using referencing management software, particularly to save time and effort in formatting sources – the part of referencing that most people find the most tedious and time consuming.

Since the previous edition of this book was published, referencing management software has developed rapidly in terms of its ease of use. It is increasingly intuitive to use, and can be downloaded free in some cases – including apps that produce a fully formatted reference in one of thousands of different referencing styles, taken from the barcode of a book or journal.

Referencing management software cannot, however, explain or teach the principles that underpin referencing, how to select the right sources, or how to use referencing to help build or develop an effective argument in an assignment.

This book does that.

Referencing in this book

The name–date Harvard style is the one chosen for referencing evidence and illustrating sources in this book. This version of Harvard is in line with British Standard (BS) guidelines, most recently BS 690:2010: *Information and documentation – Guidelines for bibliographic references and citations to information resources* (BSI, 1983–2010).

However, the 'British Standard Harvard' is different from other versions of Harvard that readers may encounter (see Chapter 9) and I certainly do not present the one shown throughout this book as the 'definitive guide' to Harvard. There is no 'definitive' guide, as BS guidelines are advisory only, and over the years have been given tweaks here and there by all and sundry. Students required to use the Harvard style of referencing in their assignments need to be aware, then, that subtle formatting variations of this style abound, even within referencing management software. It is important therefore that students follow the version of Harvard approved by their institution. But if a reader understands the 'what', 'why' and 'when' of referencing, the rest falls into place.

Part **1**

1 The 'shock' of referencing

Referencing—the basic idea · Student perceptions of referencing · Survey results and student voices · Difficult aspects of referencing · Recurring concerns of students: secondary referencing; paraphrasing; using own words and ideas; formatting; referencing the spoken word; plagiarism

Since starting at university, the focus on it has been huge and a shock.
(Undergraduate: law and politics)

I find referencing incredibly anal and not very productive to my learning efforts. I did not come to university to learn the skills of bureaucratism!
(Undergraduate: politics and international relations)

Referencing is essential, and learning to do it boosts confidence, not just in writing, but also and primarily in arguing ideas. It is a way of putting my point forward.
(Postgraduate: communications and media)

*

It is an expected academic practice that students will refer to (or cite) the sources of ideas, data and other evidence in written assignments. Referencing is the practice of acknowledging in your own writing the work of others—work that has been presented in some way in the public domain.

However, the importance given to referencing in Britain is not universal, and students from other countries studying in Britain are often surprised by the emphasis placed on it by UK higher education institutions. It can often come as a shock to home students, too:

Even though I'm in my third year, I still don't understand how to reference properly.
(Undergraduate: law)

I think the big issue with referencing is that it is not required at A-level to a very high standard and then you are suddenly expected to just know how to do it at university, without anyone teaching you.

(Undergraduate: philosophy)

Critical thinking

Referencing – the basic idea

'Referencing' is what you do; 'References' are the outcome.

The main point of referencing is to support and identify the evidence you use in your course work.

Referencing direct readers to the sources of evidence you have selected to use in your work. This is done by presenting (or 'citing') the author's or originator's name, or an identification number, in the main text of your work.

The citation in the text links with the full source detail, which is given later, either in a footnote or endnote, and/or in a list of references at the end of the assignment.

As you progress through different levels of study, you are expected to become increasingly more critical of ideas and theories, and the ways they are applied or become apparent in everyday life. Education needs ideas, arguments and perspectives to thrive, but these have to be tested rigorously and subjected to the scrutiny of others. This is done by researching, preparing and presenting work in the public domain—a formidable task for any writer or commentator, and one that can take years to achieve.

Referencing is, then, about respecting and honouring the hard work of writers and commentators by acknowledging them in your assignments. Importantly, too, referencing can also help you to write assignments that project or reflect the way *you* see or perceive things. Evidence presented and correctly referenced supports and strengthens your opinions—and converts them into arguments. However . . .

Referencing: 'a pain'?

Despite these 'worthy' reasons, many students find referencing a pain, a mechanistic chore and a complete bore. Not all do, though, as can be seen from the comments of the third student at the start of this chapter; but more on that later.

So a recurring theme in this book is how to use references to your advantage, rather then being irritated, manipulated and controlled by them. There is also referencing management software available that will remove the 'pain', particularly the boring formatting part of the process (read more about this in Chapter 7).

Specifically, this book will explain:

- the **why** of referencing—the principles underpinning referencing practice
- the **what** of referencing—what to reference, i.e. which sources to choose
- the **when** of referencing—when to reference, and when it is not necessary
- the **how** of referencing.

It will also answer recurring student questions on the thorny issue of **plagiarism**—an ongoing cause of concern to both students and institutions.

In addition to the three big referencing issues—the 'why', 'when' and 'how' of referencing—this book will also address the referencing and academic writing issues that UK and international students find particularly problematic. These issues were the subject of my surveys of student perceptions of referencing over three academic-year periods, leading to referencing and writing seminars in 2009 and 2010 at the University of Bradford.

Student quotes in this book

Between 2008 and 2010, I initiated two projects to gather the views of undergraduate and postgraduate students from 17 UK higher education institutions, on their perceptions and feelings towards referencing in academic writing (summarised in Neville, 2009; 2010). The two projects were sponsored by the government-funded *Learnhigher* and *Write Now* initiatives, both aimed at helping students become more effective learners.

As part of these surveys I offered drop-in referencing advice workshops for students at a London university, led formal referencing discussion sessions at my own university in Yorkshire, and set up an online 'Have your say' website to collect written responses from students studying at UK universities.

As a result, I gathered the views of 632 students studying across a wide range of subjects at 17 British institutions of higher education. A total of 359 undergraduates (57 per cent) and 273 postgraduates (43 per cent) were represented in the survey, and international students made up more than two-thirds (72 per cent) of the total number of respondents in the combined surveys. The quotes used in this book are all taken from comments received from students from both surveys and provide a real sense of what they felt about referencing at that time.

Before the results are summarised, here are copies of two of the questionnaires students were asked to complete. You are invited to complete one or both now to clarify the referencing issues of interest or concern to you.

Survey questionnaires

1. How do you feel about referencing?

Which one of the following four statements is closest to your true feelings about referencing? Please be totally honest about this.

Figure 1.1 Four statements exercise

1. I understand that referencing is regarded by the institution as an essential part of assignment writing and a way of avoiding plagiarism, but, to be honest, I find it rather a chore or a nuisance.

2. I regard referencing as a significant part of the process of supporting my own ideas in an assignment.

3. Referencing is an important way for me to acknowledge in my assignments the data, ideas, models and practices produced or developed by others.

4. I feel referencing in assignments is an important part of the process of agreeing with or challenging the ideas of others.

You may, for example, have mixed feelings about referencing that include elements from all four. But which of the four do you feel you would rank as 'number one' in line with your true feelings?

Tick the box against the statement closest to how you really feel about referencing. However, if none of the statements applies, you can write your own, and a space is provided for this purpose.

Space for your own statement (use the space below only if **none** of the four statements above connects with your true feelings about referencing):

2. Difficult aspects of referencing

What, if any, aspects of referencing do you currently find difficult?

If you find any of the following difficult, **please identify up to three** that present the greatest levels of difficulty. Please then rank these **1 to 3,** with **1** representing the most difficult item for you.

Figure 1.2 Difficult aspects of referencing

	Ranking
1. Being undecided whether or not a reference is always needed at a particular point in an assignment	
2. Being unsure how to cite and reference what writer B (a secondary source) has said about writer A, who is the one you are interested in	
3. Deciding **where** in the text of your assignment to locate a particular source citation	
4. Separating out your own experiences, memories and knowledge from printed or electronic sources	
5. Ensuring that the citations in the text of your assignments connect with the list of references or bibliography	
6. Listing sources in a list of references or bibliography in a way consistent with a particular referencing style, e.g. Harvard style	
7. Knowing how much of your **own** opinions or assertions to include in an assignment	
8. Deciding the right order of the source detail in any reference consistent with a particular referencing style, e.g. Harvard style	
9. Worries or uncertainty about plagiarism and referencing, e.g. about citing and summarising an author in a way that avoids plagiarism	
10. Difficulties with managing two or more referencing styles—for example, on a combined studies course, where the two subject areas require different referencing styles	

Other referencing issues

Please use the space below, if applicable, to note down other referencing issues or difficulties that concern you. If you need more space, please use separate paper.

The survey findings follow.

More detail

For some: 'no problem'

Around a quarter of the students said that they were not experiencing any referencing problems at the time of the survey. This was particularly the case with UK final-year undergraduates and postgraduate students. This was largely because they had learned what was expected of them and, more importantly why, at earlier stages of their academic careers. Two students commented as follows.

> Referencing is essential and learning to do it boosts confidence, not just in writing, but also and primarily in arguing ideas. It is a way of putting my point forward.
>
> (Postgraduate: communications and media)

> Referencing is an essential element of the assignment; what academic use is there in saying anything that is unverified or unsupported . . . I wouldn't read an unreferenced piece of work myself—it would have no credibility.
>
> (Postgraduate: classics)

. . . but a challenge for most

However, for the majority, referencing was a challenge, and certainly a chore. The intensity of feeling varied from 'hatred' to the dull ache of dislike about the whole process:

I hate referencing because I am not very good at it and find I get marks deducted for bad referencing. The thing is, I have never been taught to write an essay, let alone how to reference.

(Undergraduate: philosophy)

In all honesty, I seriously dislike referencing. It is far too troublesome for simply putting forth a point.

(Undergraduate: accounting, management and information systems)

Referencing is laborious, time consuming and dull.

(Undergraduate: chemistry)

What was causing such antipathy to referencing?

The main difficulties faced by students were in relation to unfamiliar forms of academic writing, understanding the technical complexity of the referencing styles they had encountered, integrating their own views into assignments—and avoiding plagiarism. The issue of time management was a recurring overall theme in the surveys and was aligned with the frustration of attending to the detail required by a particular referencing style.

More time ends up being spent on checking the references than the work itself, which is ridiculous!

(Foundation studies student)

It's hugely time consuming and a real pain.

(Undergraduate: English literature)

However, the referencing difficulties of all students—home and international—cannot easily be separated from other writing difficulties experienced by them, including paraphrasing, summarising, and developing a sense of ownership or authorship of their work.

Similar concerns were expressed by both home (UK) and international students, although the weighting given to them differed between groups (see Table 1.1).

Main recurring concerns for all students

- Paraphrasing and summarising the work of others
- Secondary referencing
- How to integrate own ideas and experiences into assignments
- Concerns about plagiarism
- Referencing the spoken word

Table 1.1 The main ranked referencing concerns of home and international students

Home Students	International Students
1. Secondary referencing	1. Paraphrasing and summarising
2. How to integrate own ideas and experiences into assignments	2. How to integrate own ideas and experiences into assignments
3. Paraphrasing and summarising	3. Secondary referencing
4. Formatting and organising bibliographic lists	4. Plagiarism concerns
5. Plagiarism concerns	5. Referencing the spoken word

These concerns need to be considered as interlinked, rather than as separate entities. For example, while complaints about the time consumed by formatting sources were common, these connected, as suggested earlier, with a feeling of uncertainty about the whole referencing process—were they doing it right?

This uncertainty resulted in 'assignment task drag', often at deadline times, when a number of assignments were due.

More detail

1. Secondary referencing

Secondary referencing is when you read about X (the primary source of the evidence in question) in a text that has been written by Y, or when both X and Y have been summarised by Z. The 'so-who-do-I-reference?' issue was a problem for students. When asked why the original, or primary, sources were not chosen instead of secondary ones, students frequently mentioned:

- the demands made on their time
- the difficulties in finding the primary sources
- the ease of finding secondary information on the internet.

(This topic is discussed in more detail in Chapter 3.)

2. Paraphrasing

This was the main issue of concern for international students, but was also problematic for home students, too. The issue appeared to stem from a lack of confidence about writing in English. It was common to hear comments at the referencing workshops for both home and international students, but particularly the latter, that they could not always think of alternative words or ways of expressing ideas; and some admitted to only half understanding the meanings in some required reading, so had resorted to partial copying of the more impenetrable sections of the text.

Students were often puzzled by the difference between paraphrasing and summarising, and to what extent the same words in the original text could be replicated in the summary; and how and where in the text the source should be cited and referenced—if indeed it should be at all. (This topic is discussed in more detail in Chapter 6.)

3. Integrating own ideas into assignments

The issue of integrating one's own ideas and experiences into assignments was linked to two main issues.

1. Anxiety about doing this in the first place—for example, to what extent do tutors genuinely welcome this, or is it better to just present the work of others? As one student said, 'Sometimes I have my own idea, but I am not sure whether it is similar to any author and then whether lecturers will consider my work as plagiarism or not' (postgraduate, human resources management).
2. Concern about the acceptable forms of words that could be used in assignments to distinguish one's own ideas from those of published authors. (This topic is discussed in more detail in Chapter 6.)

4. Formatting

The technical 'where-do-the-dots-and-commas-go'-type concerns were a recurring theme both in my workshops and in the online surveys.

> I am still getting used to the format of referencing, Harvard etc., and referencing for different academic works, such as books, journals etc. They are really complicated.
> (International postgraduate student)

> It can take a good portion of the day to perfect it . . . therefore one disadvantage is that it can be time consuming and may put people off.
> (Undergraduate: law and politics)

At the referencing workshops, questions were often to do with where in the assignment text a source should be located (or cited). There was confusion about whether or not first names should be cited in the text, and about the way internet sources, and sources without an obvious originator name, should be referenced. Some new students did not yet understand the process of linking the evidence in the main text of their assignment (citations) to the full reference details at the end of their work (there is more on this in Chapter 6).

5. The spoken word

International students were also unsure how to reference the spoken word, particularly what they had heard in a lecture or seminar. This issue is addressed in Chapter 11, topic 15.

6. Plagiarism

For many students in my surveys, a fear of being accused of plagiarism was at the core of their difficulties, and resulted in referencing being regarded primarily as a shield against such accusations. This, for a number of students, resulted in a cautious, defensive form of writing akin to editing, rather than authorship. Plagiarism is discussed in more detail in Chapter 5.

'Confusing'

Another survey of student and staff experiences of referencing (Pullinger and Schneider, 2014), at a university in the north of England, also found significant levels of confusion about referencing. Two students said:

> It is confusing to know which style to use as different departments and even different members of staff within the same department say different things.

> Some tutors have said that the referencing was done incorrectly, when I had used the examples given in the Library guide . . . I always dread getting an essay back because I'm worried the tutor will have marked me down for referencing.

The views of 1464 students and 91 staff members were gathered. The main issues for students were:

- understanding and managing the wide range of referencing styles in use, plus multiple variants on these
- the differing expectations from tutors, within schools, and even within modules
- the risk of inconsistent and inequitable marking because of the differing expectations of tutors
- inconsistent advice from tutors on referencing, which left them feeling confused
- the disproportionate amount of time they spent on referencing.

The survey found that tutors were often unaware of what referencing guidelines were currently offered to students at the university and the researchers found differing opinions and expectations among staff on the referencing styles used on their courses.

The survey was instrumental to change at the university. With the support of the vice-chancellor and other senior members of the institution, a Rationalising Referencing Policy was implemented that included changes to the Codes of Practice on Assessment.

All schools at the university were required to adopt a standardised institutional agreed version of the name–date (Harvard) or numeric style of referencing. Any school choosing another referencing style was required to direct students to a single and agreed guide for the style in question (referencing styles are discussed in Chapters 8–10 of this book). In addition, all marking of referencing by tutors would need to conform to the standardised institutional guidance hosted on the University Library website.

The example above suggests that changes to referencing policies and practice can happen if people take initiatives within their institution to gain the attention of senior managers. Students can make their voices heard through the student union. If you have a view about referencing, let your student union know what it is.

Summary

- The importance attached to referencing can be a shock for many new higher education students in Britain.
- Students complain about the time-consuming nature of referencing.
- However, referencing can be part of a range of writing issues that students find problematic, including paraphrasing and summarising, secondary referencing, and integrating their own ideas into assignments.
- Worry about being accused of plagiarism was a recurring concern (more on this in Chapter 5).
- Students also complain about too many referencing styles, as this can potentially result in inconsistent marking and a confusion of advice. Some universities are tackling this issue by introducing referencing policies that limit the number of styles used and by producing their own in-house versions of the main referencing styles, particularly Harvard style.

2 Why reference?

The rationale for referencing · Principles of referencing · Nine good reasons for referencing · Referencing in other countries (research findings) · International students' previous experience of referencing · A (very) brief history of referencing

Why reference? And *why* is there so much emphasis on referencing in academic writing?

It stops you spouting cow dung.

(Undergraduate: contemporary art practice)

Principles of referencing

- Referencing is part of the communication process in academic writing; it facilitates the transmission of knowledge.
- Referencing helps you to separate your own ideas and work from the work and ideas of others.

Nine good reasons for referencing

Figure 2.1 presents nine good reasons for referencing.

More detail

Tracing the origin of ideas

Academic study involves not just presenting and describing ideas, but also being aware of where they came from, who developed them, why and when. The 'when' of referencing can be particularly important. Ideas, models, theories and practices originate from somewhere and someone. These are often shaped by the social norms and practices prevailing at the time and place of their origin, and the student in higher education needs to be aware of these influences.

Figure 2.1 Nine good reasons for referencing

Referencing, therefore, plays an important role in helping to locate and place ideas and arguments in their historical, social, cultural and geographical contexts. As one student participant in my surveys commented:

> It does help to strengthen arguments, as you make reference to current arguments and debates. Without it, it would be impossible to cite the origins of the debate within the essay.
>
> (Postgraduate: sustainable development)

Learning builds on learning. However, like trying to discover the 'real' source of a mighty river, there are often many contributory networks to knowledge, and it is sometimes impossible to work back to the beginning and to the origin of an idea.

All you can do, sometimes, is to reference *a* source—one that is immediately relevant to your assignment task, and one that appears to be reliable and valid in relation to the arguments presented by you.

A web of ideas

Knowledge connects and spreads: the past connects with the present and has an impact on the future. As you build your argument in an assignment, it is rather like a spider building its web. You build carefully engineered connections between ideas. You advance an argument in one section, but then counter it with another threaded and connected group of ideas, each supported by its own referenced evidence. But you have at the centre your own position, your own place in the scheme of things—your point of view.

Finding your own voice

As mentioned in Chapter 1, students, when they enter higher education, are often confused about the gap they perceive between the conventions of academic writing and the need to make their *own* points in essays. In most science disciplines, one's own *opinion* on a topic is not what is wanted—it is evidence and factual information that is expected, and conclusions based on this.

However, with other assignment topics, where engaging with big ideas is the norm, tutors will normally encourage students to develop their own perspectives, while also emphasising the need for them to cite and refer to the work of experts. Some tutors in these disciplines will encourage personal opinions in assignments, others will not. This apparent confusion can sometimes result in assignments in these subject areas that are an unsuccessful blend of the personal and the academic. This is discussed further in Chapter 6.

However, you can strive to gain **ownership** of your own work in the following ways.

- You can decide which position or direction to take in an assignment.
- You can select evidence that allows *you* to present a strong set of arguments or descriptions.
- You can summarise or paraphrase in *your* own words what you read. Your own words are far more preferable to tutors than a plagiarised mash of the written work of others (see Chapter 5).

The perspective you take, the ideas you present, the conclusions you reach, can all be your choice; referencing helps this process. The process is summarised in the flow chart shown in Figure 2.2.

Validity of arguments

To be taken seriously, you must present valid evidence in assignments. Aristotle, around 350 BC, argued that persuasive rhetoric included *Logos*: appeals to logic to persuade an audience through sound reasoning. This is done by the presentation of reliable evidence, usually in the form of facts, definitions, statistics and other data that has an appeal to the intelligence of a particular audience. This ageless principle can be applied equally to written arguments. Referencing reliable and valid evidence in assignments appeals to the intelligence of the reader.

Referencing also enables your tutors to check for themselves the accuracy and validity of the evidence presented. In particular, they will want to ensure you are using ideas from the past in a way that is relevant or original to the assignment topic under discussion. Do not assume tutors have read everything on the subject; they may be unfamiliar with the work you cite, so may need to check it themselves.

Figure 2.2 Flow chart of argument presentation process

You can present an argument in an assignment by:

1. Stating your position early in the assignment, and presenting a clear and consistent rationale to support it.

2. Offering **reliable evidence**, or illustrative examples, to support your argument. This is evidence that you have read reputable and authoritative texts, articles, newspapers, internet sites etc.

3. Showing where this evidence has come from: by citing your sources, and listing all your sources in the references or bibliography section at the end of your assignment.

4. Demonstrating that you are aware of, and have considered, arguments that are counter to your own. You will need to summarise counter-arguments in a clear, accurate and undistorted way.

5. Being able to show why the arguments you have chosen to use are more convincing for you than others.

Spreading knowledge

Referencing also presents an opportunity for the tutor and other readers to advance their own knowledge. It gives them the possibility of tracing the sources you cite and using the same evidence for their own purposes. You may have discovered how useful bibliographies and lists of references at the end of journal articles can be in identifying other related sources for your own research. Once you start following up sources in bibliographies, it can open up a trail of knowledge that is invaluable for your assignments. One source leads to another; you begin to build your own web of learning around a subject.

An appreciation

Education needs ideas, arguments and perspectives to thrive, but these have to be tested rigorously and subjected to the critical scrutiny of others. This is done by researching, preparing and presenting work in the public domain, which, as noted earlier, is a formidable task for any writer—and one that can sometimes take years to achieve. Referencing, then, is also about giving appreciation: a modest genuflection to the work of others. It is about showing courtesy and respect, and about honouring the hard work of writers and commentators—by acknowledging them in your assignments. As one student commented:

> I see it as quid pro quo . . . If you had produced the original thought you would be pretty gutted if someone 'stole' it!
>
> (Undergraduate: theology)

Three other student-related reasons

From a student perspective, there are three other good reasons why referencing is important:

1. your reading, and influences on your work
2. marking criteria
3. avoiding plagiarism.

Your reading, and influences on your work

Tutors will be also interested in your list of references or bibliography to identify what authors or sources have been influential in moulding or shaping the direction taken by you in your research. As one student commented: 'It helps the marker see the evolution of your ideas' (undergraduate, English and philosophy). The tutors, may, as a result, offer comment on the absence or inclusion of any particular commentator or theorist in an assignment. Your sources may also occasionally help your tutors, by introducing new authors and ideas to them, thus broadening their own knowledge.

Marking criteria

The selection of relevant evidence and accurate referencing is an important element in the marking of assignments, particularly at postgraduate level. Accurate referencing can often make the difference between a pass, credit or distinction. Accurate referencing is also a tangible demonstration to your tutor of your research, intellectual integrity and the care you have taken in preparing to write the assignment.

> During my first year . . . I did not understand why lecturers made such a big deal about referencing and plagiarism. Well, today I understand that it is a crucial part of academic assignments—in fact, [it] is about educating yourself, which means researching, comparing contrasting views, being critical about what you read etc.
>
> (Undergraduate: events management and psychology)

Avoiding plagiarism

Finally, accurate referencing will help you to avoid being accused of plagiarism. Western concepts of plagiarism are based on an economic model of capitalism and the notion that someone can claim *ownership* of an idea, if it has been presented in the public domain in some tangible way. However, the explosion of global communication mediums has created difficulties in identifying original sources of ideas, and there is a grey area between deliberate cheating and carelessness with referencing—or an ignorance of it. You can read more about this in Chapter 5.

The 'language' of referencing

Each referencing style (see Chapters 8–10) has its own standardised 'language': a way of presenting information and way of communicating with others in an academic community. The standardisation of referencing practice, e.g. adopting a particular referencing style, supports this communication process. References are presented in a way that allows everyone who has learned the practice to recognise and understand the meaning of codes and formulas presented. The danger is that too many referencing styles, and the multiple variants these breed, can lead to confusion, rather than effective communication (there is more on this later, in Chapter 8).

Referencing in other countries

In my 2010 survey, which focused on international students, I wanted to learn to what extent these assumptions about referencing and plagiarism were shared in other parts of the world. Bailey and Pieterick (2008) had found that many of the new international students at their institution had not previously encountered referencing in their home countries, or it was perceived or presented in different ways than was the case in Britain.

My survey included an online questionnaire to test these findings (see Figure 2.3).

Exercise

If you are an international student studying in Britain, why not write your own comments in answer to the questions in Figure 2.3, then compare your responses with my survey findings, below?

Figure 2.3 International students' questionnaire

Questions	Your responses
Reasons for referencing: what do you think are the main reason(s) for referencing sources in written assignments on your current course(s)?	
About your previous experience of referencing: please summarise to what extent in your home country you were expected to reference sources in essays and/or reports and, if so, how were you expected to do it?	
Your response to referencing in the UK: how do you feel about referencing in assignments on your current course? What, if any, are the 'big issues' for you?	

(I also asked an additional question about their knowledge of plagiarism—see Chapter 5.)

Findings

I received 130 responses to my questionnaire from international students studying in Britain, with home countries in Africa, Asia, Europe, Latin America and the Caribbean, the Middle East, North America and Oceania. The number of students from each region is shown in Table 2.1.

Table 2.1 Geographical spread of students in the survey	
Africa: 14 students	Nigeria (7); Uganda (2); Ghana (2); and 1 student each from Tanzania, Botswana and Sierra Leone
Asia: 54	Mainland China (14); India (14); Malaysia (6); Hong Kong (5); Pakistan (4); Singapore (3); Sri Lanka (2); and 1 student each from Kazakhstan, Thailand, Burma, South Korea, Japan and Taiwan
Europe: 33	France (7); Germany (7); Poland (3); Eire (2); Romania (2); Cyprus (2); Netherlands (2); Norway (2); Italy (2); and 1 student each from Latvia, Greece, Czech Republic and Sweden
Latin America & Caribbean: 5	Brazil (3) and 1 student each from Puerto Rico and Trinidad
Middle East: 6	Jordan (2) and 1 student each from Bahrain, Brunei, Palestine and Yemen
North America: 15	USA (11); Canada (4)
Oceania: 3	1 student each from Papua New Guinea, Philippines and New Zealand

More than half of the international students reported that they had not been expected to reference sources in their home countries in the same way as in Britain, and their knowledge of what constituted plagiarism was also based on different learning experiences (see Chapter 5). A summary of their responses is presented in Table 2.2.

Table 2.2 International students: previous experience of referencing		
Level of experience N:128*	**Undergraduate** (n:45)	**Postgraduate** (n:83)
None (or very little): 19 students (15%)	**8 students** (18%)	**11 students** (13%)
Some previous experience: 52 students (41%)	**18 students** (40%)	**34 students** (41%)
Same/similar experience: 57 students (45%)	**19 students** (42%)	**38 students** (46%)

* Two of the 130 students did not respond to this part of the questionnaire, although they did complete the plagiarism awareness question (discussed later in Chapter 5).

International students with no, or very little, previous
experience of referencing (19 students: 15 per cent)

Students in this group reported that they had not encountered referencing before arriving in Britain, mainly because the predominant form of assessment in their home countries was by way of tests or exams, or because it was allegedly not expected of them by their tutors.

> I was not asked to reference sources in essays or reports in university in my home country, so it is something very new to me.
>
> (Postgraduate from China)

Some students, however, drew distinctions between what was expected at undergraduate and postgraduate levels of study on previous courses. One student wrote:

> [At] undergraduate level, referencing is not compulsory, and a large number of students are not aware of the importance of referencing. Even lecturers do not be bothered by that. However, in postgraduate level, the same level [as UK] is expected for referencing.
>
> (Postgraduate from South Korea)

Some previous experience (52 students: 40 per cent)

Students in this group stated that they had been made aware of the principles underpinning referencing in their home countries, but had had different experiences of the referencing process itself. These differences tended to fall into four groups:

1. the students who reported that they had not been required to cite sources in the text of their assignments, as is the case in Britain, but only to supply a bibliography, or list of sources consulted
2. the students who reported that referencing was required only in the final stages of their degree courses
3. the students who were aware of referencing conventions, but felt that the enforcement of these was not as strict in their home countries
4. the students who reported differences between their home countries and Britain in relation to what sources needed to be referenced; there were, for example, differences as to what constituted common knowledge and the 'ownership' of commonly accepted ideas (see Chapter 4 for more information about this).

Student comments included the following:

> Referencing is only done when doing your project dissertation.
>
> (Postgraduate from Nigeria)

> As an undergraduate in my home country . . . ideas taken from someone else had to be acknowledged (name of the author and page number), but we were not expected to use many secondary sources, and would not be penalised if we did not reference according to a specific format.
>
> (Postgraduate from France)

Referencing was expected, although the format was not very strict. Also, there was no need to reference widely accepted ideas that have been credited to a particular person, but are used frequently by the masses.

(Postgraduate from the Philippines)

Same or similar experience (57 students: 45 per cent)

A significant percentage (45 per cent) of the students in the survey reported that their experience of referencing in assignments in their home countries was identical or very similar to that in Britain. These students came from countries that included Germany, Holland, Sweden, Norway, Canada, the USA, New Zealand, Sri Lanka, Botswana, Malaysia, Ghana, Singapore, Sierra Leone, Brazil and Hong Kong.

'A new experience'

For nearly half of the students in my survey, their previous education experiences in their home countries had prepared them well for their studies in Britain. They had written essays and reports before, and had learned from previous courses how to choose, apply and reference evidence. Their previous institutions had formulated policies on plagiarism, and so these students were more likely to understand what behaviours constitute a breach of academic regulations. If English was a main language for them, they would also be 'tuned in' to the subtleties or idiosyncrasies of English speech and texts.

However, more than half of the respondents reported that managing sources in the way required on their UK courses was a new experience for them. Typically, they had moved from educational institutions in their home countries where knowledge was assessed predominantly through tests and exams, or by oral examinations, to a situation in Britain where evidence has to be presented in course-work assignments in very particular and regulated ways—and where failure to comply with these requirements might lead to accusations of plagiarism. This situation was aggravated for those still fine-tuning their English language skills and often struggling to understand the more densely written academic texts.

However, I found students from the same countries reporting different experiences. For example, there were five undergraduate respondents from Hong Kong. Two of these students gave accounts that suggested their referencing experiences in Hong Kong were the same as in the UK; two gave accounts suggesting some relevant experience (the production of bibliographies, but no in-text citation experiences); and one student reported no previous referencing experience before starting her UK course. There were similar mixed-experience responses from students from mainland China, India and Nigeria.

The results of my survey left me with an impression of a rapidly changing educational scene across the world, where referencing practices vary significantly, even within the same country. However, with increasing global links, educational institutions are learning from and sharing with one another, including how students reference evidence in assignments. For international students wanting to study in Britain, it can help if they have some pre-course preparation, particularly in the style of academic writing they will encounter here; and UK higher education institutions are establishing links with colleges and universities overseas, and running bridging courses like this. However, in the short term, variations in educational practice globally will mean that referencing and UK-style academic writing will continue to be unfamiliar processes for a significant number of international students new to study in Britain. But not just in Britain . . .

Catherine Hutchings, in her 2013 study of professionally trained mature students returning to postgraduate education at a university in South Africa, found them disorientated by the need to write in an academic way—which was a style disconnected from their previous work experiences, or even previous academic experiences. Understanding when and how to reference was a 'tumultuous path' for most (Hutchings, 2013).

Transition

All new students, home and international, face an academic transition, which can be summarised as shown in Figure 2.4.

The realisation, trial-and-error, and reflection stages are common for all students, but for students with a previous grounding in the UK expectations of academic writing, the transition to understanding and integration into the academic world is usually quicker and less stressful. For international students, the trial-and-error stage, particularly in relation to academic writing, can be difficult and prolonged.

However, the resilience, tenacity and willingness of international students to adapt to their new learning situations has been noted by several commentators, including Biggs and Watkins (1996) and Maxwell, Curtis and Vardanega (2008). From my own teaching experience, I have found that international students are quick to grasp new systems and embrace new perspectives, provided that the opportunity to learn is offered to them.

Figure 2.4 Academic transition

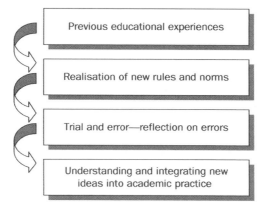

'Once upon a time': milestones in referencing history

Like every subject or topic, referencing has its own history story in the overall scheme of things. I won't bore you with the full version, but here are a few milestones in referencing history.

- Referencing can be traced back to Roman jurists who 'provided very precise references to the earlier legal treatises they drew upon' (Grafton, 1997, pp. 29–30). In other early manuscripts, annotation, glosses or explanations were included to connect the finished work to its sources.
- The invention of printing in the late fifteenth century made ideas more accessible and established the notion of an author. The growth of printing encouraged people to write, and to make a living from their ideas and talent for writing. It also encouraged the cult of personality, and the emergence and promotion of artists distinguished by their style of writing (Eisenstein, 1983). This led to writers wanting to protect their work against plagiarism.
- The Statute of Anne, which passed into law on 10 April 1710, was the first copyright act in the world; it established both copyright for the authors of books and other writings, and the principle of a fixed term of protection against piracy for published works.
- The development of printing also standardised the practice of annotation into printed footnotes. These appeared within scholarly works from the eighteenth century onwards. References appeared in textbooks in footnotes and were referred to in the text by printers' symbols, including asterisks and daggers. These influenced the growth of referencing styles from the nineteenth century onwards.
- The development and growth of universities in the nineteenth century in Europe and the USA resulted in the mass assessment of student knowledge by way of essays and examinations. There was a rigorous testing of knowledge and, as part of this, students were expected to cite the origins of ideas and offer detailed analysis and interpretation of sources. Citing and analysing the works of authors became a way for students to demonstrate their scholarly engagement with a text.
- In the twentieth century, a range of referencing styles was developed, building on these earlier foundations.

Summary

- There are nine good reasons to reference, including separating your own work from the work of others; acknowledging the work of others; providing support for and giving credibility to your arguments and ideas; and to avoid plagiarism.
- International students often have limited or different previous experience of referencing in their home countries; they were often assessed in different ways, e.g. tests and exams, or not required to cite sources in the text of their work.

- All students face an academic transition from their previous education into UK higher education institutions. This can be more challenging for some students, particularly those with little previous experience of the teaching styles, academic writing and modes of assessment encountered in Britain.

3   What to reference

> What to reference · Primary and secondary sources · Quiz: When to use primary and secondary sources · Choosing sources · Interrogating sources · Quiz: Pros and cons of using printed sources · The value of using academic journals as sources

This chapter is about the range of sources that can be referenced, and about the criteria for evaluating them.

What to reference

Typically, the sources you will use in your assignments as evidence will be from books, academic journals and websites. However, most forms of communication, including performance and the visual arts, providing they have been presented in the public domain in some way, can be referenced.

This includes an increasing range of internet sources, but can also include unlikely media, such as display boards, postcards and advertising material—all of which can be of interest to, among others, historians, sociologists, and communication and media studies students. The examples in Chapter 11 illustrate how to reference a wide range of sources.

However, there is no point in referencing anything that cannot be accessed by others who want to check the same source—particularly your tutors. So personal conversations on the telephone, and text messages, for example, can be mentioned in the main body of an assignment, but should not be referenced, unless there is some audio or written record of the discussion that can be heard or read by others, for example as an appendix item in your work. Emails—summarised or quoted entirely or partly—can be cited in the text of an assignment and referenced, providing you save, record or transcribe them in some form, and make them available to your tutor, if required.

The important points to bear in mind when selecting evidence for use in assignments concern the credibility and reliability of sources, and the importance of distinguishing between primary and secondary sources.

Primary and secondary sources

What's the difference between primary and secondary sources?

Table 3.1 Primary and secondary sources	
Primary sources	**Secondary sources**
This is evidence that comes **directly from** the creators, originators or instigators of the work or phenomenon in question	This is non-original material produced **about** the work or phenomenon, including the commentary or interpretation of others about it

Now try the quiz that follows (Figure 3.1).

Quiz: Primary or secondary source?

Figure 3.1 shows examples of sources. Decide which are primary sources and which secondary, and tick the relevant column.

You can find the answers at the end of this chapter.

Figure 3.1 Quiz: Primary or secondary source?

Source	Primary	Secondary
Articles in academic or other professional journals (printed or online) presenting new research		
Books written by the originator of a particular theory, idea, model or practice		
Newspaper reports of new research findings		
Wikipedia internet site		
Speakers at a conference presenting the results of their research		
Autobiographies		
Tutor handouts summarising the main theories and ideas associated with a subject		
Reference books, e.g. dictionary of science terms		
Biographies		
Transcripts of parliament or law court hearings		
Minutes (written records) of public or private meetings, e.g. board meetings		
Textbooks summarising the work of others		
Internet sites summarising the work of others		

(Continued)

Figure 3.1 *(Continued)*

Source	Primary	Secondary
Internet site of an author where she/he presents his/her own work		
Articles in trade magazines reporting on developments in a particular profession		
Journalist talking about the work of a particular economist, e.g. on a radio broadcast		
Reports written about a particular event by the main investigator		
An entry in an online encyclopaedia		
Transcript (written record) of an interview		
Results of an original survey presented online by the researcher		
A well-known scientist presenting his or her response to a theory, idea or other aspect of science (on radio, television, internet, or in an article, book chapter etc.)		

When to use primary and secondary sources

It is very important to know when to use primary and secondary sources in your course-work assignments (see Figure 3.2) as this knowledge and its application will greatly enhance your chances of gaining good grades.

Choosing sources

Students are faced daily with the task of choosing sources to use in an assignment to support their arguments or descriptions. An important skill in managing information is deciding which sources to choose and use.

The important thing is to choose sources that give credence, authority and support to the ideas and arguments that you present. Your tutor will suggest a range of reliable

Figure 3.2 When to use primary and secondary sources

Primary source material should be used, wherever possible, for your central definitions, main descriptions, quotations, key points, arguments, and to support assertions or important points made by you

Secondary source material can be used for lesser definitions, factual information, illustrative examples and supporting points; it can also be used in the absence of primary source material

Figure 3.3 Discriminating between sources

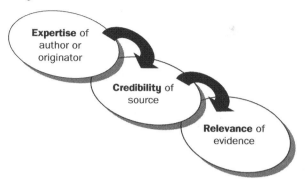

sources, and this will be your starting point, but you will also be expected to look beyond the recommended reading and to search out relevant information for yourself. If you do this, and connect relevant evidence gained from additional reading to your assignment, this can sometimes make the difference between a pass and a distinction grade for you.

In this respect, you will find that recommended books and other sources will prove—because of the accurate referencing that has gone into them—to be rich veins of additional information. The references or bibliography in a book or journal will often point you in the direction of other relevant sources.

For all sources there are essentially three cascading areas of enquiry to help you select the best to use (see Figure 3.3). The first two elements are the deciding factors if more than one source appears relevant to the point you are making.

Always choose the authors/originators that are the most reputable in their academic fields to support your arguments in your essays—these will carry the most credibility with your tutors.

Interrogating sources

Table 3.2 summarises the questions to ask when choosing sources.

Table 3.2 Interrogating sources

Relevance and bias	Currency
• To what extent is the source relevant and applicable to the assignment? • Does the information presented give a partial or restricted view of the subject? • How balanced and objective does the language in the source appear to be? • Are counter-arguments to the author's own ideas treated with respect? If not, why not?	• When was the source originally published? Are the ideas, practices, assumptions still valid? (You need to ask if the ideas expressed are a product of a particular time and place in history that no longer applies today) • Has the author revised or changed his or her views since the date of the original source? If so, do you know when and why?

(Continued)

Table 3.2 *(Continued)*

Authority	Scope
• Is the source authoritative enough to be included in the assignment? For example, is the source a credible one, e.g. a reputable publishing company, a peer-reviewed academic journal? • Do other authors refer to and discuss this source? • How credible is the source to you? (You can turn your own reservations into a starting point of critical enquiry about it)	• How universal or general are the ideas, models or practices described in the source? Do they have a limited geographical or occupational application? • Do the ideas in the source span a range of cultures or are they applicable only to particular groups?

Printed sources

Despite the rise of the internet, printed texts are still important sources of knowledge. Can you distinguish between primary and secondary sources in printed texts? What are the characteristics of printed texts you are likely to encounter during your studies? Try the following quiz.

Quiz: Pros and cons of printed sources

See Table 3.3.

1. Common sources of printed knowledge are shown in the left-hand column of Table 3.3 (numbered 1–5).
2. Comments describing these sources are shown in the right-hand column (labelled A–E).
3. Match the comment to the type of source shown. So, starting with 'Textbooks', which of the five descriptions best describes textbooks? And so on . . .

There is an answer grid for you to fill in at the end of the quiz.

Table 3.3 Quiz: Pros and cons of printed sources

Source	Comment
1. **Textbooks:** offer a broad-based foundation to the study of a subject	A: provide an in-depth focus on a particular topic, usually written by a well-regarded expert in the subject; however, this type of source can go out of date quite quickly—make sure you have the most current edition
2. **Specialist topic book (a 'monograph'):** these are concerned with a single or focused topic, e.g. liquid crystals	B: can provide a useful introduction to a subject, but can be of limited value in an academic essay because they are usually secondary, rather than primary, sources

(Continued)

Table 3.3 *(Continued)*

Source	Comment
3. **General science journals:** these publish review-type articles aimed at the general interest reader, e.g. *New Scientist*	**C:** important and up-to-date sources of information on significant developments in any field of study; they can often, though, be 'difficult reading', because of the complexity of the language and ideas
4. **Academic journals:** publish peer-reviewed articles on research and trends in the chosen subject	**D:** useful for students, as they can offer a point of comparison, sources of relevant knowledge and an exemplar for others; however, there may be no way of assessing the relative quality of the source against others of a similar nature
5. **Dissertations:** these are research reports written by postgraduate students, and held in libraries and other academic repositories	**E:** good starting points for students, providing a broad overview of a topic; however, they can go out of date quite quickly, so it is important to ensure you are reading the most current edition

Source: Moore, Neville, Murphy and Connolly (2010, p.118)

Answers: 1 = _____ 2 = _____ 3 = _____ 4 = _____ 5 = _____

Turn to the end of this chapter for the answers.

The value of using academic journals in your research

The importance and value of using academic peer-reviewed academic journals, particularly in science assignments, was highlighted in a study by Zeegers and Giles (1996). These researchers analysed essays submitted by more than 500 first-year undergraduate biology students, looking at the range of sources used. A positive correlation was found for the relationship between the number of relevant journal articles referred to in the assignment and the level of mark awarded: 'Most students who were awarded a credit grade or higher used five journal articles or more and spent on average 20 hours reading them' (1996, p.452).

The number of relevant journal articles read and the number of hours spent reading generally, and writing their assignments, appears also to have been a significant factor in the award of good marks to geography students (Hounsel, 1984), as well as psychology students (Norton, 1990).

Summary

- Sources need to be chosen for their credibility and reliability.
- Students need to be able to distinguish between primary and secondary sources.
- Primary sources should be chosen, whenever possible, to support your main ideas and arguments.
- Academic journals are an excellent source to use in assignments. They often present primary source evidence.

Quiz answers

 Primary or secondary source?

Figure 3.4 Primary or secondary sources? Quiz answers

Source	Primary	Secondary
Articles in academic or other professional journals (printed or online) presenting new research	✓	
Books written by the originator of a particular theory, idea, model or practice	✓	
Newspaper reports of new research findings		✓
Wikipedia internet site		✓
Speakers at a conference presenting the results of their research	✓	
Autobiographies	✓	
Tutor handouts summarising the main theories and ideas associated with a subject		✓
Reference books, e.g. dictionary of science terms		✓
Biographies		✓
Transcripts of parliament or law court hearings	✓	
Minutes (written records) of public or private meetings, e.g. board meetings	✓	
Textbooks summarising the work of others		✓
Internet sites summarising the work of others		✓
Internet site of an author where she/he presents his/her own work	✓	
Articles in trade magazines reporting on developments in a particular profession		✓
Journalist talking about the work of a particular economist, e.g. on a radio broadcast		✓
Reports written about a particular event by the main investigator	✓	
An entry in an online encyclopaedia		✓
Transcript (written record) of an interview	✓	
Results of an original survey presented online by the researcher	✓	
A well-known scientist presenting his or her response to a theory, idea or other aspect of science (on radio, television, internet, or in an article, book chapter etc.)	✓	

Pros and cons of printed sources

Answers: 1 = ____E____   2 = ____A____   3 = ____B____   4 = ____C____   5 = ____D____

The sources matched with their correct descriptions are shown in Table 3.4.

Table 3.4 Pros and cons of printed sources—result

Source	Comment
1. **Textbooks:** offer a broad-based foundation to the study of a subject	**E:** good starting points for students, providing a broad overview of a topic; however, they can go out of date quite quickly, so it is important to ensure you are reading the most current edition
2. **Specialist topic book (a 'monograph'):** these are concerned with a single or focused topic, e.g. liquid crystals	**A:** provide an in-depth focus on a particular topic, usually written by a well-regarded expert in the subject; however, this type of source can go out of date quite quickly—make sure you have the most current edition
3. **General science journals:** these publish review-type articles aimed at the general interest reader, e.g. *New Scientist*	**B:** can provide a useful introduction to a subject, but can be of limited value in an academic essay because they are usually secondary, rather than primary, sources
4. **Academic journals:** publish peer-reviewed articles on research and trends in the chosen subject	**C:** important and up-to-date sources of information on significant developments in any field of study; they can often, though, be 'difficult reading', because of the complexity of the language and ideas
5. **Dissertations:** these are research reports written by postgraduate students, and held in libraries and other academic repositories	**D:** useful for students, as they can offer a point of comparison, sources of relevant knowledge and an exemplar for others; however, there may be no way of assessing the relative quality of the source against others of a similar nature

4 When to reference

When to reference · Quiz: Is a reference needed? · Four questions to ask to decide if you need to reference · Six occasions when you must reference · Common knowledge · Quiz: Test your understanding of referencing

> The problem I have with referencing is that I never know when not to do it.
>
> (Undergraduate: economics and politics)

> I no longer understand when referencing is not necessary.
>
> (Postgraduate: health studies)

When to reference

When should you reference? And when is it not necessary? These are recurring questions—and can produce, unfortunately, a range of different answers from tutors. Angélil-Carter (2000), for example, found inconsistencies among staff at one higher education institution, particularly in the area of what constituted common knowledge, which does not need referencing. 'Common knowledge', however, did not always mean the same to one tutor as it did to another, even in the same subject area (more on this later in this chapter).

Knowing *when* to reference is as important as understanding *how* to reference; this can establish your credibility with your tutors.

Try the quiz that follows (Figure 4.1).

Quiz: Is a reference needed?

Do you need to reference in the situations described in Figure 4.1? Indicate **Yes** or **No** in each case.

Turn to the end of this chapter to see the answers, but—before you do—read the following.

Figure 4.1 Quiz: Is a reference needed?

Scenario a You are on a train and two professors from your university, who you recognise, are seated behind you. They begin to discuss a subject of interest to you—as you have to write an assignment on it—and you can hear their conversation quite clearly. You make a mental note of what they say, think about it yourself and later integrate their ideas into your assignment. Do you need to reference the names of the two professors?	Yes	No
Scenario b A week or so ago, you were a passenger in a car and you were listening to the car radio. A speaker—you didn't make a note of the name of the person—on a radio programme made some interesting and original remarks on a topic of interest to you. You summarise these remarks in an assignment. Do you need to reference in this situation?	Yes	No
Scenario c When you were younger—about ten years ago—you went to listen to a talk by a scientist (you can't remember who it was now), who spoke on a subject relevant to your current degree studies. Over the years you had thought about what had been said by the scientist, agreed with this viewpoint and 'adopted' it as your own opinion. You write an assignment on the topic in question and integrate this viewpoint into your work as your own opinion. Do you need to reference in this situation?	Yes	No

Do you need to reference it? Four questions to ask

There are four questions to ask about a source to help you decide if it needs to be referenced.

1. Has it been presented formally into the **public domain** in some way? (This can include print publications, internet, lectures, seminars, films etc.)
2. Has it been presented publicly in a **tangible form**? 'Tangible' in this context means in a clear or definite way. This can include printed material, the internet, a formal public talk/lecture, a public performance.
3. Does someone, or an organisation, have a claim to it or **ownership** of it? Look for a named author or writer, or the name of an organisation, including the website or host, presenting the information in question.
4. Is the information presented in the source in question **outside** the realm of 'common knowledge'? (See below for more on this.)

If the answer to all of these questions is 'yes', then the source should be referenced.

When to reference: six scenarios

Figure 4.2 summarises the occasions when you must reference a source.

Figure 4.2 When to reference

You always need to reference:

- the sources of statistics, tables, charts, data, photos and other illustrations
- when describing or discussing a theory, idea or model
- **When to reference**
- when paraphrasing or summarising another person's work
- all quotations used in your assignments
- to give **emphasis** to a particular idea, concept, model etc.
- to support your own ideas, arguments, points of view

More detail

You should always reference evidence in assignments in the situations or for the reasons that follow.

1. To inform the reader of the source of tables, statistics, diagrams, photos and other illustrations included in your assignment.
2. When describing or discussing a theory, model, practice or example associated with a particular writer, or using their work to illustrate examples in your text (this links specifically with the next two items).
3. To give authorial weight or credibility to an argument supported by you in your assignment.
4. When giving emphasis to a particular theory, model or practice that has found a measure of agreement and support among commentators.
5. To inform the reader of the sources of direct quotations or definitions taken from external sources in your assignment.
6. When paraphrasing another person's work that you feel is particularly significant, or likely to be a subject of debate.

See the following essay extract examples (in the Harvard style of referencing) of these six scenarios for when to reference.

1. To inform the reader of sources of the tables, photos, statistics or diagrams presented in your assignment (either copied in their original form or collated by you)

Example

Recent studies employing current methodologies demonstrate Oestrogen receptor (ER) concordance between needle core and surgical specimens ranging between 88 per cent to 99 per cent (Ozdemir et al., 2007; Park et al., 2009; Ough et al., 2011).

Even if the statistics are easily found and freely available in the public domain, they need to be cited and referenced, as stating the origin of the data is important for establishing the credibility of the source.

2. When you describe or discuss a theory, model or practice associated with particular writers, or when using their work to illustrate examples in your text

Example

Bill Gates, the founder of Microsoft, at the 2008 World Economic Forum in Davos, argued that capitalism has benefited the lives of many, but it has not helped billions of the world's poorest people. He has encouraged companies to think beyond just making large financial profits, to making more positive social contributions. However, he recognises that if profit oriented organisations are going to get more involved in helping to alleviate social problems, they need to gain some kind of 'return' or commercial advantage. This is at the core of what he has called 'creative capitalism' (Microsoft, 2008).

3. When you want to give authorial weight or credibility to an argument supported by you in your assignment

Example

Handy (1995) has argued that federalism is a way of making sense of large organisations, and that the power and responsibility that drives federalism is a feature of developed societies and can be extended into a way forward for managing modern business. In relation to power, Handy argues that 'authority must be earned from those over whom it is exercised' (p.49). Respect must be earned from employees, and not expected simply because of one's rank.

4. When giving emphasis to a particular theory, model or practice that has found a measure of agreement and support among commentators

Example

As the behavioural response of communication apprehension (CA) is to avoid or discourage interaction with others, it is not surprising that CA has been linked to feelings of loneliness, isolation, low self esteem and the inability to discuss personal problems with managers or others (McCroskey, Daly, Richmond and Falcione, 1977; Daly and Stafford, 1984; Richmond, 1984; McCroskey and Richmond, 1987; Scott and Rockwell, 1997).

In the above example, the student cites five sources, all saying much the same thing, to emphasise and give credibility to an important point summarised in the assignment. The use of multiple authors can add weight to a summary, particularly if the idea is a controversial one. However, citing six relevant authors is the suggested maximum for this purpose, and citing two or three is the more usual practice.

5. To inform the reader of the sources of direct quotations or definitions in your assignment

Example

Cable (2001) argues that Freeman became ever more resentful of the way he was treated by publishers. It appears he felt that his Oxbridge education should have accorded him more respect from his contemporaries. He talked 'bitterly of a certain titled young gentleman who treated him as an equal on The High in Oxford but who, on Saxmundham railway station, refused to acknowledge him' (p.5). However, Cable argues that this snobbishness was also in Freeman's own character, so he was particularly sensitive when the snubs were directed at him!

If the quote is taken from a printed book or journal, you always need to include the page number in the citation so the reader can go straight to that page to find it. If it is an electronic source, the URL address, which will be listed in the full reference, should take the reader to the relevant web page or screen.

   If the quotation is by a well-known person, and is included only to add colour and general interest to your writing, it can be cited, but does not need to be given a full reference entry—for example, 'If music be the food of love, play on' (Shakespeare: 'Twelfth Night', L.i.1). But, if in doubt, always supply a full reference entry for this type of quotation.

6. When paraphrasing another person's idea or definition that you feel is particularly significant or likely to be a subject of debate

> **Example**
>
> We all perceive the world around us in ways that are often unique to us through a series of personal filters, and we 'construct' our own versions of reality (Kelly, 1955).

Note: In this example the student paraphrases an idea that Kelly originally outlined in 1955. The inverted commas around the word 'construct' suggest this is a significant word used by Kelly to describe a key concept. By citing the source, the student is, in effect, saying, 'This is Kelly's idea; I am just paraphrasing it.'

When you don't need to reference . . .

Over-referencing is where the identity of the academic writer becomes completely lost in a jumble of other people's ideas and quotations. To avoid this, you should be aware that there are four situations when you do **not** need to reference.

These are:

1. when presenting historical overviews
2. when presenting your own experiences
3. in conclusions, when you are repeating ideas previously referenced
4. when summarising what is regarded as 'common knowledge'.

(See also Chapter 6, 'Referencing and writing', on over-referencing.)

Historical overviews

You do not need to reference information drawn from a **variety of sources** to summarise what has happened over a period of time, when those sources state much the same things and when your summary is unlikely to be a cause of dispute or controversy.

In the example that follows, the student summarises the topic generally, and has used for this purpose a number of different and reliable sources, which all agreed on the reasons for the growth in call centres.

> **Example**
>
> The growth in call centres in the West was encouraged by economic and technological factors. From the late 1970s the growth of the service sector focused the attention of large organisations on communication with customers in more cost-effective and streamlined ways. This growth of a service-sector economy connected with advances in telecommunications and changes in working practices in Western companies. The logic of call centres was that a centralised approach and rationalisation of organisational operations would reduce costs, while producing a standard branded image to the world.

However, if the student had used just one source for the summary, this should be cited and referenced. A general introduction like this could also lead on to using specific and cited evidence on particular features of the topic, in this case the growth of call centres.

Your own experiences and observations

You do not need to reference your own previously unpublished experiences or observations, although you should make it clear that these are your own. For example, you could use the first-person term 'I' to do this, although not all tutors encourage this style of personal writing. If you are discouraged from writing in the first person, you could say something like, 'It has been this author's [or this writer's] experience that . . .'.

If, however, you have had your work published in a journal, book or other source, you could cite your own published work in support of your own experiences, points of view or arguments (again, see Chapter 6 for more on this).

Summaries or conclusions

You do not need to reference again if pulling together a range of key ideas that you have already introduced and referenced earlier in the assignment. For example, it can be good practice in writing, particularly in a long assignment, to summarise ideas before moving on to another line of discussion. Also, when you reach the concluding sections of your assignment and begin to draw together your arguments, you would not need to cite sources previously referenced, unless you were introducing new material or introducing a new perspective drawn from previously cited sources.

Common knowledge

This is the most problematic of the four situations, as there can be disagreement among lecturers on what constitutes common knowledge. Students are likely to encounter 'common knowledge' that is:

- in the public domain generally
- specific to their area of study.

One definition, applicable to common knowledge in the public domain, is:

> Information that is presumed to be shared by members of a specific 'community': an institution, a city, a national region, the nation itself . . . a particular race, ethnic group, religion, academic discipline, professional association, or other such classification.
>
> (Hopkins, 2005)

This definition requires you to think about who is reading your text—would the likely and intended readers accept what you say as 'common knowledge'?

In the public domain, within a particular societal context, you are using common knowledge when sharing and expressing generally undisputed facts circulating freely, publicly, and when there is unlikely to be any significant disagreement with your readers about your statements or summaries of this information. See, however, the earlier comment about statistics. Even if statistics are easily available online or elsewhere, you need to cite their source to allow others to find them and decide for themselves whether or not you are using them in the right context.

This contextualisation of common knowledge also applies to academic writing. Pecorari (2013) emphasises the importance of knowledge shared between writer and intended reader because of their shared academic experiences. In an academic context, common knowledge can be where a writer communicates mutually accepted knowledge to the intended reader.

Every subject has its own set of implicitly agreed codes, labels, assumptions, jargons, formulas or symbols that you will not need to define, explain or reference. These points of understanding may be implicit, soon become clear, or may be negotiated early on in courses between tutors and their students.

However, students new to higher education would be wise to reference sources liberally at first, rather than frugally, until they have established the common knowledge 'ground rules' on their particular course. What constitutes common knowledge in a particular subject would be a very useful discussion point between students and their personal or course tutors.

Quiz: Test your understanding of referencing

Look at situations listed in Figure 4.3 that can occur when writing assignments, and decide if a reference is needed at that point in the assignment.

Figure 4.3 Quiz: Test your understanding of referencing—is a reference needed?

1. You include tables, photos, statistics and diagrams in your assignment; these may be items directly copied or that have been a source of collation for you	**Yes**	**No**
2. When describing or discussing a theory, model or practice associated with a particular writer	**Yes**	**No**
3. You summarise information drawn from a variety of sources about what has happened over a period of time, and the summary is unlikely to be a cause of dispute or controversy	**Yes**	**No**
4. To give weight or credibility to an argument that you believe is important and that you summarise in your assignment	**Yes**	**No**
5. When giving emphasis to a particular idea that has found a measure of agreement and support among commentators	**Yes**	**No**
6. When pulling together a range of key ideas that you have already introduced and referenced earlier in the assignment	**Yes**	**No**
7. When stating or summarising obvious facts, and when there is unlikely to be any disagreement with your statements or summaries	**Yes**	**No**
8. When using quotations in your assignment	**Yes**	**No**
9. If you copy and paste items from the internet where no author's name is shown	**Yes**	**No**
10. When paraphrasing or summarising in your own words another person's idea that you feel is particularly significant or likely to be a subject of debate	**Yes**	**No**

Turn to the end of this chapter to see the answers.

Summary

- Four questions to ask to decide if a source should be referenced are: Is it in the public domain? Is it presented in a tangible form? Has someone ownership of it? Is it outside of common knowledge?
- Common knowledge can include undisputed facts commonly shared with others in a particular community or society. In an academic context, it can include subject knowledge implicitly or explicitly agreed with a particular reader—for example, your course tutor.
- However, it wise to cite and reference all sources you are unsure about until you are more confident as an academic writer.
- Sources that must always be referenced include all data and statistics; all summaries or paraphrasing of other people's theories, ideas, arguments, models and practices; all quotations; and any source that supports your own arguments and points of view. This last point is a particularly important element in your development as an effective academic writer.

Quiz answers

 Is a reference needed?

Scenario a

You are on a train and two professors from your university, who you recognise, are seated behind you. They begin to discuss a subject of interest to you—as you have to write an assignment on it—and you can hear their conversation quite clearly. You make a mental note of what they say, think about it yourself and later integrate their ideas into your assignment. Do you need to reference the names of the two professors?

Comment

The answer is a qualified **No**. The ideas were not presented publicly in a formal or tangible way. However, you would want to check if either of the professors *has* written about the subject. If they have done, you should cite and acknowledge their work in your assignment. If they have not, you would still need to check who has written on the subject and refer to their ideas in your work.

In any assignment you are free to include an 'Acknowledgements' section that can include mention and give thanks to people who have helped you in some way, e.g. proofreaders, other students who you discussed the assignment with, a personal tutor, learner support adviser—and these two professors!

Scenario b

A week or so ago, you were a passenger in a car and you were listening to the car radio. A speaker—you didn't make a note of the name of the person—on a radio programme made some interesting and original remarks on a topic of interest to you. You summarise these remarks in an assignment. Do you need to reference in this situation?

Comment

The answer is **Yes**. The talk is given publicly by someone who has clearly prepared for the event. The ideas are 'owned' by that person and are presented in a tangible (clear/real) way. If you didn't make a note of the name of the speaker at the time, you should make an effort to trace him or her by using the internet to locate the radio programme in question and to identify the speaker.

Scenario c

When you were younger—about ten years ago—you went to listen to a talk by a scientist (you can't remember who it was now), who spoke on a subject relevant to your current degree studies. Over the years you had thought about what had been said by the scientist, agreed with this viewpoint and 'adopted' it as your own opinion. You write an assignment on the topic in question and integrate this viewpoint into your work as your own opinion. Do you need to reference in this situation?

Comment

The answer is **No**. There is a difference between what you read, saw or heard recently (as in scenario b) and what happened in the more distant past. This example raises the issue of the origins of ideas. We use ideas from the past all the time. Other people raised these ideas in the past; we listened and have woven them into our lives, gradually taking ownership of them, and have eventually forgotten who it was that influenced us in the first place. The people who influenced us were in turn influenced by named and nameless others over the centuries.

However, as an academic writer you will want to research who *has* published work on the topic in question. As you attended a public talk, the chances are that there is published work on the subject. So if you learn of an author who *has* written in a way that validates your own opinions on the issue, you would be wise to cite and reference him/her, if only to demonstrate your reading on the topic.

Test your understanding of referencing

Figure 4.4 Test your understanding of referencing. Quiz answers

	Yes	No
1. You include tables, photos, statistics and diagrams in your assignment; these may be items directly copied or that have been a source of collation for you	✓	
2. When describing or discussing a theory, model or practice associated with a particular writer	✓	
3. You summarise information drawn from a variety of sources about what has happened over a period of time, and the summary is unlikely to be a cause of dispute or controversy		✓
4. To give weight or credibility to an argument that you believe is important and that you summarise in your assignment	✓	
5. When giving emphasis to a particular idea that has found a measure of agreement and support among commentators	✓	

(Continued)

Figure 4.4 *(Continued)*

6. When pulling together a range of key ideas that you have already introduced and referenced earlier in the assignment	**Yes**	**No** ✓
7. When stating or summarising obvious facts, and when there is unlikely to be any disagreement with your statements or summaries	**Yes**	**No** ✓
8. When using quotations in your assignment	**Yes** ✓	**No**
9. If you copy and paste items from the internet where no author's name is shown	**Yes** ✓	**No**
10. When paraphrasing or summarising in your own words another person's idea that you feel is particularly significant or likely to be a subject of debate	**Yes** ✓	**No**

5 Plagiarism

When you start university referencing and plagiarism is completely hyped up to the point that I was really concerned that anything I wrote might be seen as plagiarism. After all, some things are difficult to say in other words.

(Undergraduate: geography with business)

A fear of plagiarism now forces students to research any and every idea they might wish to include in a paper/assignment . . . I no longer understand when referencing is not necessary.

(Postgraduate: health studies)

I'm just scared about referencing wrongly and having marks deducted for it or accidentally being punished for plagiarism.

(Undergraduate: economics)

What is plagiarism?

There is certainly no one universally agreed definition in Britain, and every institution of higher education develops its own interpretations of what it is—and isn't—based on discussion and debate among academic staff. For example, it can be argued that all imitative learning is plagiarism; other people's ideas *should* inspire us.

I had an architecture professor that had a mantra: 'plagiarise, plagiarise, plagiarise!' By which he meant, not only to take inspiration from others' work, but also don't waste time reinventing the wheel. Take the parts and pieces that work well, that inspire you, and make it part of your own new work, and of course, credit the source when you can. He wouldn't, on the other hand, ever want us to reproduce another's work in whole and try to pass it off as our own.

(Dachis, 2010)

We use ideas from other people all the time, weave them into our working and academic lives, gradually taking ownership of them until we eventually forget who influenced us in the first place; referencing becomes difficult, if not impossible, in some situations (see Lensmire and Beals, 1994; Pennycook, 1996; Angélil-Carter, 2000).

However, plagiarism, in an academic context, refers to a particular set of actions. Try the quiz that follows (Figure 5.1) to test your understanding of plagiarism.

Quiz: Is it plagiarism (1)?

Figure 5.1 Quiz: Is it plagiarism?

	Yes	No
1. You see a useful article on an internet site that will be helpful in your assignment; no author's name is shown. You copy 40 per cent of the words from this source, and substitute 60 per cent of your own words. You don't include a source, as no author's name is shown on the site.	Yes	No
2. You summarise a point taken from a leaflet given to you by someone in the street—for example, about a civil liberties issue—without citing the source.	Yes	No
3. You are part of a study group of six students. An individual essay assignment has been set by a tutor. Each member of the group researches and writes a section of the essay. The work is collated and written by one student, and all the group members individually submit this collective and collated work.	Yes	No
4. You discuss an essay assignment with a classmate. She has some interesting ideas and perspectives on the topic, which you use in your essay. But no reference to your classmate and her ideas is included in your essay.	Yes	No
5. Your command of written English is not as good as you would like it to be. You explain carefully to another student what you want to say in an essay. The student writes it on your behalf, and you then submit it.	Yes	No
6. You see a quotation in a book and copy the quotation out word for word into your assignment and do not cite the source.	Yes	No
7. You find some interesting photos on a website. No photographer's name is given. You copy the photos or illustrations, and paste them into your assignment.	Yes	No
8. You want to give a historical overview of something that has happened over a long period—for example, general employment trends. You read three or four general textbooks on the topic. They all say much the same thing, so you summarise in your own words and do not cite the sources.	Yes	No
9. You have an assignment to write and you do the research for it. In the process of writing the assignment, a new way of looking at the subject suddenly occurs to you, which you feel is unique. You put forward this 'unique' perspective on the subject and submit the assignment. However, you discover a day or two later that someone else has already published the same idea and perspective a few years earlier.	Yes	No

Now read the following case study (based on a real incident).

Case study

You and your friend are international students studying in Britain. You are both from a country where examinations are the main way of assessing knowledge. It is common practice in your home country to anticipate what questions will be presented in exams and to memorise answers to those questions. In Britain, in preparation for an exam, you and your friend do the same thing. With broad hints from tutors, and a survey of past exam papers, you anticipate what questions will be asked in the forthcoming exam. You work together, discussing the likely topics, and think about how and what you would write in the exam. You work out together what you feel are good answers to likely questions, and memorise what you will write.

On the day of the exam, you are seated a few rows apart from each other. A question you anticipated does appear on the exam paper, and you both write the answer you have memorised. However, when the tutor is marking the exam papers, he finds two almost identically worded answers. The tutor is suspicious that you and your friend have colluded to commit plagiarism. Is the tutor right? Is this a case of plagiarism?

Tick your answer: **Yes** _____ **No** _____

> Note down here why you answered as you did. If you need more space, please use a separate piece of paper.

Answers to and comments on the plagiarism quiz and case study now follow (see Figure 5.2).

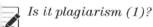

Is it plagiarism (1)?

Figure 5.2 Is it plagiarism? Quiz answers

	Yes	No
1. You see a useful article on an internet site that will be helpful in your assignment; no author's name is shown. You copy 40 per cent of the words from this source, and substitute 60 per cent of your own words. You don't include a source, as no author's name is shown on the site.	✔	
2. You summarise a point taken from a leaflet given to you by someone in the street—for example, about a civil liberties issue—without citing the source.	✔	
3. You are part of a study group of six students. An individual essay assignment has been set by a tutor. Each member of the group researches and writes a section of the essay. The work is collated and written by one student, and all the group members individually submit this collective and collated work.	✔	
4. You discuss an essay assignment with a classmate. She has some interesting ideas and perspectives on the topic, which you use in your essay. But no reference to your classmate and her ideas is included in your essay.		✔

(Continued)

Figure 5.2 *(Continued)*

	Yes	No
5. Your command of written English is not as good as you would like it to be. You explain carefully to another student what you want to say in an essay. The student writes it on your behalf, and you then submit it.	✓	
6. You see a quotation in a book and copy the quotation out word for word into your assignment and do not cite the source.	✓	
7. You find some interesting photos on a website. No photographer's name is given. You copy the photos or illustrations, and paste them into your assignment.	✓	
8. You want to give a historical overview of something that has happened over a long period—for example, general employment trends. You read three or four general textbooks on the topic. They all say much the same thing, so you summarise in your own words and do not cite the sources.		✓
9. You have an assignment to write and you do the research for it. In the process of writing the assignment, a new way of looking at the subject suddenly occurs to you, which you feel is unique. You put forward this 'unique' perspective on the subject and submit the assignment. However, you discover a day or two later that someone else has already published the same idea and perspective a few years earlier.		✓

 Was this plagiarism? Case study

As you will recall from the case study, the tutor is suspicious that you and your friend have colluded to commit plagiarism. Is he right? Is it a case of plagiarism? Read the comments that follow.

- This begs the question 'What is collusion in an academic context?' One UK university department, in relation to students working together, defines it thus: 'If two or more students work on an assignment together, produce an agreed piece of work and then copy it up for individual submission, then this is normally collusion' (University of Sheffield, 2013).
- Collusion, then, implies an intentional act—for example, students have been set an individual assignment and know, or should know, that the work they submit needs to be individually written. If they then produce an assignment together and submit it as an individual piece of work, they could be accused of plagiarism.
- In the case study there is no intention to deceive, but there is an expectation by the institution that students will submit individual responses to an exam question. So in this case the tutor had grounds for suspicion that the work was copied.
- However, it would be obvious from the layout of the examination room and invigilator's report of the examination, that no copying by any means had taken place (this is why mobile phones are usually banned from exam rooms).
- In the situation described in the case study, it is likely that the students would be commended for working so cooperatively in preparation for the exam, but it is likely, too, that the tutor would advise them to think of separate ways of responding to exam questions to avoid any future misunderstandings and to encourage individual responses to assessment tasks. The institution could also be criticised for setting exam questions so narrowly framed that students can easily memorise answers to them.

So, to return to the question 'What is plagiarism?', the remainder of this chapter takes the form of a Q&A on this topic, with another quiz at the end to see if you can spot plagiarism.

The questions that follow are often asked by new students on higher education courses in Britain.

1. What is plagiarism?

Plagiarism is one of a number of practices deemed by universities to constitute 'a lack of academic integrity'. These include the following.

Collusion, as mentioned earlier, can occur when two or more students agree ways to produce and submit work that should have been produced through individual and not collective effort. Illustrative examples include:

- when A gives his or her work for B to copy, and B then submits this as his or her own efforts
- when an assignment is written collectively, but then copied and submitted by each of the people concerned as their own individual work
- when students communicate with one another during an exam to share answers
- impersonation of another person in an exam.

Falsification: where the content of assignments—for example, statistics—has been invented or falsely presented by a student as their own work.

Replication: where a student submits the same, or a very similar, piece of work on more than one occasion to gain academic credit.

Taking unauthorised notes into an exam (see also collusion, above, if these were shared with others).

Obtaining an unauthorised copy of an exam paper (see also collusion, above, if this were shared with others).

(**Source:** adapted from Jones, Reid and Bartlett, 2005)

Plagiarism

The scenarios outlined above are premeditated acts done with a clear intention to deceive or with a disregard for institutional rules governing academic integrity. However, plagiarism, in an academic context, refers to a more nuanced set of actions.

Plagiarism can be pre-planned, or a more impulsive and risk-taking response to a particular situation—for example, running out of time to submit an assignment or frustration at being unable to paraphrase a particular piece of text. It can also occur because of a lack of attention to institutional rules about plagiarism.

Three main forms of plagiarism

As already stated, each institution develops its own definition of plagiarism, and it is likely your college or university has already attempted to make you aware of theirs. But in general, there are three main forms.

1. Copying or presenting another person's work (with or without their consent), and claiming or pretending it to be your own. This includes essays or reports acquired from assignment writing sites and then presented as your own work.
2. Paraphrasing another person's work, but not giving due acknowledgement to the original writer or organisation, including internet sites, publishing the work.
3. Presenting arguments that use the copied words of another, blended with your own, with or without acknowledging the source (see question 3, below).

2. Why do colleges and universities make such a big issue of plagiarism?

Today the open plains of social media are places where information is readily shared. Indeed, sites encourage it, and many users of these sites think nothing of live streaming or copying their own and others, work, and sending it in all directions. It is almost a sign of 'social failure' if you do post your work on to the internet and it is not copied and sent on to others.

It can be difficult, then, for people who have grown up tuned in to—and embracing— social media to wonder what all the fuss is about. Why should it be so different in education? Why is plagiarism described by some universities as 'theft' or 'stealing'? There are three main reasons for this (see Figure 5.3).

Figure 5.3 Three main reasons why universities condemn plagiarism

More detail

Plagiarism is not true learning; it is contrary to nurturing independent thought and action

Cynics will probably roll their eyes at this one, as education 'big ideas' can become lost in a bureaucratic fog if we allow it to happen. But the best universities see themselves as places where ideas can be ignited into action. They want students to become independent thinkers, to contribute to that process within the institution—and beyond in whatever sphere of work and life their studies lead them. And plagiarism is the antithesis of independent thinking.

Ethical issues

The education values framework summarised above is also built on the view that academic advance comes from transparency of research and investigation: making clear to others the process by which ideas emerge, and thus can be tested, debated and challenged. Transparency equates with honesty of action, so the idea of plagiarism—taking someone else's work and claiming it as one's own—is anathema to the moral values that underpin the best forms of higher education; values that most lecturers wholeheartedly endorse and many embrace.

Academic research is also a time-consuming and rigorous process. Before an academic article is cleared for publication it is subjected to detailed scrutiny by the writer's peers and publication editors. Writers, understandably, become protective of the work that has cost them dear, in terms of time and effort, so do not want others presenting it as their work when it is not. Students do understand this:

> I guess if I wrote something I was proud of and that I really had invested a lot of time [in], I'd be pretty mad if someone took a paragraph of mine and said it was theirs.
>
> (Quoted in Power, 2009, p.654)

However, students may wonder why they have to reference a Facebook page, a snapshot or a poster with the same degree of rigour as they would an academic journal article. The response of institutions to this is that to create distinctions between sources is a recipe for confusion and constant arguments about what should or should not be referenced. All published work is therefore treated in the same way (see also 'Stigma', below). It also connects with the transparency argument above: you need to show clearly the sources of your ideas; making qualitative distinctions between what you deem to be worthy or not worthy of referencing is a slippery slope into plagiarism.

Unchallenged acts of plagiarism also give out a message that this type of behaviour is acceptable both within and outside the institution. Universities do not want to be seen to be condoning deceptive behaviour that may well have negative future consequences in the workplace or elsewhere for their graduates.

Stigma

Third, and more pragmatically, universities do not want to be associated with acts that breach copyright, and invoke legal actions against them or the plagiarist. Western concepts of plagiarism are based on an economic model of capitalism and the notion that someone can claim ownership of an idea if it has been presented (published) as work in the public domain. Published work is subject to copyright law, and everyone, including lecturers, within the university needs to respect these laws, not only to protect their own reputations, but those of their employers. An institution that became associated with plagiarism, leading to bad publicity and/or a civil court action against one of its employees or students, would be tainted and stigmatised by association—as would the student or employee.

There are 'plagiarism watchers' who watch and report online serious breaches of plagiarism in the global academic community; their blogs can go viral if a university is compromised by serious breaches of copyright law committed by staff or students (see the Weber-Wulff blog, 'Copy, shake and paste', at http://copy-shake-paste.blogspot.co.uk/).

3. Are there levels of plagiarism?

Life is not just black and white, and most experienced tutors recognise different levels of plagiarism. This can range from the blatant and unreferenced copying of great chunks of someone else's work into assignments (which usually ignites the fury of even the most placid of lecturers) to the much greyer areas of, often unintended, plagiarism arising from students attempting to paraphrase set reading they don't really understand—and resorting to the partial copying of extracts from texts they find particularly unfathomable. It can also arise from students struggling to summarise a text in a way that is different from the original. And it can occur from students simply not understanding the why, when or how of referencing—or what referencing is *for*.

Howard (1995) attempted to categorise the different forms of plagiarism into three classes: (1) cheating, (2) non-attribution and (3) 'patch-writing'. The first is done deliberately, while the second usually results from a lack of experience of academic writing in general and referencing conventions in particular. The third results when a student tries to put together assorted copied text, combined with their own words, to make up the whole. Sources may be cited and referenced, and the end result may even be a harmonious combination of text, where the plagiarised elements go undetected unless scanned by referencing management software, but what can often result, particularly from inexperienced writers, is a mixture of unevenly written sentences that sets alarm bells ringing in the heads of tutors. This patch-writing moves the students concerned into a grey area betwixt paraphrasing and plagiarism, and can lead to tutor criticism of their work or, worse, loss of marks.

4. What percentage of students plagiarise?

Nobody really knows. There is a general impression among lecturers and university administrators that it is a growing problem (see Pecorari, 2013), but estimates of the scale of plagiarism in higher education institutions vary considerably. However, it is easy to get carried away by the belief that plagiarism is rife, and that all students are 'at it'. It is not, and they are not. Jude Carroll, who has researched and written widely on this subject, reminds us that 'most students do not plagiarise' (Carroll, 2007, p.31) and it is worth keeping this always in mind.

Plagiarism research has focused on two main ways of estimating the extent of plagiarism: asking students directly, and looking at the incidence of plagiarism detected and reported by tutors—although both can be crude and inaccurate measures. Students may not want to admit to plagiarism, or don't recognise (or accept) what they do as a breach of institutional regulations. And there is a relative dearth of tutor-focused surveys, as tutors (and institutions) can be reluctant to engage in research that might open a Pandora's box for them, in the form of tabloid newspaper 'shocking revelations' headlines.

A UK study, by Dennis (2005), of 80 undergraduate and postgraduate students on computer science degree programmes found a quarter of respondents admitting to activities the institution regarded as plagiarism, which were largely to do with copying, or partial copying, from printed or web-based sources.

Jones, Reid and Bartlett (2005) also found that one in five of 171 students, from both engineering and psychology undergraduate degree courses at one UK institution, admitted copying and pasting material from websites into assignments without crediting the sources.

In another UK study (Barrett and Malcolm, 2006), 182 mainly postgraduate students, on computer science, automotive engineering and electronics courses, were asked to summarise a number of research papers in an essay. Their assignments were submitted to text-matching software (more on this in Chapter 7) with a view to giving feedback on how original their words appeared to be. A threshold of 15 per cent of matching text was used, as it was considered inevitable that some words and sentences would recur. It was found that just over a quarter (26 per cent) of assignments were above the threshold. These students were shown their work, with the copied passages highlighted, and given an opportunity to resubmit the work. For many students it was revealing how much text they had copied, wittingly or unwittingly, without attribution to the original sources. On resubmission, the incidence of text matching had dropped to 3 per cent overall, as the students rewrote text in their own words.

As mentioned earlier, plagiarism is a global phenomenon. For example, a study in Australia at two universities found that more than three-quarters of undergraduates and half the postgraduates admitted to acts of plagiarism at some point in the course of their studies. This tended to be mainly for not referencing all sources used and for unauthorised sharing of work with other students (Maslen, 2003, summarised in Bennett, 2005, p.138).

Pecorari reported a survey (by Ellery, 2008) of assignments submitted by South African students, where plagiarism was found in a quarter of the 151 essays checked, and where, in another study (by Pickard, 2006), more than 70 per cent (72 per cent) of lecturers over a 12-month period reported finding plagiarism in students' assignments (Pecorari, 2013, p.24).

5. Why do students plagiarise?

Plagiarism is not a new phenomenon. Hart and Friesner (2004) point out that studies of cheating behaviour in the USA date back to the 1940s. They cite studies from the early 1940s, which suggested that, even then, nearly a quarter of students admitted to some form of cheating behaviour. Twenty years later, a study by Bowers (1964) suggested that three-quarters of a sample group of 5000 students had admitted some form of academic cheating at some point in their studies.

Pressure to succeed

The financial investment involved for all students, and particularly for international students—often faced with five-figure sums to pay for courses—can put them under intense pressure to succeed. One commentator (Potts, 2012) suggests that ghost-writing sites are 'thriving' in the wake of 'desperate' students, thrown off balance by unforeseen circumstances, to succeed at any cost:

> Things go wrong at university—family bereavements, personal crises, simple time mismanagement—and the sheer stomach-turning, throat-constricting panic of being unable to produce an assignment on deadline leads vulnerable students down this costly path.
>
> (Potts, 2012)

Time and money

With the introduction of tuition fees, many students have had to take out loans to survive financially. *Times Higher Education* reported in 2013 that nearly two-thirds of higher education students were working part-time to supplement their loans. They were also working increasingly longer hours—90 per cent of students spent up to 20 hours a week working; a big increase from 2012, when only just over half of working students were working more than 11 hours a week (*Times Higher Education*, 2013).

Bennett (2005), in his study of students at a London university, found a link between financial hardship and minor forms of plagiarism. Students were obliged to take on part-time work to support themselves, creating time-pressurised situations where copying work, rather than paraphrasing it, was seen as a shortcut to producing assignments on time.

Time pressures are a recurring theme in plagiarism research (see Pecorari's survey of the literature, 2013). Dordoy (2002), for example, found the most common reasons cited by students for plagiarism and other forms of cheating were related to motivation to achieve higher grades, linked to time-management issues, and the temptation provided by easy access to material via the internet.

'Not serious'

Other studies (Aggarwal et al., 2002; Culwin, 2002; Introna et al., 2003) suggest that students regard copying small amounts of material without citing the source as a not particularly serious breach of academic integrity. Power (2009), in her study of US students, found a disconnect between the attitudes of teaching staff and students towards plagiarism:

> Many understand what their professors are telling them about plagiarism, but they are much less clear about why it is such an important issue. The concept of intellectual property is not intrinsic to most of these students; it is imposed on them by authorities or other people in power outside of themselves.
>
> (Power, 2009, p.654)

The rules of the game

For international students the concept of plagiarism can be different from their previous experiences, and it can take time to learn and adjust to the new situation in Britain. What is regarded in Britain as plagiarism—for example, quoting from sources extensively without referencing them—can be viewed as perfectly normal in other countries, even within Europe (Sherman, 1992; McCourt Larres, 2012).

In my own 2009/2010 survey of student perceptions of referencing and plagiarism (summarised in Chapter 1), 122 international students responded to an online questionnaire on the differences, if any, between how plagiarism is perceived and dealt with in their home countries and the situation in Britain (130 questionnaires were received, but eight were incomplete, so not collated).

Twenty per cent of respondents stated that they had no, or very little, prior knowledge of plagiarism from previous education experiences in their home country. Just over a third (35 per cent) of students stated that they came from countries where plagiarism was discouraged, but where the emphasis was different or perceived as not as strict as in Britain. The remainder, 44 per cent, felt there was no difference, or very little, in the way plagiarism was perceived and dealt with in their home countries; and one student (from Singapore) felt plagiarism was dealt with more seriously in his home country (Neville, 2010, pp.17–18).

However, it should be remembered that this survey was about perception, which does not always equate with reality. A much closer look at the way evidence is managed in the countries concerned would be needed before any firmer statements could be made about the preparedness of international students to reference sources in the way expected of them in Britain.

6. Can institutions of higher education do more to prevent plagiarism?

Plagiarism prevention, rather than prosecution, tends to be the approach adopted by most British universities, although all will take action to discipline offenders, usually by failing the assignment or module, or even expelling students for persistent plagiarism. All have guidelines setting out their own institutional definitions of plagiarism and what the academic implications are for students who transgress. Institutions also use text-matching software to detect where copied text has been copied and pasted into assignments (see Chapter 7 for more detail on this).

As seen earlier, plagiarism can result from students struggling to write assignments against time pressures, often in a second language for them.

The entry standard for English language for international students to study in Britain in higher education tends to lie between score six and seven (but sometimes lower) in the International English Language System (IELTS), which is somewhere between 'competent user' (band 6) and 'good user' (band 7) of English (see Table 5.1).

Table 5.1 IELTS bands

Band 6: competent user	Band 7: good user
Has generally effective command of the language despite some inaccuracies, inappropriacies and misunderstandings. Can use and understand fairly complex language, particularly in familiar situations.	Has operational command of the language, though with occasional inaccuracies, inappropriacies and misunderstandings in some situations. Generally handles complex language well and understands detailed reasoning.

Source: British Council (2015)

So a score of 6.5 is somewhere between 'competent' and 'good'. Students in both bands can fall prone to 'misunderstandings', are still only at the stage of understanding 'fairly complex' to 'complex' language, and are in a situation that is new, rather than 'familiar'. Students with an IELTS score of 6, or lower, starting degree courses will certainly encounter 'complex' academic texts, which can be hard to summarise or paraphrase, particularly if only half understood.

In addition, there was big expansion of students entering higher education from the late 1990s onwards, often from family backgrounds not familiar with higher education practices. This has also created challenges—and responsibilities—for institutions to support all of their students, but particularly those who need help with academic writing.

Institutions recognise that students often need support—it is not a sign of 'inadequacy' if they do, as academic writing can be challenging to the most proficient of writers. All institutions of higher education in Britain now offer learning support to students in some form. This support can also include collaboration between university student support services (*Learnhigher*, 2015) to produce high-quality writing resources for students (*Learnhigher* material can be found at http://www.learnhigher. ac.uk/writing-for-university/academic-writing/).

Learner support can also include the provision of informal drop-in writing centres, and peer-writing support and mentoring schemes (Write Now, 2007). Unfortunately these projects, and non-revenue-generating parts of a college or university, can often be subject to short-term funding, or vulnerable to financial cuts imposed externally on institutions. New students will normally be advised on arrival as to what learning support services are available, but the institutional library would be a good place to find out if you are unsure.

Pecorari notes that, 'the very best prevention for patchwriting is good teaching . . . Teaching students not to misuse sources means teaching them how to write academic texts which use sources appropriately' (2013, p.99).

Assessments

Universities are also looking at the types of assessment they set, and making these more individual and project based, or written under supervised conditions. They are also looking more critically at the way referencing is taught and are reinforcing the message that good referencing is 'an indication of worthy membership of the academic community' (Hart and Friesner, 2004, p.93).

'Judge us by our deeds'

Institutions are also regulating their own teaching, typically by peer evaluation, so that lecturers, for example, do not plagiarise by giving lectures accompanied by unreferenced handouts and PowerPoint slides.

Some universities (as reported in Chapter 1) are developing referencing policies that aim to streamline the number of referencing styles found within the institution and ensure consistency of marking. Some have developed their own in-house version of Harvard and other referencing styles, and both staff and students are expected to use these. This can bring clarity to students on what is expected of them when citing and referencing sources, and gives staff a tangible and approved benchmark for marking assignments.

Helping students to integrate and connect with the academic community of an institution of higher education at an early stage of their studies can benefit all concerned. This is important, as Bennett (2005) has linked the incidence of plagiarism in one university to students feeling a lack of connection or affiliation with the institution. In a situation of alienation or emotional disconnection, students may reject the academic values of their university. An alienated student may not be overly concerned about upsetting the sensibilities of the institution by plagiarising work; it simply becomes a pragmatic means to an end, to getting through the course and gaining the best grade possible.

7. How can plagiarism be avoided?

There are two main ways of avoiding plagiarism in assignments.

First, when you refer to, summarise or restate another person's work—including theories, models, practices or ideas—you should give acknowledgement to that person, by citing the source in the text of your assignment and presenting a list of references at the end of your work.

Second, if you quote directly from a source you should always use quotation marks (or indent lengthy quotations in your text) to distinguish between the actual words of the writer and your own words. If you quote directly from texts you should always cite your sources and present full details of these in your list of references.

Quiz: Is it plagiarism (2)?

Read the following extract from a journal article. Then look at the four examples after it, which attempt to transfer the information from the extract into assignments. Decide which, if any of these, amount to plagiarism.

The extract

> For thousands of years, outsiders have regarded China as a xenophobic country. However, the stereotypes have been changing since China opened up its economy in 1979. Now, the encouragement of foreign direct investment (FDI) and international technology transfer (ITT) lies at the heart of economic relations between foreign countries and China. The international flows of capital, information and technology facilitate the economic growth of China and the influence of multinational enterprises (MNEs). The boom in FDI and ITT has brought to the fore the issue of intellectual property rights (IPRs) as a major topic in the economic development of China. Although a historical review shows that the germination of the concept of IPRs in China goes back more than 100 years, in reality no effective system of intellectual property protection (IPP) existed until very recent times.

Source: Yang, D. and P. Clarke, 2004. 'Review of the current intellectual property system in China', *International Journal of Technology Transfer and Commercialisation*, **3**(1), pp.12–37.

Now decide which, if any, of the following are plagiarised.

Example 1

This essay is about intellectual property (IP) in general and about the situation in China today, and about China's relationship with the West in relation to this issue.

For thousands of years, outsiders have regarded China as xenophobic. However, the stereotypes have been changing since China opened up its economy in 1979. Now, the encouragement of foreign direct investment (FDI) and international technology transfer (ITT) is at the centre of economic relations between foreign countries and China. The global flows of capital, information and technology have helped the economic growth of China and the influence of multinational enterprises (MNEs). The boom in FDI and ITT has brought to the forefront the issue of intellectual property rights (IPRs) as a major topic in the economic development of China. Although history shows that the germination of the concept of IPRs in China goes back more than 100 years, in reality no effective system of intellectual property protection (IPP) existed until very recent times.

Is this plagiarism?   **Yes** _____ **No** _____

Example 2

Outsiders have long regarded China as a xenophobic country. However, the stereotypes have been changing since China opened up its economy in 1979. Yang and Clarke (2004) argue that now the encouragement of foreign direct investment (FDI) and international technology transfer (ITT) lies at the heart of economic relations between foreign countries and China. They state:

> The international flows of capital, information and technology facilitate the economic growth of China and the influence of multinational enterprises (MNEs). The boom in FDI and ITT has brought to the fore the issue of intellectual property rights (IPRs) as a major topic in the economic development of China. (p.12)

Although a historical review shows that the germination of the concept of IPRs in China goes back more than 100 years, in reality no effective system of intellectual property protection (IPP) existed until very recent times.

Is this plagiarism?   **Yes** _____ **No** _____

Example 3

This essay is about intellectual property (IP) in general and about the situation in China today, and about China's relationship with the West in relation to this issue. For centuries China has been regarded by the outside world as a rather closed and insular country. However, Yang and Clarke (2004) argue that now things are changing, and particularly so since 1979, when China decided to open up its economy. Since then, foreign direct investment (FDI) and international technology transfer (ITT) are important connecting links between China and the rest of the world. Now the flows of capital, information, technology and the influence of multinational enterprises (MNEs) have stimulated the Chinese economy. But these developments have also caused attention to focus on the issue of intellectual property rights (IPR). Although the concept of IPR goes back more than a hundred years, there has been no effective system of intellectual property protection (IPP) until recently.

Is this plagiarism?   **Yes** _____ **No** _____

Example 4

This essay is about intellectual property (IP) in general and about the situation in China today, and about China's relationship with the West in relation to this issue. For centuries China has been regarded by the outside world as a rather closed and xenophobic country. However things are changing. Since 1979, China has loosened, opened and stimulated its economy by foreign direct investment (FDI), international technology transfer (ITT)—and from the influence of multinational enterprises (MNEs). However, these developments have also focused attention on the issue of intellectual property rights (IPR) and until recently in China there has been no effective system of intellectual property protection (IPP).

Is this plagiarism?   **Yes** _____ **No** _____

Answers to this quiz can be found below, after the chapter summary.

Summary

- Plagiarism is when the work of others is presented or misrepresented as one's own.
- Plagiarism is an ongoing concern to institutions of higher education. This is because of the perceived immorality of the deed (some call it 'stealing'); implied rejection by students of the learning values of the institution; and the fear of bad publicity, or even litigation in the worst cases, for copyright infringements.
- Some commentators have argued that there are levels of plagiarism culpability, from pre-planned and deliberate cheating, to unintended plagiarism caused by a lack of knowledge about correct referencing practice.
- The scale of plagiarism within higher education is unknown, although it is a global phenomenon.
- There are many reasons why students plagiarise, but time issues, problems with academic writing, including poor referencing practice, and financial pressures to succeed at all costs, are the recurring reasons suggested by students and researchers.
- Institutions of higher education have a big part to play in preventing plagiarism. In particular, there is a clear responsibility to provide academic writing support to their students, particularly to help with referencing.
- Understanding and applying the principles and practice of referencing are the best safeguards against allegations of plagiarism.

Quiz answers

 Is it plagiarism (2)?

Example 1

Yes, this is plagiarism. It is almost identical to the original and there is no attempt to identify the source.

Example 2

Yes, this is plagiarism. Although the authors have been cited, and some of their words directly quoted, the student simply copies a large part of the original, and the implication is that the sections outside the quotations are predominantly the student's own words—which they are not.

Example 3

No, this is not plagiarism. The original source is acknowledged and the student has made a good effort to summarise the extract in his or her own words.

Example 4

Yes, this is plagiarism. Although this is a very good summary of the original extract, it is plagiarism as the original authors are not cited. The original source containing the specialist work of the authors must be acknowledged. It is only when knowledge becomes so publicly well known (or 'common knowledge') that summaries of undisputed facts can be presented without referencing the sources.

Sentences two and three of the student's summary can be regarded as common knowledge, as the information in these could be derived from a general reference book. However, the remaining sentences reflect the specialist knowledge and work of the authors, who should have been cited at the end of this section. If in doubt, always cite your sources.

6 Referencing and writing

> *Introduction to citing sources · Types of evidence · Presenting evidence exercise · Stylistic approaches to citing sources · Citing secondary sources · Elements to include in a reference · Bibliographies and references · Introduction to academic writing · Paraphrasing and summarising · Paraphrasing exercise · Examples of academic writing, including a full-length essay*

> I am not against referencing, but with the degree to which it is over-emphasised I fear it will defeat the objective of education—to train the mind to think.
> (Postgraduate: information systems, organisation and management)

As seen in the last chapter, referencing sources correctly is a key defence against accusations of plagiarism. It is also, and primarily, a means for building reasoned arguments in assignments—which will gain you the best marks and grades. So this chapter will demonstrate how referencing can be integrated into your academic writing to support the points, ideas and arguments you want to include in your assignments.

The chapter is divided into two sections:

1. Referencing
2. Academic writing.

Both referencing and academic writing are inseparable but, for the purposes of this chapter:

- the **Referencing** section looks at the practical issues of citing sources in the main text of your writing, and producing a list of references or a bibliography
- the **Academic writing** section offers advice on summarising and paraphrasing in a way that avoids plagiarism, and presents examples of effective academic writing.

Referencing

Citing sources in your assignment

Examples in this section are in the Harvard style (see Chapters 8 and 9).

In the main text of your assignment, you give a partial reference (called a **citation**). This signals to the reader that the evidence you have just featured in your assignment is the work of another. The citation therefore is normally the last name of the **originator**, followed by the year of publication of the evidence concerned.

An originator is an author or, if no author(s) is (are) named, the name of an organisation, newspaper, journal etc. If there is no obvious name of an originator, the title or part of a title can be used instead.

You then give full details of the source at the end of the assignment in a 'References' or 'Bibliography' section. You can abbreviate lengthy organisational names in the citations provided that you explain the citation in the full reference (see the example that follows). Citations are shown in bold below to emphasise them here, although there is no need to do this in an actual assignment.

> Although **Handy (1994)** has argued that education is the key to economic success for individuals, organisations and nations, a majority of adults in the UK have yet to be convinced or persuaded of this argument. In 1999 only forty per cent of adults had participated in any sort of formal learning in the previous three years. Of these, a significant majority was from social class groups A, B and C. Only a quarter of adults from semi-skilled or unskilled work backgrounds had involved themselves in formal education (**Tuckett, 1999**). The consequences for people without qualifications who lose their jobs are often serious. A study of long-term unemployed people in Yorkshire found that sixty-one per cent had no educational qualifications, and a significant number of these had special learning needs (**YHES, 1998**). There would appear to be a link too, between lack of qualifications, poor health and a disengagement from participation in political or civic life, and which could aggravate the situation of unemployment for the people concerned (**Hagen, 2002**).

Citations in the text

The way you present citations in your assignment is not a neutral act; it is a way of signalling to the reader your position, response or attitude to the evidence selected.

Exercise: Introducing evidence

Look at the six numbered writing extracts in Table 6.1, which are taken from student assignments. They fall into two broad clusters (cluster A and cluster B) in terms of the way they present evidence.

Table 6.1 Introducing evidence

1. The potential benefits of water immersion on muscle strain injuries include: preventing inflammation and oedema, transporting blood from interstitial and intramuscular space to intravascular space, reducing the permanent scar tissue, and aid in the transportation of waste products away from the injured site (Wilcock et al., 2006).

2. In order to make confident recommendations the cohort would have to be increased, either by including more retrospective data, or by incorporating data from other trusts. These figures are however supported by current research, with Park et al. (2009) noting ER concordance rates as high as 99% between needle core and surgical samples, and Mann et al. (2005) reporting a concordance rate of 86%.

(Continued)

Table 6.1 *(Continued)*

3. Hill (2004) has argued that international trade liberal countries enjoy higher GDP growth rates than those that close their economies, and that falling trade barriers and encouragement of foreign direct investment (FDI) are the 'twin engines' to accelerate a nation's prosperity.

4. In Giddens's view, the three key elements of globalisation that have been particularly important for the development of international trade have been, firstly, the growth of the Internet, and spread of ideas, and transfer electronically of money; secondly, the collapse of Communism and subsequent easing of geographical and political barriers; and third, the growth of global regulatory agencies (Giddens, 1999).

5. Studies among depressed patients found that anxiety can be alleviated with relaxation gained from massage, although for some patients there may be an emotional imbalance straight after the treatment, e.g. people feeling fearful and weepy in the short term (Hollis, 1988, p.33).

6. Rachlin (2000) asserts that the function of habit in human life is to regulate our behaviour, avoid impulse decisions, and offer us a measure of emotional security in a rapidly changing world.

Can you identify which extracts are similar in the way they present evidence? Group them into Cluster A and Cluster B, using the answer grid in Figure 6.1.

Figure 6.1 Introducing evidence: answer grid

Cluster A	Cluster B
Number = Number = Number =	Number = Number = Number =

Comment

Extracts 1, 2 and 5 present factual evidence gathered from research studies. Verbs, such as 'noted' and 'found', or summarising results, as in 1, signal that this type of information will be presented and that the evidence cited provides relevant support to the points being made.

Extracts 3, 4 and 6 present more interpretative ways of looking at the evidence. The words 'has argued', 'In X's view' and 'asserts' signal to the reader that there are likely to be other interpretations of the topic under discussion.

It is important therefore to use the most appropriate verb to introduce evidence in assignments. In this respect, there are often value judgements to be made about the evidence you want to use. Your role as an academic writer is to:

- select relevant primary and, if appropriate, secondary evidence to support the points you are making (see Chapter 3)
- ask yourself what role the evidence plays in your assignment; you then choose the most appropriate verbs or ways to introduce the evidence in your text (see Table 6.2 for examples of presenting verbs)
- link your evidence to the point you wish to make in your assignment.

Table 6.2 Presenting verbs

Author X ...	
Factual orientation	**More subjective**
Found	Argues
Showed	Asserts
Discovered	Proposes
Demonstrated	Considers
Identified	Debates
Recorded	Estimates
Noted	Criticises
Observed	Feels
Correlated	Believes
Tested	Contends
Selected	Thinks
Surveyed	Appeals
Measured	Points out

And this leads author X to ...

Conclude
Explain
Identify
Describe
Define
Label
List
Name
Defend
Classify
Justify
Interpret

Stylistic approaches to citing sources

You can introduce Harvard-style citations into the text stylistically in a variety of ways. For example:

> 1. There emerged by the end of the twentieth century two broad approaches to the management of people within organisations.
>
> (Handy, 1996)

This introduces a point of view, and the way the evidence is presented and cited suggests that Handy is a major proponent of this perspective. The citation in this example is at the end of a sentence. However, this is not the only way of citing an author. The student could have started with the citation, as follows:

2. Handy (1996) observes that by the end of the twentieth century two broad approaches to the management of people within organisations had emerged.

Or, if wanting to include Handy as an exemplar of this proposition:

3. Some commentators, notably Handy (1996), have observed that by the end of the twentieth century two broad approaches to the management of people within organisations had emerged.

Or:

4. Two approaches to the management of people within organisations had emerged by the end of the twentieth century (Handy, 1996; see also Brown, 1999, and Clark, 2000).

In example 4, above, a major source—Handy—has been advanced, with two (in this case, fictitious) supporting sources, which are presented in chronological order.
Or:

5. Charles Handy, among others, has noted that by the end of the twentieth century two broad approaches to the management of people within organisations could be observed (Handy, 1996).

There is no one right way of citing authors. It depends on the type of evidence chosen (see earlier in this chapter), the context of the sentence, and the style of writing adopted at any particular point in the assignment.

Two key points regarding citing sources

1. Always give credit to the authors/source originators who have provided you with evidence.

2. Make sure you place the citation in the sentence in a way that makes clear the authorship or origin of the source you have consulted.

Exercise: Where do you think the citations should go?

The second point in the 'key points about citations' concerns where in the text of your assignment you should locate a citation.

Look at the following extract from a science report. Where do you think the citations should go? Put an **X** in the text where you think evidence should be cited.

Breast cancer represents 23 per cent of all female cancers, and it is by far the most frequent cancer among women in both the developed and developing world. Although mortality rates remain much less than incidence rates, breast cancer is

> also the most frequent cancer-related death in women. Sex steroid hormones play a major role in the growth and development of the mammary gland, and a clear correlation between pathogenesis of breast cancer and cumulative exposure to oestrogens has been demonstrated.

The answer to this exercise can be found at the end of this chapter.

Secondary referencing: citing secondary sources

There is a 'golden rule' in most referencing styles: always cite and reference what *you* have read (see Chapter 12, 'Frequently asked questions', question 4, for exceptions, i.e. Vancouver referencing style).

This can cause difficulties, though. A significant number of students in my referencing surveys had difficulties with secondary referencing (see Chapter 1). If you find problems with secondary referencing then, typically, you will be reading a chapter in a book and the author will mention an interesting piece of research done by someone else, or that provides a useful fact for your assignment. The author then provides a citation naming another writer or writers.

What to do in this situation?

You can find and read the source mentioned and check out the accuracy of the summary given by the secondary source author—this is the recommended option. You can then refer directly to this author, as you have read the source yourself. However, there are circumstances when it could be appropriate to use the secondary source:

- if you find it difficult to find or gain access to the primary source
- if you are confident the secondary source is reliable and accurate in the way the primary author has been summarised, paraphrased or quoted, and
- if you do not need to go into any great depth of analysis on what the primary author has written.

For example, in the book *Licensed to Work*, by Barrie Sherman and Phil Judkins (1995), there is a reference to another writer, Ivan Illich, who talks about 'shadow work', meaning the tasks in society that were once the responsibility of extended families and close communities.

If the Sherman and Judkins book was used as a secondary source, your citation must make this clear. So, using the Harvard referencing style, you could write:

> Ivan Illich (1981), as summarised by Sherman and Judkins (1995, p.121), has suggested that 'shadow work', a term he coined, which means . . .

Or:

> Illich (1981) has coined the term 'shadow work', meaning the tasks in society that were once the responsibility of extended families and close communities (in Sherman and Judkins, 1995, p.121).

Or:

Sherman and Judkins, in their book (1995, p.121), refer to the work of Ivan Illich (1981), who coined the term 'shadow work' as being . . .

With the name–date Harvard and APA referencing styles, it is necessary only to give details of the source you looked at. If anyone wanted to read Ivan Illich's book to pursue his ideas in more depth, they could look at *Licensed to Work* and find the full reference details there. (For more on referencing secondary sources in footnote-related referencing styles, see Chapter 12, question 4).

How many references should I use in an essay?

This is a common question and the answer is 'as many as necessary, and no more'. A university tutor commenting on student work wrote:

> A few students had produced impeccably referenced gobbledegook, seemingly on the basis that if it moves, cite it! . . . Any rhythm that the resulting prose might have possessed had been destroyed through being referenced to death.
>
> (Sanders, 2009)

If you are clear in your mind what you want to say, prove or discuss, then the number of citations and references will follow your evidence. You will not be judged by the *number* of references, but by the quality, reliability and relevance of them to your work. Over-referencing can be counter-productive, as this student in my survey recognised:

> Authors' views one after another, without any of your own thoughts in between, leads to your work appearing as a thicket of speech marks and parentheses.
>
> (Undergraduate: Japanese studies and politics)

A 'thicket' of sources can be presented in assignments because, in the view of another student:

> It is considered that if there are a lot of references then the person has done more research, which is not necessarily true. I think an assignment must be more of your own work, and not an entire literature review. Your own ideas must be valued.
>
> (International student, studying management)

What elements need to be included in a reference entry?

You need to give the reader enough information to help them easily and quickly find the source you have cited. If another person wanted to look at your source and check it for themselves, could they find it easily with the information you have supplied?

The essential information that should be included is as follows.

- **Originator or creator of the source:** this should be the starting point for the reference. The originator or creator can be the name, nickname or nomenclature of the author, writer or editor, or the name of a government or government body, an organisation, institution, group or website/website host.

Then include . . .

- **Date (year):** this is the year of origin of the information, and other specific dates, if relevant—for example, the exact publication dates in the case of newspapers, journals or magazines.
- **Title:** title and subtitle of the source in question. If the creator/originator of the source is unknown, the reference can be started with the source title.
- **Specific identifiers:** for example, the nature of the source, e.g. [DVD], volume and edition numbers, and page numbers.
- **Where the source can be found:** this can be the location and name of the publisher/originator; or, in the case of the internet, a web URL or DOI.

However, the position in the reference of these elements can vary according to the referencing style you are required to use (see Chapters 8–10).

References or bibliography?

Your choice of sources cited in your assignment will be included at the end of your assignment in an alphabetical list of sources headed either 'Bibliography' or 'References', unless you have been asked by your tutor to include both in the assignment (some styles of referencing refer to these lists respectively as 'Works Consulted' and 'Works Cited').

What is the difference between a list of 'References' and a 'Bibliography'?

The terms are often used synonymously, but there is a difference in meaning between them.

- **References** are the items you have read and specifically referred to (or cited) in your assignment.
- A **bibliography** is a list of everything you read in preparation for writing an assignment. A bibliography will therefore contain sources that you have cited *and* those you found to be influential, but decided not to cite. A bibliography can give a tutor an overview of which authors have influenced your ideas and arguments, even if you do not refer to them specifically.

Table 6.3 summarises the differences between these two terms.

Table 6.3 References and bibliographies

Bibliography (or 'Works Consulted')	References (or 'Works Cited')
If you wish to list the sources you made specific reference to (cited) in your assignment, **and** give details of other sources consulted (but not directly cited), then you can include all the sources under one subheading: '**Bibliography**'.	If, however, you have cited—made specific reference to—all the sources you consulted in the assignment, your list will be headed '**References**'. If you make a point of reading selectively, it is likely that you will make use of everything you read and refer directly to it in your assignment. In that event, it will be fine to just have a 'References' list, instead of a 'Bibliography'; it will certainly not go against you.

The list of references at the end of the assignment for the extract shown earlier containing just four citations would look like this, and in this alphabetical order:

References

Hagen, J. 2002. *Basic skills for adults*. Birmingham: The Guidance Council.

Handy, C. 1994. *The empty raincoat*. London: Hutchinson.

Tuckett, A. 1999. Who's learning what? *Guardian*, 18 May, p.13.

YHES: Yorkshire and Humber Employment Service. 1998. *Survey of clients aged 25+ unemployed for two years or more*. London: Department for Education and Employment.

You can also look at the list of references at the end of this book to see how sources are displayed; see also Chapter 9.

Academic writing

This section of the chapter looks at the way academic writing connects with referencing, and includes an exercise and examples of effective science and non-science writing.

Academic writing is defined by its close attention to detail. Academic writers usually have to submit their work to the close scrutiny of their peers, so they pick their words carefully, use jargon if they feel it will be understood by their intended readers, and will typically leave room for disagreement or discussion by their cautious use of language.

Academic writing style, then, is usually more akin to the considered language of the law courts, rather than the zippy prose of the tabloid press or social media sites. But this presents a paradox for students. In a fast-moving world, where succinct, even abbreviated, reading is increasingly the norm, reading academic texts forces you to slow down—and to reach often for the dictionary.

Paraphrasing and summarising

Chapter 1 highlighted the difficulties that both home and international students have encountered when paraphrasing and summarising the work of others—an issue that often connects with their lack of confidence about writing in English (see also Chapter 5). In my surveys, one of the main issues for home and international students was the difficulty of thinking of alternative words to the texts they needed to paraphrase:

> If you are a foreigner it is difficult to use diverse paraphrasing and to express things with your own words. This for me is mainly a language problem.
>
> (Undergraduate from Italy)

So what is the difference between paraphrasing and summarising? And what does successful paraphrasing or summarising look like?

Summarising is about the general, while paraphrasing is about the particular (see Table 6.4). You would summarise, for example, a chapter of a book, but paraphrase a section of that chapter.

Table 6.4 Summarising and paraphrasing

Summarising	Paraphrasing
Summarising involves writing an account, in one's own words, of the main, broad and general meanings of a text.	Paraphrasing involves close attention to a **particular section** of a text and attempting, in one's own words, to capture the essence of the original.

It can sometimes be difficult, if not impossible, to avoid using some of the author's original words, particularly those that describe or label phenomena. However, you need to avoid simply copying what the author has written. Choose words that you feel give a true impression of the author's original ideas or action.

Exercise: Which of the following is the most successful attempt at paraphrasing the extract?

Read the following extract from a journal article. It can help to underline key or main point sentences as a starting point for paraphrasing any text.

> So what is the point of referencing? It can be argued that the main purpose of referencing is to facilitate the collective development and transmission of academic knowledge. This development and transmission is powered by human endeavour and communication; referencing is one element in this communication process, and can allow writers to separate their ideas from the work of others. It also helps other scholars trace the origins of ideas and thus build links across knowledge.
>
> (Neville, 2012)

Decide which of the examples in Figure 6.2 is the most successful attempt at paraphrasing the extract.

Figure 6.2 Which of these is the most successful attempt at paraphrasing the extract?

Paraphrasing attempts	Your comments
Student 1 It has been argued that the main purpose of referencing is to facilitate the development of knowledge. This development process is driven by human communication and endeavour, and referencing is one part of this. It allows writers to separate their ideas from the work of others and helps other scholars trace the origins of ideas and thus build links across knowledge.	
Student 2 The point of referencing is to 'facilitate the collective development and transmission of academic knowledge' (Neville, 2012). He also says that 'development and transmission is powered by human endeavour and communication; referencing is one element in this communication process, and can allow writers to separate their ideas from the work of others'. Referencing also helps others to trace the origin of ideas, which helps to build knowledge.	

Figure 6.2 *(Continued)*

Student 3 Neville (2012) has argued that the main aim of referencing, which is a form of academic communication, is to help writers share knowledge in a way that separates out the ideas of one writer from another. Referencing also helps scholars to identify where ideas came from and how they have developed over time.	
Student 4 Referencing is an essential part of academic writing because it assists the spread and communication of knowledge. It helps writers to separate their own points from those made by others, and it makes it easier to identify the originators of ideas and how these ideas have developed over time.	

See the comments at the end of this chapter.

Tips for paraphrasing

- Highlight the key point or points in the text.
- What is main point or idea in the text—the one upon which the others are built?
- Start your paraphrasing with a rewrite of the main point or idea, but in your own words.
- Then rewrite the other supporting points in your own words.
- Then re-read the original to make sure nothing essential is missing.
- Make sure you have referenced the source of the original extract.

Introductions

The introductions to assignments are particularly important for setting the right tone and direction to your work, and for beginning to establish your credibility as an academic writer.

Exercise: Essay introduction

Look at the following introduction to an essay on household debt. If you were a tutor marking this, what feedback would you give to the student? The student was asked to 'Discuss the causes of rising household debt and its implications.' Think about the way it is structured and organised, and the evidence it provides. Note down your thoughts in the space that follows the extract.

Discuss the causes of rising household debt and its implications.

There is clear evidence of rising debt and that its implications are serious for the individual health of people affected and for both the short and long term economy of any country.

We should remember, though, that debt of itself is not necessarily a problem. The Finance Guide (2013) states:

The concept of debt is not that of modern times rather it is very old. It has its roots deepened in the ancient past. It is known to have emerged when people just started to engage themselves in various barter-related trades. It was also functional at the advent of world's oldest known human civilisation established in Sumeria.

So we need to remember that debt is only a problem when expenditure continually outpaces income and where interest rates on the debt increasingly adds to the sum owed (Roper, 2000; Davis, 2010; Atkins, 2011).

Household debt in Britain rose by 314% to £1,437bn in 2013 from £347bn in 1990 (*This is Money*, 2014). The 35 to 44 year-olds are the age group with the highest level of debt (Financial Inclusion Centre, 2010) although AgeUK found nearly a quarter of older people, over 50, were paying more than £85 a week to pay off debts (AgeUK, 2013).

The ten most common causes of debt are (1) low income, (2) bad budgeting, (3) divorce, (4) depending on credit cards, (5) gambling, (6) illness, (7) little or no savings, (8) lack of financial communication, (9) spending future money, and (10) not knowing the basics about finance (Bank Tracker, 2014). Debt Round-Up (2014) also sees overspending, large family size, poor investment and inflation as adding to the difficulties.

What feedback would you give this student? Write your comments in the spaces provided below. If you need more space, note down the headings on a separate piece of paper and make your notes there.

Structure and organisation

Use of evidence

Other points

 Exercise: Essay introduction—comment

The introduction shifts from household debt to debt in general, so the student needs to keep the essay subject—household debt—clearly in focus the whole time.

The essay also starts with: 'There is clear evidence of rising debt and that its implications are serious for the individual health of people affected and for both the short and long term economy of any country.' However, no source is cited in support of this 'clear evidence'. An alternative approach would have been to state that evidence will be introduced, but later in the essay, and to refer specifically to 'household debt' in the introduction. For example, the student could have written:

> This essay will show that there is clear evidence of rising household debt and that its implications are serious for the individual health of people affected and for both the short- and long-term economy of any country.

The student also needs to put the discussion into a geographical context—for example, stating which countries will be featured in the discussion. It is implied (in paragraph 4) that it will be Britain, but if that is the case this needs to be stated early in the introduction. For example, the student could have written:

> . . . and for both the short- and long-term economy of any country. This essay will focus on household debt in Britain, but it will make comparisons with the situation in the USA and with selected countries in Western Europe.

A significant number of secondary sources are presented in the extract—for example, 'This is Money', 'Bank Tracker' and 'Debt Round-Up'—rather than using primary sources for this important statistical and lifestyle information. Where did these secondary sources get their information from? The student should be looking at the origins of this information and using these instead, if at all possible.

The debt causal information is also presented largely in terms of individual shortcomings, but is that the full story? Are there wider political and socio-economic issues that should be considered and introduced—for example, inflation, global world recession, cuts to welfare provision?

The student also uses age-related information from two different sources separated by three years, e.g. Financial Inclusion Centre (2010) and AgeUK (2013), yet conflates the information into one sentence. The situation for older adults, aged 55-plus, as reported by AgeUK in 2013, may have been different in 2010. It would have been better to have used one source offering comparative information focused on one particular year or period.

Three citations—Roper, 2000; Davis, 2010; Atkins, 2011—are used to support a statement about when debt can become a problem. However, the explanation presented is hardly surprising and would be regarded as common knowledge (or common sense) to most people. Why were three sources used to support a non-contentious statement like this? This is an example of common knowledge—and a prime example of unnecessary referencing.

There is also a long quotation inserted, supported by a secondary source: the Finance Guide (2013). However, the information could easily have been summarised into a single sentence. For example:

> Debt has been a part of life ever since people started to trade and barter with one another.

Again, such a statement would amount to common knowledge, so would not need to be referenced. Copying chunks of other people's work into your own assignments, even if you do cite and reference it, will gain you few marks. Quotations should always be introduced to assignments *very selectively* and to make a particular impact—for example, to introduce an author's distinctive 'voice' into your work, or to emphasise a key point you are making.

Good examples of referencing and writing in action

In this section you will find two examples of academic writing that demonstrate the effective use of evidence and referencing.

1. Science writing

The first extract is an introduction from a third-year biomedical science undergraduate dissertation (used with the student's permission). The student has tested a particular hypothesis in relation to the diagnosis of breast cancer. It is not necessary to understand the science—the point of this example is to demonstrate how referencing has been used to support the student's work.

Science writing can be different from the more persuasive/argumentative forms of academic writing, in that science students typically present evidence of observations and findings. Theories and models can certainly be challenged, but usually only by evidence produced from research by the student or by others. Quotations and personal opinion are rarely used in science writing.

Referencing in science reports usually serves to:

- introduce and identify the sources of previous research and research findings as a way of setting the scene; the work of science pioneers can be acknowledged in this process

- explain and justify the methodology used in the current reported research
- match current reported research findings against those from previous research
- link or explain any anomalies, differences or similarities between the current results and those of other research studies
- identify ongoing research that connects with the student's own findings.

So as you read the following extract, note:

- how evidence is introduced by the student (e.g. the author position—see the exercise earlier in this chapter, page 66)
- how the student presents the source of all statistics, research, guidelines and hypothesis.

1.0 Introduction

Breast cancer represents 23 per cent of all female cancers, and it is by far the most frequent cancer among women in both the developed and developing world (World Cancer Report, 2014). Although mortality rates remain much less than incidence rates, breast cancer is also the most frequent cancer-related death in women. Sex steroid hormones play a major role in the growth and development of the mammary gland, and a clear correlation between pathogenesis of breast cancer and cumulative exposure to oestrogens has been demonstrated (Hevir et al., 2011).

Section 1.01: Oestrogen and progesterone receptor status

Evaluation of the hormonal status of a breast tumour represents a central component of the pathological evaluation of breast cancer. Deroo and Korach (2006) have found that oestrogen receptors (ER) are over expressed in around 70 per cent of breast cancer cases and are known to contribute to tumorigenesis. Deroo and Korach have noted, too, that binding of oestrogen with ER stimulates proliferation in mammary cells, with oestrogen metabolism producing genotoxic by-products that reduce genome stability.

ER status is therefore a well-studied marker for prognosis and predicted response to endocrine therapy, with research findings consistently revealing a clear association between ER positivity and response to the competitive antagonist tamoxifen (Leake et al., 1981; Kuukasjärvi et al., 1996; Johnston, 2010). Progesterone receptor (PR) co-expression has seen an historical association with response to hormonal therapies in ER-positive breast cancer, with the reasoning that ER and PR co-expression describes a functionally complete signalling pathway (Hefti et al., 2013). Indeed, J. Wittliff (1984) stated that the majority of women with ER+/PR+ tumours responded favourably to endocrine therapy. This figure declined to roughly a third with ER+/PR- tumours, with only 10 per cent of ER-/PR- tumours responding favourably.

It is current protocol in the Harrogate District Hospital (HDH) Histopathology laboratory to assess the ER status of all primary breast cancer specimens in order to inform recommendations to treat with tamoxifen. Current guidelines recommend PR testing on all ER negative cases (Royal Collage of Pathologists, 2005) based on previously established findings that PR positivity indicates a potential response to tamoxifen in the absence of ER expression (Dowsett et al., 2006). The value of such analysis is, however, under criticism based on current reasoning that ER-/PR+ tumours represent a non-reproducible sub-type (Hefti et al., 2013). This hypothesis was investigated during this audit.

In this extract the student introduces the background to his research audit. The first sentence launches us directly into the topic under discussion and reminds us of its importance to women across the world. The student introduces the background to the diagnosis of breast cancer and current guidelines on practice. Referencing is used to identify sources of previous research and the outcomes from this.

The student introduces and cites sources of criticism of this practice and makes it clear that the hypothesis shaping the criticism will be investigated. You may have noted how evidence was presented. For example, 'Deroo and Korach (2006) have *found*' and later, '*noted . . .*', which suggests there is a body of evidence leading to this conclusion. However, in science, and in other realms of knowledge, hypotheses are rarely 'proved' to be beyond further testing of ideas.

2. Persuasive writing

Persuasive writing is when you write to persuade others towards a particular view-point. It requires you to have a clear point of view and persuade others to it by the use of sound reasoning and convincing evidence.

A number of students in my research, studying in disciplines where this type of essay is likely to be set, felt constrained from expressing personal opinion in their work for fear of being accused of plagiarism. Two students wrote:

> The need to reference every proposition or idea diminishes the opportunity to develop my own ideas for fear of not having properly referenced all knowledge in the assignment.
>
> (Postgraduate: European and international business law)

> Sometimes I have my own idea, but I am not sure whether it is similar to any author and then whether lecturers will consider my work is plagiarism or not.
>
> (Postgraduate: human resources management)

The most successful persuasive academic writing is often a blend of objectivity and subjectivity, presenting both the 'big picture' and the telling detail. It has the structure of a good story: with a beginning, middle and end; and like any good story it has something of the writer in it. The real person behind the keyboard is not lost in a forest of jargon, interminable sentences, multiple references, endless footnotes and statistics.

But is this easier said than done? The problem for many students is that they simply do not know what an effective essay *looks* like.

So what does such an essay look like?

The following essay was submitted by a student, Jonas Juenger, for an essay-writing competition sponsored by the *Learnhigher* Centre of Excellence in Teaching and Learning (CETL) network. The set title was 'What is the point of referencing?', and there was a maximum word count of 1500. Jonas's essay is a good example of an essay that:

- uses sources to develop, and not just reflect, arguments
- demonstrates accurate referencing in the Harvard style
- is well structured and well written
- blends Jonas's own experiences with other evidence, so is a good example of a student 'finding their own voice' in assignments, and
- above all, answers the essay question.

Exercise

As you read, I suggest you underline or mark any section you feel is a particular example of Jonas writing in his own voice. How does he assert his own identity into the text at these points?

Look, too, at the sections in the essay **when** Jonas references sources of evidence—ask yourself **why** is he referencing on these occasions. You may like to re-read Chapter 4 to remind yourself of when to reference.

Look for examples of critical analysis—this is where the writer moves away from just describing phenomena to being more analytical of them. What does Jonas do at these points in the essay?

The paragraphs are numbered to help with the commentary that follows, but normally assignments would not be numbered in this way.

Now read Jonas's essay . . .

What is the point of referencing?

1. The reasons why accurate referencing is essential for academic work are not immediately apparent, particularly for students new to higher education. This essay will, therefore, examine why referencing is an integral part of academic writing and in the process address the question, 'What is the point of referencing?'

2. There have been countless times when I finished an assignment and then spent another day on referencing. At the start of my university studies this seemed like a useless exercise without any additional value, since my assignment was already written. In the first year of my studies I knew only one reason for it: if I don't reference properly, I'll be marked down. But with a few more years of academic experience I now appreciate why referencing is essential—and the main reason is not because tutors punish deviation from the guidelines.

3. There are three main reasons for referencing. First, referencing helps student writers to construct, structure, support and communicate arguments. Second, references link the writer's work to the existing body of knowledge. Third, only through referencing can academic work gain credibility.

4. This essay will discuss these three aspects of referencing in detail, examine their validity, identify how referencing affects a writer's writing style, and show how referencing helps students to present their own ideas and opinions in assignments.

Constructing, supporting and communicating the argument

5. Becker (1986) believes the construction of arguments is the most important function of referencing systems. There are four dimensions to this. First, drawing on existing literature, authors can construct their own arguments—and adopting a referencing system supports this process. Second, it helps to structure the existing information and arguments by linking published authors to their respective works. Third, referencing helps writers identify sources and gather evidence, as well as show the relationships between existing knowledge. Finally, referencing also provides a framework to enable writers to structure their arguments effectively by assessing, comparing, contrasting or evaluating different sources.

6. However, merely reiterating existing research, rather than producing innovative contributions, is inadequate for most academics. It is important for every academic writer to avoid this narrow-minded argumentation trap; academic works are not only about compiling existing arguments, but adding new perspectives, finding new arguments or new ways of combining existing knowledge. For example, Barrow and Mosley (2005) combined the fields of human resources and brand management to develop the 'Employer Brand' concept.

7. When the argument has been constructed, it needs academic support—and only references can provide this required support. We all know that academic works are not about stating opinions, as that would be akin to journalistic comment, but arguments are supported by evidence, and only arguments with sufficient and valid support are credible. Hence arguments are only as strong as the underlying evidence: arguments relying on questionable sources are, well, questionable.

8. Referencing also enables writers to communicate their arguments efficiently. The referencing framework allows them to produce a holistic work with different perspectives, while still emphasising their own positions; quotations, for example, help the reader to differentiate the writer's opinions from those of others. Again, if arguments are badly referenced, readers might not be able to distinguish the writers' own opinions from those of their sources. Especially for academic beginners, referencing helps them to adapt to the precise and accurate academic writing style required for degree-level study. Neville (2007, p.10) emphasises this issue of writing style, and identifies the quest to 'find your own voice' as one of the main reasons for referencing. In academic writing, this requires the development of an individual style that is neither convoluted nor convivial in tone, but that is clear, open but measured, and is about identifying and using evidence selectively to build and support one's own arguments.

Science as network of knowledge, interlinked by referencing

9. Immanuel Kant said, 'Science is organised knowledge.' This short quote brilliantly captures my next point: the primary mission of science and other disciplines is not to promote individual achievements, but to establish a connected, collective and recognised body of knowledge. This is the most fundamental reason for referencing from a theoretical point of view. Hence some authors identify this as the principal reason for referencing: 'The primary reason for citation [. . .] is that it encourages and supports the collective construction of academic knowledge' (Walker and Taylor, 2006, pp.29–30).

10. The writer's references are links to this network of knowledge. Without these links, an academic work would operate within an academic vacuum, unrelated to existing academic knowledge. A writer needs to contextualise his or her work to show how it relates to current research and debates. References also indicate in which particular knowledge network the writer operates. And these links to existing knowledge enable the reader to follow the writer's link to the existing knowledge network to gain a more in-depth insight.

11. Referencing not only connects a student writer's work to existing research, but clearly distinguishes the writer's own contributions from established arguments. Failing to indicate that ideas are taken from the existing body of knowledge would be plagiarism. This is one of the five principles of referencing identified by Walker and Taylor (2006). Neville also identifies the link to existing knowledge as one of the main reasons for adopting a referencing style; he highlights 'tracing the origin of ideas', 'spreading knowledge' and 'indicating appreciation' (2007, pp.9–10), which is my next point.

12. Referencing a work indicates that the writer finds the referenced material important: hence references create 'academic clout' in an assignment. In the global academic community a well-cited article will find more recognition. However, this practice is not without its critics. Thody, for example, calls this the 'sycophantic' use of referencing—and it can certainly be used to 'flatter your mentors' (2006, p.186). And Thompson calls this 'ritualized obeisance to the reigning authorities' (2003, p.27). So the important issue here is not about selecting references for their expediency value, but for their enduring quality. Writers have to link their work to a recognised and credible knowledge network—and this becomes increasingly important in contemporary society, with vast amounts of information readily available. References indicate in which knowledge network the writer operates—if the references are untrustworthy, changeable sources, the writer's work can be seen only as untrustworthy and changeable. This brings us to the next point: credibility.

Credibility

13. Martin Joseph Routh said in 1878: 'You will find it a very good practice always to verify your references, sir!' Correct referencing enables the

reader to do exactly that: check sources and verify conclusions. The issue of credibility is identified by commentators as a key issue in referencing. Nygaard, for example, identifies credibility as the main reason for referencing: 'The goal of referencing is to enhance [. . .] your credibility as an author' (2008, p.177). Neville came to the same conclusion, that 'to be taken seriously, [a writer] needs to make a transparent presentation of valid evidence' (2007, p.10). Also the Academic Learning Support from Central Queensland University (2007) sees the credibility of arguments as the primary motive for correct referencing.

14.   References allow the reader to trace the source of the writer's arguments, consult the original independently and verify whether the writer's usage of the sources is valid. Some readers, for example, interested in a point in question, might want to verify the writer's interpretation of a referenced work. The quality of references is, therefore, extremely important for the credibility of an academic work. Arguments are only as good as the underlying references—untrustworthy and unreliable sources can even invalidate an argument, while reliable and dependable sources strengthen the writer's argument.

15.   Finally, the writer's selection of sources also demonstrates whether the writer has evaluated all important arguments and has a thorough understanding of the subject. Only a credible work that takes all important arguments into account will find acceptance in the academic world.

Conclusion

16.   So what is the point of referencing? I have argued that there are three main aspects why academic writers have to adopt a referencing system: First, it helps to structure, support and communicate arguments. Second, it links the work to the existing body of knowledge, although it is also important for writers not merely to present the ideas of others, but to contribute where possible with innovative ideas of their own. Third, only referencing can give the argument credibility—and this is a particularly significant element for success in the academic world.

References

Academic Learning Support, 2007. Division of Teaching & Learning Services, Central Queensland University. *Harvard (author–date) referencing guide.* Rockhampton, Queensland: Central Queensland University.

Barrow, S. and R. Mosley, 2005. *The employer brand.* Chichester: John Wiley & Sons.

Becker, H.S. 1986. *Writing for social scientists.* Chicago: University of Chicago Press.

Neville, C. 2007. *The complete guide to referencing and avoiding plagiarism.* Maidenhead: McGraw-Hill/Open University Press.

Nygaard, L.P. 2008. *Writing for scholars.* Universitetforlaget.

Thody, A. 2006. *Writing and presenting research.* London: Sage Publications.

Thompson, A. 2003. Tiffany, friend of people of colour. *International Journal of Qualitative Studies in Education*, 16(1), pp.7–30.

Walker, J.R. and T. Taylor, 2006. *The Columbia guide to online style.* 2nd edn. New York: Columbia University Press.

Comments on the essay

1. Examples of student's own voice in the essay

Paragraph 2 is an example of Jonas talking directly to us. He tells us about his early experiences of referencing—one that will be shared by many students—and how his perceptions changed as he gained more experience of academic writing. He uses the first person term 'I' at this point, so we are left in no doubt that this is his authentic voice speaking directly to us.

But how acceptable is this form of personalised writing in an academic assignment? As stated earlier, it is impossible to generalise, as it depends on the subject and the attitude of the tutor marking the assignment. Some tutors will not accept this type of personal engagement within an essay, but others will—particularly if, for the most part, the essay is presented in a traditional way, using the third-person style of writing.

The use of personal experiences, if done discretely, can add a lighter style to an academic essay of this type, and make a link between theory and everyday reality. However, your own comments, when included in an essay, will need to make direct connections between your own experiences, and the theories, ideas and practices you are discussing. You need to ask yourself, 'What do my experiences add to this discussion?' In this case, Jonas uses his own experiences as a bridge to the points he makes in paragraph 3 and onwards. This also encourages us to identify with the writer and gain a sense of the person behind the keyboard.

Jonas's own voice emerges briefly again at the beginning of paragraph 9, when he writes, 'Immanuel Kant said "Science is organised knowledge." This short quote brilliantly captures my next point . . .'.

He reminds us here that the points being made are *his*; he has selected them and has taken ownership of them. Jonas uses this technique again at the end of paragraph 11, as a bridge to paragraph 12. And, in his Conclusion, we are again reminded, with the opening to the second sentence, 'I have argued', that it has been *this* particular student, Jonas Juenger, who has selected and presented the evidence in the essay.

The **selection** of evidence is, in fact, one of the main ways that you can assert your own voice in an assignment: you look for evidence that supports your arguments, and the viewpoints you feel are relevant and important; referencing thus becomes your servant rather than your master.

A writer's own unique **style** of writing is another way of adding individuality to an academic essay. In this essay Jonas uses the repetition of words effectively to reinforce and make points. For example:

Paragraph 7: 'Hence arguments are only as strong as the underlying evidence: arguments relying on questionable sources are, well, questionable.'

Paragraph 12: 'If the references are untrustworthy, changeable sources, the writer's work can only be seen as untrustworthy and changeable.'

He also uses a number of quotations to add authority to the points that he wants to make (see paragraph 9), and to add some stylistic 'colour' to his text (paragraph 13).

2. When to reference

Jonas uses evidence:

- when describing and discussing theories associated with particular writers (see the examples in paragraphs 5 and 11)
- when presenting an illustrative example (see the example in paragraph 6)
- in support of points made (see the examples in paragraphs 8, 11 and 13)
- to cite the source of quotations (see the examples in paragraphs 9, 12 and 13).

You may have noticed that Jonas includes two unreferenced quotes in paragraphs 9 and 13. However, as was mentioned in Chapter 4, if the quotation is by a well-known person, and is included to add stylistic 'colour', credibility, a way into an idea, or for general interest, the name of the source should be cited, but it does not need to be given a full reference entry. However, if in doubt, always supply a full reference.

3. Example of critical analysis

Critical analysis is about looking at a subject from a range of perspectives, and following or creating logical arguments. There is a choice of six directions you could take:

1. **agreeing** with a particular point of view, and giving good reasons to support it
2. **rejecting** a particular point of view, but again using reliable evidence to do this
3. **conceding** that an existing point of view has merits, but that it needs to be qualified in certain respects, and stating what these are
4. **proposing** a new point of view, or reformulating an existing one, backed with supporting evidence
5. **reconciling** two positions, which may seem at variance, by bringing new perspectives to bear on the topic
6. **connecting** or **synthesising** different ideas, so that new approaches and points of view can be advanced.

(Source: adapted from Taylor, 1989)

In the essay, we find examples of critical analysis that connect with the above items 1, 3 and 4.

We can find an example of **agreement** with a particular point of view in paragraph 5: 'Becker (1986) believes the construction of arguments is the most important function of referencing systems.'

Jonas then presents four reasons in support of this argument. But then, in the following paragraph, he **proposes** another fifth dimension to the discussion:

It is important for every academic writer to avoid this narrow-minded argumentation trap; academic works are not only about compiling existing arguments, but adding new perspectives, finding new arguments or new ways of combining existing knowledge. (Paragraph 6)

He comes back to this key point in paragraph 9, and reinforces the idea of combining knowledge for the greater good:

> The primary mission of science and other disciplines is not to promote individual achievements, but to establish a connected, collective and recognised body of knowledge.

In paragraph 12, Jonas writes:

> Referencing a work indicates that the writer finds the referenced material import-ant—hence references create 'academic clout' in an assignment. In the global aca-demic community a well-cited article will find more recognition.

He partially concedes the point, but then moves on to qualify it:

> However, this practice is not without its critics. Thody, for example, calls this the 'sycophantic' use of referencing—and it can certainly be used to 'flatter your mentors' (2006, p.186). And Thompson calls this 'ritualised obeisance to the reigning authorities' (2003, p.27). So the important issue here is not about selecting references for their expediency value, but for their enduring quality. (Paragraph 12)

Your own voice

We have seen in this chapter an example of how a student combined his own experi-ences with referenced evidence to engage with an essay question.

Our experiences are drawn from many sources and it can sometimes be difficult, if not impossible, to reference all that have influenced us. We cannot always remember where we read, heard or discussed a particular idea. And sometimes our statements in assignments may be a fusion of our own instincts or viewpoint and what someone else has written or said.

In an assignment tutors want evidence of your general ability to research a topic, develop ideas critically and correctly reference your sources when this is needed. And, in an otherwise well-referenced essay, most tutors will appreciate that the occasional unreferenced statement is a genuine attempt by you to express your ideas or interpret events in your own way.

Summary

- The main point of referencing is to support and identify the evidence you use in your assignments or course work.
- Citations are partial references indicating the source of evidence presented at that point in your text.
- Citations always link with the sources detailed in a list of 'References' or 'Bibliography'.

- Don't cite just to demonstrate your reading; use evidence selectively.
- Choose the most appropriate presenting verb to introduce your evidence—does the evidence 'suggest', 'prove', 'illustrate' etc. the point you are making?
- Be careful when paraphrasing. It is easy to drift into plagiarism, particularly if you do not cite the source, or copy the words of others without treating them as a quotation.
- It can help to highlight the main point, or points, in the extract you are paraphrasing and use this as a starting point for your own interpretation, in your own words.
- In science writing, referencing is the means of providing essential background information on previous research and connecting your own findings to this earlier research.
- In the more persuasive forms of academic writing, referencing is an important resource for giving credibility and support to your arguments.
- In particular, the *selection* of evidence is an important way of asserting your own voice and identity in an assignment.

Exercise results

Exercise: Where do you think the citations should go?

> Breast cancer represents 23 per cent of all female cancers, and it is by far the most frequent cancer among women in both the developed and developing world. Although mortality rates remain much less than incidence rates, breast cancer is also the most frequent cancer-related death in women **X (World Cancer Report, 2014).** Sex steroid hormones play a major role in the growth and development of the mammary gland, and a clear correlation between pathogenesis of breast cancer and cumulative exposure to oestrogens has been demonstrated **X (Hevir et al., 2011).**

This extract contains two types of information. The first two sentences present a general introduction to the topic, while the final sentence summarises the results of relevant research. The statistical information contained within the first two sentences needs to be referenced, so the citation is placed at the end of the second sentence. The source of the data is therefore clarified and the citation also creates a useful reading 'break' between both parts of the extract, which then become more obvious in their information differences.

Exercise: Which of the following is the most successful attempt at paraphrasing the extract? Comments:

Student 1

It has been argued that the main purpose of referencing is to facilitate the development of knowledge. This development process is driven by human communication and endeavour, and referencing is one part of this. It allows writers to separate their ideas from the work of others and helps other scholars trace the origins of ideas and thus build links across knowledge.

Comment: This includes a large proportion of the original words from the extract, so is a poor example of paraphrasing—and is also plagiarism (see Chapter 5), as no source is cited.

Student 2

The point of referencing is to 'to facilitate the collective development and transmission of academic knowledge' (Neville, 2012). He also says that 'development and transmission is powered by human endeavour and communication; referencing is one element in this communication process, and can allow writers to separate their ideas from the work of others'. Referencing also helps others to trace the origin of ideas, which helps to build knowledge.

Comment: Although the original source is cited, there is far too much use of direct quotation in this example, and very little attempt to summarise the original extract.

Students often resort to quoting directly from an extract if they are not sure what it means, or cannot think of other ways to rephrase it. But a deeper level of learning can come from thinking hard about a text and rephrasing it in your own words.

Student 3

Neville (2012) has argued that the main aim of referencing, which is a form of academic communication, is to help writers share knowledge in a way that separates out the ideas of one writer from another. Referencing also helps scholars to identify where ideas came from and how they have developed over time.

Comment: This is a good example of paraphrasing. The source has also been cited.

Student 4

Referencing is an essential part of academic writing because it assists the spread and communication of knowledge. It helps writers to separate their own points from those made by others, and it makes it easier to identify the originators of ideas and how these ideas have developed over time.

Comment: This is also a good attempt at paraphrasing, but the source is not cited, so it is another example of plagiarism. If you paraphrase the work of others, you must acknowledge the sources by citing them in your text, and referencing them in full at the end of your assignment. Failure to do this is plagiarism (see Chapter 5).

7 Referencing and the digital world

The internet and referencing · Referencing management software (advantages and disadvantages) · Text matching software · Choosing internet sources · Discriminating between sources · How to cite and reference a website

In the first and second editions of this book, the importance of note taking for recording sources was emphasised and some note-taking ideas were featured.

The need for note taking is no less important today, but many students now use smartphones to do the job. Free apps, such as Evernote and Pocket, can be downloaded and used for taking and making notes, recording lectures, taking screenshots, and sharing these with others. For students who still prefer paper-based ways of note taking, there are some excellent resources to be found on the *Learnhigher* website (look for 'Research Skills—notetaking') at http://www.learnhigher.ac.uk/research-skills/.

In 2014—the twenty-fifth anniversary of the World Wide Web—there were 2.4 billion users of the web worldwide, and in 2013, in Britain, 36 million adults (73 per cent) used the internet every day (gov.uk, 2014).

The second decade of the twenty-first century has also seen a phenomenal growth in hand-held internet-connected devices. In 2015 around 2 billion internet-connected smartphones were being used worldwide, with an estimated growth to nearly 3 billion by 2017 (Srivastava, 2014). In Britain alone, in 2013 nearly 90 per cent of young people were using a smartphone or tablet to go online—an increase of more than 100 per cent in just three years (gov.uk, 2014). The internet is a major source of information for students, although its easy accessibility makes it a tempting source of content to plagiarise (see Chapter 5).

In education, the creation and growth of educational digital technology and software to support teaching and learning is now a major export commodity for the UK. In 2014, educational technology (edtech) developed in Britain was worth £17.5 billion a year in a global edtech and e-learning market estimated to be worth more than £60 billion (Anderson, 2014). The growth of referencing management software (RMS) has been an important part of this market.

Referencing management software (RMS)

There have been rapid advances in the way students can digitally manage their referencing on and offline. In particular, the chore of formatting can be removed with the use of RMS. A few years ago students would normally have encountered RMS and used it only within their college or university. They still can and will, but now an increasing number of RMS packages are free to download and intuitive to use, with the result that increasing numbers of students are using this software both inside and outside their institutions to manage and reference information for their assignments.

Most universities provide RMS resources free for students to use within their premises or enable them to purchase the software themselves, often at a discounted price. The most commonly used RMS tools offered to students within UK universities at the time of writing were EndNote, RefWorks and Reference Manager software, but other RMS packages are widely available as free downloads for anyone to use. These include the intuitive Zotero and Mendeley packages, and for the more computer savvy, BibTex, used in association with LaTeX documents, to help organise references and create bibliographies. LaTeX is a typesetting program that converts plain text files to formatted documents; it is widely used for the preparation of dissertations with mathematical and foreign characters.

A free referencing app, RefMe, introduced in October 2014, had been downloaded by 500,000 people by the December of that year (Anderson, 2014). Its linkage to smartphones was a major element in its popularity, as these can be used to photograph a book or journal barcode, the data from which will produce a citation and formatted reference in a chosen referencing style. The app can also be used on any PC or tablet as a way of organising referencing lists and generating citations in any of the 6500 referencing styles on its database.

Advantages

A student in my 2009 referencing survey—very much in a minority at that time—wrote about the advantages of using referencing management software:

> Throughout the Masters and PhD I have used Endnote software to assist with organisation of references and this has transformed the way I work. I can input and access references throughout my work with ease, which has taken away the negative aspects I used to complain about.
>
> (Doctoral student: geography)

For students looking for straightforward help with citing and formatting lists of references, RMS tools are invaluable for saving time and taking the chore out of the citation and formatting side of referencing. RMS tools also allow you to build an electronic library of sources that can be subdivided into separate folders linked to particular assignment tasks. This bibliographic list can be used to draw up a list of references, which are quickly and easily imported into a Word document.

Features of RMS

Features common to RMS resources are:

- internet search for a wide range of online resources (books, journals, reports, articles etc.), and a facility for easily importing these into your own online research library
- a way of organising your references as you read, rather than leaving it until the last minute—RMS will help you find relevant evidence, then produce a citation and full reference entry for any source you decide to use in your work
- a citation in a chosen referencing style can be produced for any item in your library and these can be imported directly and easily into your assignment; most referencing styles, including those linked to particular journals and publishers, are available
- conversion of all resources imported into a full reference in a referencing style of your choice
- alphabetical sorting of sources in lists ready to be imported directly into a list of references in any assignment
- editing features, so you can make changes at any time to references already entered.

Some RMS tools can also offer:

- a 'cite while you write' facility
- social networking opportunities, and a chance to link up with other students researching the same subject
- the opportunity to make notes on PDF documents as you read them
- search facility across multiple resources
- a way of sharing resources with others—particularly useful if you are working on group projects.

There are a number of useful RMS comparison sites that you can visit to gain an overview of what the different RMS packages can offer the independent student, although most students are likely to take advantage of the RMS plus the training and support offered at their institutions.

A useful RMS comparison table can be found at the University of Oxford: the Oxford LibGuide Reference Management Comparison Table, available at http://ox.libguides.com (choose 'Managing your references', under 'Reference Management', on the left-hand side of the screen, then 'Comparison Tables' at the top of the screen).

Limitations

RMS does, however, have its limitations, and, arguably, no one package can offer all that students need for fully integrated information search and easy transfer of information into citations and full reference lists. A search for sources using RMS may not, for example, produce a comprehensive list of resources—some key books in your subject area may not be featured.

You may find, too, that a fine-tuning of the full reference entry produced by the RMS is needed before or after you import it into your assignment. For example, although you might choose Harvard referencing style, the RMS may produce an entry that does not completely match, in its formatting detail, the Harvard style expected by your institution (for reasons outlined in Chapters 8 and 9).

However, the main point of limitation about RMS is that it helps you only with the technical citation and formatting side of referencing. It does not help you to understand the principles underpinning referencing and the avoidance of plagiarism. And it cannot help you discriminate between one source and the next. If you are so inclined, your essay could still end up as a confused tangle of unsuitable sources; the RMS tool will just make the task easier for you. However, the tool will undoubtedly make your life easier if you do understand *why* you should reference, *when* you need to reference, and *what* evidence to select for inclusion in your assignment.

Text matching software

Another product of the rapid growth in educational technology and software over the past decade is text matching software, now used by many colleges and universities to detect and deter plagiarism, and as a teaching aid for helping students develop their referencing knowledge and skill.

Software, such as Turnitin, and Data Match can compare a text with a database of billions of web pages, and will highlight passages that have been copied in. This software can be introduced to students by institutions as a deterrent for detecting unreferenced copied text, although arguably the most effective use of it is when it is used for teaching purposes, supported by individual discussion with tutors (Davis and Carroll, 2009). In this situation, students, supported by tutors, typically check their assignments against the software to highlight and change copied areas, to help them identify issues with copying and referencing.

This approach seems to be producing some positive results. Cohen (2007), for example, found that trial use of Turnitin among Business and Economics students had encouraged them to use more of their own words in assignments, and had highlighted copied sections that needed to be cited and referenced.

McKie (2014) reported on the use of Turnitin to help students improve their academic writing, particularly paraphrasing. One student wrote:

> We used Turnitin with a sample of our written work. It was really good, because I could see the areas I had plagiarised in a different colour. The Study Advisor (leading the session) then explained about the importance of paraphrasing, i.e. putting text into your own words, and how this is a good way to avoid plagiarism.
>
> (McKie, 2014, p.9)

Bailey and Challen (2015) offered final-year undergraduate students the opportunity to check their projects against Turnitin. Those that did found it helpful to see what matching text was highlighted, and then to check why it was there. On most occasions it highlighted quotations that were properly supported by references. However, its use did generate some anxiety, as students wondered if it would highlight inadvertent plagiarism in their work, although most wished it had been introduced to them much earlier in their courses.

If you haven't heard about the text matching software used by your institution, ask your librarian or personal tutor about it, and particularly about the opportunity for checking an assignment against it before you submit it formally for marking. Work can be uploaded and a report is quickly generated, colour coded to highlight the degree of overlap between the text submitted and the database. A close match, for example, between text and database is coloured red, usually indicating direct copying, although this may not be plagiarism if the passage has been properly cited and referenced.

If you find you do have the opportunity to check your work against this software before submission for marking, it is best to do so in discussion with a tutor or learning support adviser, who will be able to advise about referencing or rewording any dubious sections of text.

Choosing internet sources

The web is a rich source of information for students. It is also, for many, their first choice. It can and does provide a useful starting point for ideas and the pursuit of ideas, so reliable internet sites can certainly be used, cited and referenced in assignments. How can you evaluate them?

The use of the digital object identifier (DOI) now to identify and track sources gives one indicator, at least, of their permanence. But there are other ways of checking sites. Drawing on the work of Munger and Campbell (2011) and Rumsey (2008), Table 7.1 presents questions, in regards to originator, site credibility, content and site design, that can be asked of all internet sites to help evaluate their credibility.

Table 7.1 Evaluating the credibility of websites

Ownership and aim	Content
Who is taking 'ownership' of the information presented? Is there a contact address, telephone number and email address?	Do your tutors or librarians recommend this site?
Why has this site been established—is it clear from the introduction?	Were you linked to this site from a reliable source?
Who is the sponsor of the site—who pays for it?	Is the information up to date? Is the site updated regularly?
Who is the intended readership for the site?	Are sources properly referenced? Does the site tell you where a particular theory, idea, statistic or other data has come from, i.e. its original source?
Are there any biases or possible hidden agendas in the site?	
Is it trying to sell you something? If so, *be cautious* of it.	Are the links provided working? (*A site that is not being updated should not be trusted.*)
Is it clear who is the originator or author for the item you want to cite? Does the author have any academic or professional affiliation?	What reasons for including the links shown are given?
	Does the site include advertising? If so, might this influence the objectivity of the material?
	Are there spelling and grammatical errors? (If there are, *beware.*)

How to reference a website

There are many examples of website referencing in Chapter 11, but here is the basic idea.

Citations

Never cite a URL or DOI in the text of your assignment unless it is absolutely necessary, e.g. when no other features identifying the source are shown. Instead, you should cite the name of the writer, if shown; use the pseudonym shown, if necessary. If the writer's name is not shown, cite the name of an organisation hosting the site.

Full reference

Generally, the following elements are listed in the order in which they appear in a full reference entry. However, there may be occasional exceptions to this rule. This may be because of particular referencing style guidelines, or because of the nature of the source or the context in which it is to be used in an assignment.

You can include:

- originator—this can be a named writer or, if there is no named writer, the person or organisation taking the main responsibility for the source; it can include the name of the website, e.g. Biz/ed
- year the information was published online
- title of the work viewed or downloaded
- name of publisher or type of online source if not obvious—for example, [blogpost]
- specific date the information was placed on the site, if shown
- online address, e.g. the URL or DOI
- name of database, if applicable
- other identifying features, if needed
- date you viewed or downloaded the information—say which; if you looked at the source online, you state when you 'accessed' or 'viewed' the information or, if you downloaded a file, you state 'downloaded' on the date in question.

The order in which these elements will appear will depend on the referencing style and type of source, but if you include all or most of this information you will not go far wrong.

Example (in Harvard style)

> **Citation**: (Kirk, 2014)
> **Reference:** Kirk, T. 2014. *Physics Study Guide*. Oxford University Press. Available at http://www.ebooks.com/1784809/physics-study-guide-2014/kirk-tim/ [downloaded 15 March 2015].

Summary

- Referencing management software (RMS) can support students with their referencing. It can save time by producing a correctly formatted list of references that can easily be imported into a document.
- RMS also helps students identify sources, build a library of resources and share them with others.
- However, it cannot help students choose which sources to use in assignments, and it cannot teach the principles that underpin referencing practice.
- Choosing credible internet sources to use in assignments is an important part of the referencing process.
- Text matching software is used by all institutions to detect and deter plagiarism, although it also makes an important contribution to the teaching of academic writing, including referencing.

Part  2

8 Referencing styles (introduction)

> *Referencing styles within UK higher education · Types of referencing style · Why so many referencing styles? · Is there referencing style confusion? · Student opinions*

All referencing styles are built on the same idea of citing evidence in the text of an assignment, either with a source name or number allocated to it. The name or number connects with the full source details in a footnote, endnote or reference list.

However, there are variations in the way sources are formatted, according to the referencing styles adopted by the institution.

There are many referencing styles—as mentioned in Chapter 7, RefMe referencing management software (RMS) features 6500—but this includes the styles required by academic journal and book publishers, who will all have their own referencing guidelines for authors (usually derived from one of the more common styles, e.g. Chicago, APA, Harvard). Fortunately, colleges and universities have adopted a smaller range of referencing styles, although arguably still over-large in number.

Referencing styles within Britain

There are an estimated 14 referencing styles found within colleges and universities in Britain and they fall into three main types, as outlined in Table 8.1. Although one institution might, in theory, host all 14 styles, typically a large university would host eight of these, spread across a wide range of subject areas.

Table 8.1 Referencing style types

In-text name/date styles	Consecutive numbering	Recurrent numbering
These styles cite the name(s) of author(s) or organisation(s) in the text with the year of publication (or page number for MLA style)	This style uses superscript numbers in the text that connect with notes and/or references in either footnotes or chapter/assignment endnotes (usually the former)	This style uses bracketed (or superscript) numbers in the text that connect with a list of notes and/or references at the end of the chapter/assignment

(Continued)

Table 8.1 *(continued)*

All sources are listed alphabetically at the end of an assignment and labelled 'References', 'Reference List', 'Work Cited, 'Works Consulted' or 'Bibliography', according to the style	**This system uses a different and consecutive number for each reference in the text** A list of sources is included at the end of the assignment, which lists all the works referred to in the notes ('References'; 'Works Cited') Some tutors may also require a list of all works consulted in preparation for the assignment (i.e. a 'Bibliography' or 'Works Consulted')	**The same number can recur, e.g. if a source is mentioned more than once in the text** Your tutors may also require you to include a bibliography, which could include additional sources consulted, but not directly referred to in the text

The three main types divide into specific styles, each with their own guidelines, as summarised in Table 8.2.

Table 8.2 Names of referencing styles

Name–date styles	Consecutive numbering	Recurrent numbering
• Name–date (Harvard) • APA • MLA • MHRA • Chicago • Council of Science Editors (CSE)	• British Standard BS690: (Running Notes) • MHRA • Chicago • Oxford: OSCOLA	• British Standard BS690: (Numeric) • Vancouver • IEEE • Council of Science Editors (CSE)

The Chicago and Council for Science Editors (CSE) styles are more commonly used in the USA, although can be found within UK institutions. These styles offer the choice between a name–date referencing style *or* a numbering style, although the two styles must not be mixed within an assignment. Similarly, while MHRA style is usually associated with a consecutive numbering approach, it also offers a name–date style alternative to users.

Why so many styles?

Referencing styles can become adopted because of recommendations from the librarian at the institution, or because of departmental affiliations to style guides produced by an organisation representing the interests of a professional group or discipline, for example APA.

Other reasons for the adoption of a particular style include departments imitating departments across institutions; an arbitrary past decision by someone in a department, probably now long gone; or because of an institutional or departmental decision to standardise practice.

Gibaldi has argued that the referencing styles adopted by institutions and departments can be shaped by the kinds of research and scholarship undertaken. He suggested that, in the sciences and business disciplines, the name–date referencing style, usually the Harvard style, is often used to give prominence to the year and general timeliness and currency of the research; whereas with the humanities it is often more important to guide the reader to exactly the right author and page, so a telling detail can more easily and speedily be found (Gibaldi, 2003, p.143).

Spot the difference

Although there are clearer differences in the way sources are cited in the text of an assignment, spotting the style differences between full reference entries, as shown in Table 8.3, can make an interesting party game! You try it. (I am using the British Standard guidelines for the version of Harvard seen in the example below—but more on this later.)

Table 8.3 Comparison of styles

Harvard	Pecorari, D. 2013. *Teaching to avoid plagiarism: how to promote good source use.* Maidenhead: Open University Press.
APA	Pecorari, D. (2013). *Teaching to avoid plagiarism: How to promote good source use.* Maidenhead: Open University Press.
MLA	Pecorari, Diane. *Teaching to Avoid Plagiarism: How to Promote Good Source Use.* Maidenhead: Open University Press, 2013. Print.
Vancouver	Pecorari D. Teaching to avoid plagiarism: how to promote good source use. Maidenhead: Open University Press; 2013.
MHRA	Pecorari, Diane, *Teaching to Avoid Plagiarism: How to Promote Good Source Use* (Maidenhead: Open University Press, 2013)
IEEE	D. Pecorari, *Teaching to Avoid Plagiarism: How to Promote Good Source Use.* Maidenhead: Open University Press, 2013.

A confusion of styles?

Is there a confusion of referencing styles within colleges and universities?

One in ten students in my research surveys made a particular point of mentioning this. Two students commented:

> I wish there weren't so many styles of referencing and [there were] one standard referencing style for all courses.
>
> (Undergraduate: applied sciences)

> It would be better if there were just one style throughout all academic disciplines, as it is really confusing.
>
> (Postgraduate: theology)

The issue was particularly significant for undergraduate students on combined studies courses who might encounter not only two or more referencing styles, but also differences in the ways styles were interpreted by their tutors:

> I am expected to use two different systems within my course. This can become somewhat confusing!
>
> (Undergraduate: communication studies)

> The different systems are confusing, and lecturers often have different preferences so that one essay may need to be referenced in one way, while another is almost completely different.
>
> (Undergraduate: classics and ancient history)

> Because my course is spread across many schools, they each have different ways that they like work referenced and they never specify which referencing style they want.
>
> (Undergraduate: environmental studies)

However, even within departments that had adopted one particular style, some students found that the way they had been taught or had learned referencing within an institution conflicted with what some tutors expected:

> When seeking guidance from lecturers each uses a variation of the business school's recognised system . . . the core [referencing] guide . . . goes against what your lecturers say.
>
> (Undergraduate: business management & IT)

> I also find that different tutors want you to reference in different ways, even though we are informed to use Harvard referencing.
>
> (Undergraduate: education)

> We are told to use the Harvard style of referencing and have had library seminars on this. However . . . tutors have said that the way I have done it is not correct. The way they say it should be done is different to how I've understood I'm supposed to do it.
>
> (Postgraduate: dental hygiene)

Student support advisers in higher education institutions are aware of the referencing style problems that students face. In a referencing style survey I organised in 2005, student support staff in UK institutions expressed their own concerns on this issue:

> Different lecturers recommend different styles of Harvard to their students; it is difficult to get consistency across schools, let alone the university!

> The non-Harvard system used in one of our faculties is described as MLA, but uses numbered notes.

> Students who take psychology and sociology modules, usually 1st and 2nd years, do get confused between the two systems (Harvard and APA) that they are asked to use. They are very similar but the psychologists get upset if their system (APA) is not used.
>
> (Quoted in Neville, 2007, p.45)

Since my 2005 survey, a number of UK universities—for example, Coventry, East London and Leeds—have introduced referencing policies to limit the number of referencing styles within the institution and ensure that those that are promoted conform to particular referencing style guides, either produced internally or externally.

Because there is no definitive version of the Harvard referencing style (see the next chapter), Leeds and Coventry universities, for example, have produced their own customised versions of the Harvard referencing style, which all staff and students use as the official standard for courses adopting Harvard.

Pressure to change and limit the number of referencing styles within an institution of higher education often comes from staff in their libraries or learning support centres (see the example cited in Chapter 1). However, as suggested earlier, if students are concerned about the number of referencing styles they are encountering, they can make their views known to senior managers. This is best done collectively through their student union, who could ask management to explain the rationale for the styles adopted by departments, and if there has ever been any institutional review of referencing. The head of library and information services is likely to be the best first point of contact for individuals or groups of students concerned about this issue.

Summary

- There are an estimated 14 referencing styles to be found within higher education in Britain, although typically a large university would host around eight styles.
- They fall into three groups: in-text name–date styles (for example, Harvard style), and the footnote-related recurrent number and consecutive number styles.
- Students can find the range of styles they encounter confusing, particularly those on combined studies courses, who may have to learn how to apply two or more styles.
- Some institutions have limited the number of referencing styles and have produced their own definitive versions of Harvard style to avoid confusion.

Harvard and other name–date referencing styles

> Why 'Harvard'? · Harvard referencing: the basic idea · Pros and cons of using Harvard and other similar styles · Examples of Harvard referencing · APA style and examples · MLA style and examples · Chicago style and examples · MHRA style and examples · CSE style and examples

This chapter presents an overview of the main name–date referencing styles applied within UK further and higher institutions of education, particularly the Harvard style. It will present a brief overview, with comparative examples, of these styles. With the exception of Harvard, you are advised to consult the referencing guides mentioned later in the chapter for each of the styles introduced.

With the exception of Harvard, all other name–date referencing styles—for example, APA—have detailed manuals you can consult, so there seems little point in duplicating these here. (See also the frequently asked questions in Chapter 12 for questions often asked about Harvard and other name–date styles.)

Hurrah for Harvard!

Despite the apparent proliferation of referencing styles in higher education, and the difficulties this can cause to students (see Chapter 8), the Harvard style of referencing appears to be predominant across a range of both science and non-science disciplines in UK universities (Neville, 2007, p.43). A recent survey of courses at a university in the north of England (Pullinger and Schneider, 2014) found 74.5 per cent using Harvard, with 14 per cent using MHRA and the remainder using other styles.

Why 'Harvard'?

Does it originate from Harvard University in the USA? An article in the *British Medical Journal* (Chernin, 1988) suggests it emerged from a referencing practice developed by Edward Laurens Mark, a professor of anatomy and director of Harvard University's zoological laboratory, who in turn appears to have been inspired by a cataloguing system in the Library of Harvard's Museum of Comparative Zoology. However, another writer (Grafton, 1997, p.31) has identified an even earlier contender: a thirteenth-century example of in-text referencing!

Harvard referencing style: the basic idea

In Chapter 6, the way citations could be introduced into an assignment, and how sources are organised into a list at the end of the work, was illustrated. But just to remind you, the basic idea of the Harvard style is to:

- use citations (a partial reference) in the text of your assignment by citing a name and year of original publication of the source next to the evidence in question; the name is the last or family name of the author(s), or an organisational name
- list all references in full and in alphabetical order at the end of an assignment
- ensure that the name used in the citation connects with the name used to start the full reference entry.

Example

> **Citation:** (Carroll, 2007)
>
> **Reference:** Carroll, J. 2007. *A handbook for deterring plagiarism in higher education.* Oxford: Oxford Centre for Staff and Learning Development.

Pros and cons of the Harvard style

The **pros** are:

- most useful when all sources are printed, and these have one or more designated authors
- easy to follow the chronological progress of a particular debate
- for manual formatting, it is easy to add or subtract in-text citations and references
- relatively easy to learn; easy to teach
- familiar—recognisable from many book and journal articles
- no distraction from the text to look at footnotes or endnotes.

The **cons** are:

- useful when citing and referencing sources without authors and/or dates
- can be awkward for citing television, radio and other audio-visual sources
- long-winded for citing secondary sources
- in-text citations are normally counted in assignments on most degree courses, as the student takes 'ownership' of evidence cited; this can add significantly to the word count.

The biggest drawback of Harvard

The biggest drawback of Harvard, however, is that there is no definitive benchmark for this style, unlike the others featured in this chapter that have prescriptive referencing style guidebooks to assist writers. The nearest to a guidebook in Britain for the Harvard style can be found in a range of British Standard Institution (BSI) publications (1983–2010), the most recent of which is BS ISO 690:2010: *Information and documentation—Guidelines for bibliographic references and citations to information sources.*

But, as the BS document says, 'The examples used in the International Standard are not prescriptive as to style and punctuation' (BS/ISO 690:2010, p.1). The important thing, BS emphasises, is to be consistent.

This has resulted in a wide range of variants in the online and printed guides produced by institutions and within referencing management software (RMS).

Although most Harvard style guides, including within RMS software, conform to the way BS guides present the order of elements within a reference entry, you will find variations of formatting presentation from one version to the next. Pullinger and Schneider (2014) illustrated this in their conference presentation by asking, which one of these (see box) is the correct version of Harvard?

(a) Smith, A., Jones, R. and Edwards, J. (2014). How to reference. 2nd ed. Oxford: Oxford University Press.

(b) SMITH, A., R. JONES and J. EDWARDS. 2012. How to reference. 2nd ed. Oxford: Oxford University Press.

(c) Smith, A. et al. 2012. How to reference. 2nd ed. Oxford: Oxford University Press.

Source: Pullinger and Schneider (2014)

The answer is 'they are all correct', in that they can all be found as examples of Harvard style in referencing guides.

Harvard style in this book

As stated earlier, students need to follow their own institutional guidelines on the way Harvard style is presented in their assignments. In this book, in the full reference entries, I have adopted the version suggested by British Standard. The British Standard guideline version of Harvard shows the year of source publication without brackets, for the reasons given in Chapter 12, 'Frequently asked questions', question 16, and this interpretation has been the benchmark for the Harvard examples in this third edition.

However, most versions of Harvard copy the APA referencing style practice of enclosing the year of publication in round brackets. For example:

Murray, R. (2013). *Writing for academic journals.* Maidenhead: Open University Press.

This is most probably because the Harvard and APA styles are very similar—almost identical—in the way many sources are formatted, so that the more advisory British Standard Harvard style version has tended gradually over the years to hybridise with the prescriptive APA version.

Your list of references or bibliography

In the 'References' or 'Bibliography' section at the end of an assignment the basic format for listing references in the Harvard style is shown, as follows.

- All sources are listed in alphabetical order by last name or name of originator; and, as stated earlier, the citation connects with the alphabetical item in the reference.
- Where there is a named author, start with the surname/last name/family name. This is followed by the first name or initials of the first author. For subsequent authors, British Standard guidelines show the first name or initials preceding the family/last name. For example: Coleman, A. and A. Chiva, 1991. *Coping with change—focus on retirement.* London: Health Education Authority.
- Compound and hyphenated last names, such as Russell-Harris, should be alphabetised by the first part of the compound, e.g. Russell.
- Alphabetise the prefixes Mac, Mc and M' in that order: MacDougall, comes before McAllister, which comes before M'Cardy. For guidelines on referencing foreign names, see 'Frequently asked questions', Chapter 12, question 17.
- If the name of author is shown on the source specifically as 'Anon', this goes alphabetically into the list. If there is no author or originator's name shown, and 'Anon' is not presented in lieu of an author's name, a title for printed material can be substituted (the title will also be used in the citation). The first letter of the first proper title word can be the guide to placing it alphabetically in the list of references.
- If you are including several works by the same author, they are listed in chronological order, with the earliest work first. For example:

    Huws, U. 1993. *Teleworking in Britain: a report to the Employment Department.* Research Series No. 18, Oct. 1993. London: Department of Employment.

    Huws, U. 1996. *eWorking: an overview of the research.* London: Department of Trade and Industry.

    Huws, U. 1999. *Virtually there: the evolution of call centres.* London: Mitel Telecom Ltd.

- If you have references with the same first author, but different second and third authors, arrange these alphabetically in the reference list by the order of surnames of these following named authors.
- As stated earlier, if you do not have the name of an author, start with the name of the originator. This can be an organisation name, e.g. BBC, or the name of a website, e.g. HubPages.
- Author name is followed by the year of publication. With books, the year of publication should be easy to find: just look at the copyright page, which usually follows immediately after the main title page. All the information you need should be there, including name of publisher, where published, when first published and edition. Always show the edition number for the source you looked at—although the edition is different from the impression or reprinted number. Look for the year of the edition and ignore the impression number years. So, 'Seventh edition by Oak Knoll in 1995. Reprinted 1997, 1998, 2000, 2002' would be shown as 1995 in your reference—ignore the reprint years.
- However, in some older books the date of publication may be missing. In this event, put either (n.d.) or (no date). With internet sources, look for the year the item was

placed on the site (often to be found at the bottom of the home page) or, in the absence of this, the year when the site was last updated—or, if unsuccessful with either of these two, the year you looked at the information.

- This is followed by the title of the source, which is italicised (or underlined if you are not using a word processor). The main source would be, for example, the title of a book, name of the magazine, journal or newspaper, item title from an internet site, broadcast production source, title of video or CD-ROM etc.
- If your source is a chapter from an edited book, you then give the name or names of the editors of the book, followed by the title of the edited book, underlined or in italics. The initials or first name(s) of the editor(s) should precede the last name(s) (see the example in 'Chapter from an edited book' that follows).
- With book references, you give details of the publisher. You first give the name of the town or city where the source was published, followed by the name of the publisher.
- In the case of a journal article, you finish with the reference details of volume, edition/issue number (if shown) of the journal and the page number(s) of where the article can be located within the journal.

Examples of the Harvard style of referencing

Printed book (one or more authors)

- Start your full reference with the last name of the author(s) so it connects with the citation; then give the initials or first name(s) of the author(s).
- Year of publication comes next.
- Next, give the title of book, in italics.
- Finally, give the place of publication and name of publisher.

Example:

> **Citation:** (Wilmore, 2000)
>
> **Reference:** Wilmore, G.T.D. 2000. *Alien plants of Yorkshire.* Kendall: Yorkshire Naturalists' Union.

Chapter from an edited book

- Start the full reference entry with the last name of the chapter's author, followed by initials, then state year of publication.
- Then give name(s) of editor(s). To distinguish editor(s) from the name of the writer of the chapter, indicate a single editor by the abbreviation (ed.) or two or more editors by (eds.).
- State full title of book, in italics. It is helpful to then give a chapter number.
- Finally, give place of publication and name of publisher.

Example:

> **Citation:** (Nicholls, 2002)
> (Cite the name of the writer of the chapter or section in the edited book.)
>
> **Reference:** Nicholls, G. 2002. Mentoring: the art of teaching and learning. In: P. Jarvis (ed.) *The theory and practice of teaching*, chap. 12. London: Kogan Page.

Referencing journal articles

- Start with the name(s) of author(s) in the way illustrated in the box that follows.
- Then, year of publication.
- Title of article (this can be in inverted commas if you wish).
- Name of the journal or magazine (in italics).
- Volume number and part number (if applicable), and page numbers. The volume number can be in bold.

References to journal articles do not include the name of the publisher or place of publication, unless there is more than one journal with the same title, e.g. *International Affairs* (Moscow) and *International Affairs* (London).

Example:

> **Citation:** (Bosworth and Yang, 2000).
>
> **Reference:** Bosworth, D. and D. Yang, 2000. 'Intellectual property law, technology flow and licensing opportunities in China'. *International Business Review*, 9(4), pp.453–477.

Example of referencing a web source

- Never cite a full URL address in the text of your assignment—always cite the name of someone, or an organisational name/name of the website.
- Start with name of author, if shown.
- If no individual named author is shown, give the organisational name or name of the website.
- Give the year the article was written or last updated, if shown. If not shown, give the year you viewed the item, but think about whether you should be using an undated website as a source (see Chapter 7).
- Show the full URL/DOI address.
- Give the full date when you viewed the site [in square brackets].

Example:

> Khan, J. 'Chief Executive's Introduction', *Barnardo's Annual Review and Accounts*, 2014, p.5. Available at http://www.barnardos.org.uk/what_we_do/who_we_are/corporate_information.htm [viewed 27 March 2015].

American Psychological Association (APA) referencing style

Many psychology departments, and psychology-related courses, in the UK require that referencing in assignments be prepared according to American Psychological Association (APA) style. This section will give you basic information on the APA style. However, for more detailed guidance, and additional examples, you should consult the APA publications *Concise Rules of APA Style, APA Style Guide to Electronic References* or the latest edition of the APA *Publication Manual*. The APA referencing style pages of its website can be found at www.apastyle.org/index.aspx.

Examples of APA referencing

As with the Harvard style, 'citation' in the APA style means a partial reference in the main body of the assignment; 'reference' means the full source details in a list of references at the end of an assignment.

There are often only small differences between APA and Harvard styles, with the most noticeable being in relation to the wording of web sources.

- Note the way the second and subsequent lines of APA references are always indented by five character spaces.

Book (one or more authors)

Citation: (Murray, 2005)
Reference: Murray, R. (2005). *Writing for academic journals*. Maidenhead: Open University Press.

- Note how a stop follows after the year in the full reference, which is always presented in brackets.
- See also 'Frequently asked questions', Chapter 12, question 7, for citing and referencing multiple authors within APA style.

Chapter from an edited book

Citation: (Nicholls & Jarvis, 2002)
Reference: Nicholls, G. & Jarvis, P. (2002). Teaching, learning—the changing landscape. In P. Jarvis (Ed.) *The theory & practice of teaching*. London: Kogan Page.

- Note the use of the word 'In' preceding the name of the editor(s) and title of the edited book.
- (Ed.) = editor; use a capital E.

Referencing journal articles

Citation: (Torrance, Thomas & Robinson, 1993)

Reference: Torrance, M., Thomas, M. & Robinson, E.J. (1993). Training in thesis writing: An evaluation of three conceptual orientations. *British Journal of Educational Psychology*, 61, 170–84.

- The main source, in this case the name of the journal, is always italicised, as is the volume number.
- Present the volume number and edition in numerical form only. Do not use the abbreviation 'vol.' before the number.
- Use commas after the title and volume number.

Referencing web sources

- Note the use of the term 'retrieved (date) from', preceding the web address.
- Use the year shown for the last updating of the site, and the date you visited the site and retrieved the information.

Citation: JISC Info Net (2014)

Reference: JISC Info Net (2014). *Developing digital literacies*. Retrieved March 5, 2015 from http://www.jiscinfonet.ac.uk/infokits/digital-literacies/

See more comparative examples of APA style later in this chapter.

Modern Language Association of America (MLA) style of referencing

The Modern Language Association of America (MLA) was founded in 1883 at a time when modern languages were beginning to be established in the curriculum alongside classical languages. This referencing style is still widely used in Britain on language and related studies degree courses. The MLA has developed its own style of referencing and this is outlined in its guide, the *MLA Handbook for Writers of Research Papers* (at the time of writing, this book was in its seventh edition). Although this referencing style also cites the name of the author or originator in the text, it differs from Harvard and APA in the following ways.

Citations

- Although the author(s) name(s) are shown in the text, this is followed by **page number(s)** (instead of year of publication), e.g. (Handy 149) with no punctuation between author's name and page number(s). Where no page number is available, just give the author's name.

- If two authors have the same name, you can add initials to distinguish between them in the text, e.g. (K. Smith 53).
- When summarising an author's ideas made over a number of different pages, this can be done within brackets, as follows (Handy 29, 67, 113).
- If you cite two or more works by the same author, you can include a full, shortened or abbreviated title, depending on its length, e.g. (Handy, Beyond Certainty 44–45), or refer to the specific title in the text of your assignment, e.g. Handy, in 'Beyond Certainty', asserts that . . . (44).

References (or Works Cited)

- The full list of references at the end of the text is also labelled and presented in a different way to Harvard and APA. It is labelled **Works Cited** (equivalent to 'References'), or **Works Consulted** (equivalent to 'Bibliography'), and the second and subsequent lines of a full reference entry are indented by five spaces (a hanging indent), with double spacing between lines.
- Sources in Works Cited are listed alphabetically, but with regards to Works Consulted, MLA allows for either one list of sources in alphabetical order *or* sources divided into sections and items alphabetised in each. For example, a Works Consulted list might be divided into primary and secondary sources, or arranged by subject matter, or different types of source, e.g. books, journals, websites.
- The last name of a single author, or lead author, is followed by his or her full first name(s), and not just the initial letters of these. However, this is reversed if two or three authors are listed. With second and third authors, the first names precede the last; see two source examples below:

Gibaldi, Joseph. *MLA Handbook for Writers of Research Papers*, Sixth Edition. New York: MLA, 2003. Print.

Loach, Ken. (Director) and Sally Hibbin (Producer). *Raining Stones*. London: Channel Four Television (FilmFour), 1993. DVD.

- If the first name of the writer is not shown on the title pages of books or other sources, then just their initials can be used instead. For example, some writers use only their initials, e.g. A.J. Cronin, T.S. Eliot. However, the MLA handbook suggests that you may include first names if you feel the additional information would be helpful. This is done in the following way:

Rowling, J[oanne] K[athleen];

As the example shows, the remainder of name is enclosed in square brackets.

- In the source title, the first word, nouns, verbs and adjectives are capitalised. The first word after a colon in the title is capitalised. Titles are italicised.

- The publisher's name can be shortened, e.g. W.W. Norton can be shortened to Norton. If the publisher's name is commonly abbreviated, or the abbreviations are likely to be familiar to the readership, they can be used instead of the full title, e.g. MLA, BBC.

The year of publication is featured towards the end of the full reference, usually followed by page numbers and essential additional bibliographic information—for example, supplementary information about a multi-volume work, such as number of volumes and the dates between which the volumes were published. Note that the type of source is also included at the end of the reference, e.g. 'Print', 'Web', 'CD', 'LP', 'Film', 'Television'.

Example:

> Durant, Will, and Ariel Durant. *The Age of Voltaire*. New York: Simon, 1965. Vol. 9 *The Story of Civilisation*. 11 vols. 1935–75. Print.

More examples of MLA style references

Referencing a chapter from an edited book

> **Citation:** (Segalen 51)
>
> **Works Cited:** Segalen, Martine. "The Household at Work". *The Experience of Work*. Ed. Craig Littler. Aldershot: Gower, 1985. 50–71. Print.

The title of the chapter is placed within double inverted commas; 'Ed.' is an abbreviation for 'Editor'; the reference ends with details of page numbers of the chapter in the book, and the medium, e.g. 'Print'.

Referencing an article in a journal

> **Citation:** (Murray 229)
>
> **Works Cited:** Murray, Rowena. 'Writing Development for Lecturers Moving from Further to Higher Education". *Journal of Further and Higher Education*, 26.3 (2002): 229–39. Print.

The numbers refer to **volume** 26 of the journal, and **issue** 3. The year is enclosed in brackets for a scholarly journal, the page numbers are shown, and 'Print' indicates the nature of the source.

Web sources

The seventh edition of the *MLA Handbook for Writers of Research Papers* advises that URLs are no longer required in full reference entries because using search engines for titles and authors' names can be just as productive. URLs should be given only if a normal web search is unlikely to locate the source. If a URL is included it should be enclosed in angled brackets, following the date of access, a stop, and a space; see examples below.

Web source (URL not included)

> **Citation:** (GovUK)
>
> **Cited Works:** Gov.UK. *Government Digital Inclusion Strategy*. London: UK Government Digital Service, 2014. Web.

Web source with URL

> **Citation:** (Anderson)
>
> **Cited Works:** Anderson, Elizabeth. 'New App Means Students Can Create Essay Footnotes and References in Seconds.' *Telegraph* 2 Dec. 2014. Web. 5 Mar. 2015. <http://www.telegraph.co.uk/finance/businessclub/technology/11266263/New-app-means-students-can-create-essay-footnotes-and-references-in-seconds.html>.

The Chicago (reference list) style

The benchmark for this referencing style, which is more commonly used in the USA than in Britain, is the current edition of *The Chicago Manual of Style*. While the Chicago style is normally associated with in-text number and footnote referencing, it does provide an in-text author-name option, which is often used in the physical, natural and social sciences.

Citations

As with the name–date Harvard and APA styles, you give a shortened reference in the text of your work with the last name of the writer(s), or organisational name (or abbreviation), plus year and, if necessary, page number(s), e.g. (Goman 1989, 59), or (Fairbairn and Fairbairn 2001), or (MLA 2009).

If a source has one to three authors, mention their last names in the citation. For four or more names, list the first name with et al., which replaces the others, e.g. (Brown et al. 2009).

References

At the end of the text, you include a 'Reference List' of all your sources, listed in alphabetical order. So the three citation examples shown above would be listed thus:

Fairbairn, Gavin and Susan Fairbairn. 2001. *Reading at university: A guide for students.* Maidenhead: Open University Press.

Goman, Carol Kinsey. 1989. *Creative thinking in business: A practical guide.* London: Kogan Page.

MLA: Modern Language Association of America. 2009. *MLA handbook for writers of research papers.* New York: MLA.

- Use the full name(s) of the author(s)/organisation. With the first author, start with his or her surname, followed by first name; for subsequent authors, list their first name(s) first (see the Fairbairn and Fairbairn example above).
- The year of publication follows the author(s) name(s), but is not placed in brackets.
- The book title is shown in italics.
- List *all* the author names in the full reference, regardless of how many there are.
- The second and subsequent lines of the full reference are indented (five character spaces).
- Capitalise the first letter of the first word, any proper noun, major word and first letter of the first word of any subtitle.

Other Chicago (reference list) style examples

Journals (two examples)

Murray, Rowena. 2002. Writing development for lecturers moving from further to higher education. *Journal of Further and Higher Education* 26, no. 3: 229–39.

Bosworth, David and Deli Yang. 2000. Intellectual property law, technology flow and licensing opportunities in China. *International Business Review* 9, no.4: 453–477.

- As with book titles, start with first author's surname, followed by first name, but for subsequent authors, list their first name(s) first, as shown in the second example above.
- Capitalise all the words of the journal title, which should be shown in italics. For article titles, capitalise the first and last letter of the first word, any proper noun, major word and the first letter of the first word of any subtitle.

Internet sources

E-Logistics 2003. *Call centres—an inexorable flight?* <http://www.elogmag.com/magazine/29/call-centres.shtml> (Accessed March 20, 2015).

- Start with named author(s), if shown; if not, start with name of website.
- Show title of item in italics.

- Show URL in full—to take reader straight to the screen in question. Enclose the URL within angled brackets.
- Give date of access to the information: month, day, year.

MHRA referencing style

The Modern Humanities Research Association (MHRA) is normally associated with the numerical-footnotes style of referencing (see the next chapter), and most students would use this numerical-footnote style for their assignments.

However, the 'author–date system', as it is called by MHRA, is also permitted for referencing purposes. For more information, consult the latest edition of the MHRA style guide, *A Handbook for Authors, Editors and Writers of Theses*, but what follows is a summary of the main points regarding MHRA (author–date) referencing.

MHRA in-text citations

The name(s) of authors, year of publication, and, if relevant, page number is located at an appropriate place in the text, e.g. 'It has been argued (Brown, 2008) that . . .

If you use the author's name in the sentence to introduce the evidence, you do not need to include it again in the citation brackets, e.g. 'Brown has argued that . . . (2008: 201)'.

MHRA references

Like other styles, MHRA requires an alphabetical list of references to be placed at the end of a text. The format recommended by MHRA, using three books as examples, is as follows:

> Murray, N. and G. Hughes. 2008. *Writing Up Your University Assignments and Research Projects: A Practical Handbook*. (Maidenhead: Open University Press)
>
> Moore, Sarah and others. 2010. *The Ultimate Study Skills Handbook*. (Maidenhead: Open University Press)
>
> Sinclair, Christine. 2007. *Grammar. A Friendly Approach*. (Maidenhead: Open University Press)

- The names of up to three authors should be given in full. If there are more than three names, show the first, followed by 'and others' (see example above).
- The title should be used as shown on the title page, unless it is very long, in which case it can be abbreviated; use a colon to separate main title from any subtitle.
- Capitalise the first word of the title, then all principal words, including first word in a subtitle or after a colon.
- If a list includes more than one work published by an author, a long dash is substituted for second and subsequent entries, e.g.

Hampden-Turner, C. 1990. *Corporate Culture.* (London: Hutchinson)
_____ 1990. *The Seven Cultures of Capitalism.* (London: Piatkus Books)

Note the following

- The full reference starts with the last name of the author, followed by the initial letter(s) of their first or personal names; this order is reversed for second and subsequent authors. (The MHRA style also allows for the full first name of an author to be used instead of initials, if preferred by the writer—or required by a tutor.)
- Title in italics and the use of capital letters in title for all proper words.
- Location: town/city of publisher and name of publisher in brackets.
- No full stop at the end of the reference.

Journals

> Murray, R. 2002. 'Writing development for lecturers moving from Further to Higher Education', *Journal of Further and Higher Education*, 26 (3): 229–39

- The title of the journal should be italicised.
- The title of the article is set within inverted commas.
- Use numbers only to indicate volume and item of the journal. The example shown above gives the volume number, 26, and the item and page numbers, (3): 229–39, respectively.

Website

- The main source item cited is italicised.
- The website address is shown within angled brackets.

> *The Mary Webb Society* <http://www.marywebbsociety.co.uk/> [accessed 8 March 2015]

Council of Science Editors (CSE) referencing style

Some UK university science departments have adopted the Council of Science Editors (CSE) style, although it is more commonly used within the USA. Guidelines for referencing are shown in *Scientific Style and Format: The CSE Manual for Authors, Editors and Publishers*. The CSE style guide offers writers the choice of using either a name–date or recurrent number style of referencing. As with other name–date styles, the author(s) names(s) and year of origin are cited in round brackets in the main text, e.g. (Brown 2008). The sources cited are listed alphabetically in a listed headed 'Works Cited' at the end of the text.

Example:

Citation: (Pines 1997)

Works Cited: Pines J. 1997. Localization of cell cycle regulators by immuno-
fluorescence. In: Dunphy W. vol. ed. Methods in enzymology. vol. 283:
Cell cycle control. New York: Academic Press. p.109.

- Only the first word of book and article titles, along with their subtitles and proper nouns, are capitalised.
- Titles are not italicised.
- No commas are used to separate the author's last name from the initial(s) of his or her first name.
- Use full stops to separate the elements of a source.
- Indent the second and subsequent lines of a Works Cited entry.

Comparison of name–date styles

The examples in the tables that follow illustrate the differences between several different name–date referencing styles.

Table 9.1 Book: single author	
Harvard	Schumacher, E. F. 2000. *Small is beautiful: Economics as if people mattered, 25 years later . . . with commentaries*. USA: Hartley and Marks Publishers.
APA	Schumacher, E. F. (2000). *Small is beautiful: Economics as if people mattered, 25 years later . . . with commentaries*. USA: Hartley and Marks Publishers.
Chicago	Schumacher, E F. 2000. *Small is Beautiful: Economics as if People Mattered, 25 Years Later. . . with Commentaries*. USA: Hartley and Marks Publishers.
MLA	Schumacher, E F. *Small is Beautiful: Economics as if People Mattered, 25 Years Later . . . with Commentaries*. USA: Hartley and Marks Publishers, 2000. Print.
MHRA	Schumacher, E F, *Small is Beautiful: Economics as if People Mattered, 25 Years Later . . . with Commentaries* (USA: Hartley and Marks Publishers, 2000)
CSE	Schumacher E F. 2000. Small is beautiful: economics as if people mattered, 25 years later . . . with commentaries. USA: Hartley and Marks Publishers.

Table 9.2 Chapter from an edited book

Harvard	Smith, A.1979. 'Early ideas of work and the economy': In A. Clayre (ed.) *Nature an industrialization*. Oxford: Oxford University Press/Open University Press.
APA	Smith, A. (1979). Early ideas of work and the economy. In A. Clayre (Ed.), *Nature and Industrialization*. Oxford: Oxford University Press/Open University Press.
Chicago	Smith, A. (1979). Early Ideas of Work and the Economy. In A. Clayre (Ed.), *Nature and Industrialization*. Oxford: Oxford University Press/Open University Press.
MLA	Smith, Adam. 1979. "Early Ideas of Work and the Economy". In *Nature and Industrialization*, edited by Alasdair Clayre. Oxford: Oxford University Press/Open University Press. Print.
MHRA	Smith, Adam, 'Early Ideas of Work and the Economy', in *Nature and Industrialization*, ed. by Alasdair Clayre (Oxford: Oxford University Press/ Open University Press, 1979)
CSE	Smith A. 1979. Early ideas of work and the economy. In: Clayre A, editor. Nature and industrialization. Oxford: Oxford University Press/Open University Press.

Table 9.3 Journal article

Harvard	Parikh, R. M. 2014. 'Survey of engineering students' use of internet', *International Journal of Information Communication Technologies and Human Development*, 6 (2), pp. 45–55.
APA	Parikh, R. M. (2014). Survey of engineering students' use of internet. *International Journal of Information Communication Technologies and Human Development*, 6 (2), 45–55.
Chicago	Parikh, R. M. (2014). Survey of Engineering Students' Use of Internet. *International Journal of Information Communication Technologies and Human Development*, 6 (2), 45–55.
MLA	Parikh, Radha M. 'Survey of Engineering Students' Use of Internet'. *International Journal of Information Communication Technologies and Human Development* 6.2 (2014): 45–55. Web.
MHRA	Parikh, Radha M., 'Survey of Engineering Students' Use of Internet', *International Journal of Information Communication Technologies and Human Development*, 6 (2014), 45–55
CSE	Parikh RM. 2014. Survey of engineering students' use of internet. IJICTHD 6:45–55.

Note: Journal titles are generally abbreviated within the CSE style. You can gain access to a list of journal abbreviations through the Web of Science website.

Table 9.4 Website—using a DOI to locate the source

Harvard	Hutchings, C. 2013. Referencing and identity, voice and agency: adult learners' transformations within literacy practices. *Higher Education Research & Development*, 33 (2), 312–324. DOI:10.1080/07294360.2013.832159
APA	Hutchings, C. (2013) 'Referencing and identity, voice and agency: adult learners' transformations within literacy practices', *Higher Education Research & Development*, 33 (2), pp. 312–324. DOI: 10.1080/07294360.2013.832159
Chicago	Hutchings, Catherine. 2013. 'Referencing and Identity, Voice and Agency: Adult Learners' Transformations within Literacy Practices'. *Higher Education Research & Development* 33 (2): 312–24. DOI:10.1080/07294360.2013.832159
MLA	Hutchings, Catherine. 2013. 'Referencing and Identity, Voice and Agency: Adult Learners' Transformations within Literacy Practices'. *Higher Education Research & Development* 33 (2): 312–24. DOI:10.1080/07294360.2013.832159
MHRA	Hutchings, Catherine. 'Referencing and Identity, Voice and Agency: Adult Learners' Transformations within Literacy Practices'. *Higher Education Research & Development* 33.2 (2013): 312–324. Web.
CSE	Hutchings, Catherine. 'Referencing and identity, voice and agency: adult learners' transformations within literacy practices'. HERD 33 (2013). 312–24. <http://dx.DOI.org/10.1080/07294360.2013.832159>

Note: When using DOI links to sources, it is not necessary to state the date the information was 'viewed', 'accessed' or 'retrieved' from the web, as is the case when referencing URLs. This is because DOI links offer a consistent way of tracing and retrieving web sources, unlike the URL links that can often disappear, particularly those linked to more ephemeral items.

10 Numerical referencing styles

Consecutive and recurrent number referencing styles · Examples of consecutive numbering styles: British Standard; MHRA; Chicago; OSCOLA · Pros and cons of consecutive numbering styles · Abbreviations · Footnote referencing: example · Introduction to recurrent referencing styles: British Standard; Vancouver; IEEE; CSE · Examples of recurrent referencing styles

Introduction

In Britain there are two main types of numerical referencing style: consecutive and recurrent (see Table 10.1).

Table 10.1 Numerical referencing styles

Consecutive	Recurrent
These styles link consecutive numbers in the text to footnotes or end-of-chapter notes; it is sometimes referred to as the 'running notes' style or system	These styles feature a number linked to a particular source, sometimes referred to as the 'numeric' style or system; it is called a 'recurrent' style as the same number can recur in the text if the source is used more than once

More detail on these referencing types

Consecutive numbering style

The consecutive numbering style of referencing uses a superscript (or bracketed) number in the text—for example, in superscript: [1] for the first source, [2] for the second source, and so on.

This style uses a different number for each source in the text each time it is cited.

These numbers connect with citations at the bottom of the page, in footnotes, or at the end of the assignment, headed 'Endnotes' or 'Notes' depending on the referencing style. The full reference details of sources are shown against the numbers in the numerical order they appear in an assignment.

A full list of sources, in alphabetical order, either titled 'Bibliography' or 'References' (or 'Works Cited'), according to the referencing style (or instructions of a tutor) normally appears at the end of the assignment, as this is a way of bringing together all the sources referred to in the text.

The British Standard BS ISO 690:2010 (Annex A) offers a summary guide to how this style should generally be presented. British universities have often used British Standard recommendations to produce their own institutional guides to numerical referencing, usually for the benefit of departments that have not affiliated to another specific referencing style featured in this chapter. These specific referencing styles can be summarised as follows.

The Modern Humanities Research Association (MHRA)

The Modern Humanities Research Association (MHRA) guidelines are often adopted by arts and humanities departments as a benchmark for writing style and referencing in disciplines such as English Literature, and other language and culturally related studies. Students who are asked specifically to follow MHRA style guidelines should consult the MHRA style guide, *A Handbook for Authors, Editors and Writers of Theses* (2013), or the MHRA referencing guide produced by the institution. Footnotes or endnotes can be used (be guided by your institution on which is preferred).

The Chicago style

The Chicago style of footnote referencing is widely used in the USA, and increasingly within Britain, too, as more publishers and university departments adopt it as their preferred referencing style. For detailed information, use the latest edition of the University of Chicago book or website:

- book—*The Chicago Manual of Style: The Essential Guide for Writers, Editors and Publishers* (2010)
- website—http://www.chicagomanualofstyle.org/tools_citationguide.html.

OSCOLA

Students on law degree or related courses will learn a referencing style that is particular to this subject, which is usually the Oxford Standard for Citation of Legal Authorities (OSCOLA). This is the style used by the *Oxford University Commonwealth Law Journal*, which contributed to its development. Examples of legal referencing will be shown later in this book: see Chapter 11 (section 16, 'Legal sources').

More information, and a pdf document on the OSCOLA style, can be found at the following website: Oxford Standard for Citation of Legal Authorities at http://denning.law.ox.ac.uk/published/oscola.shtml.

Pros and cons of the consecutive number styles of referencing

The pros

There is a long tradition of using footnotes in essays, which, arguably, imparts an air of authority and credibility to the evidence presented (Grafton, 1997).

The advantage of this referencing style is that it can be used for both authorial notes and to cite sources. Page numbers can be included in these footnotes or endnotes, so the text of your assignment remains uncluttered with source names, dates and page numbers. It is also particularly useful for referencing secondary sources, as details of both secondary and primary source can be given in the notes rather than in the text.

The reader can also immediately identify the source on the same page it is mentioned without having to turn to the References or Bibliography. Grafton (1997) argues that the use of footnotes enables writers 'to make their texts not monologues, but conversations, in which modern scholars, their predecessors, and the subjects all take part' (p.226). They serve, therefore, as an opportunity for the writer to add authorial comments away from the main text.

The cons

In mechanical terms, the main disadvantage of the style is that it can be awkward for a student to manually format last-minute additions and changes, although referencing management software has virtually eliminated the problems this once caused—another good reason to use it (see Chapter 7).

Some readers also find footnotes distracting from the text. Grafton (citing Hilbert, 1989) quotes Noël Coward in his remark that, 'Having to read a footnote resembles having to go downstairs to answer the door in the midst of making love' (Grafton, 1997, p.70, fn.16).

Students also need to take care when placing numbers in the text, to ensure it is clear to the reader what sources are referred to.

Guidelines for consecutive number styles of referencing

The following extract from an essay demonstrates the consecutive number style of referencing, following British Standard recommendations, and how it is particularly useful for dealing with secondary sources. The numbers in the text are linked to the footnotes at the foot of each page, as shown here.

Extract

This willingness to listen, negotiate, and respond to adult learners is, however, more related to empathy, than 'charisma', a term used by Jarvis[1] to describe the characteristics of inspirational teachers. However, the use of this term: 'charisma', because of the connotations of magnetism or aura that flow from it, may be an attribute hard for many teachers to attain. Empathy with the learner, on the other hand, is attainable by the majority of teachers and in the longer term is, arguably, more durable and appreciated by a wider range of students.

---

[1]Jarvis, P. Teaching styles and teaching methods. In P. Jarvis (Ed.) *The theory & practice of teaching.* London: Kogan Page, 2002, pp.22–30.

As emphasised earlier, empathy involves listening, negotiation, treating others equally and attempting to equalise the power relationship that can exist between teachers and students. It also requires teachers to be honest with students and to give something of themselves to their students. They need to give this essence of self, paradoxically, in both a humble and bold way. Richard Hoggart asserts that all teachers should be wary of charismatic 'show off' displays, and compares the approach to a 'Pied Piper of Hamelin' teaching style. He points out that shiny-eyed devotion from a class, because of peacock teaching styles, can be addictive for the teacher. But this could also be perceived as an abuse of power, particularly when vulnerable and suggestible adults are involved. He encourages tutors to strive toward assisting students to stand on their own feet and '*be critical or . . . ironic about us and towards us.*'[2]

As stated earlier, at the end of the essay you would prepare either a Bibliography— which is an alphabetical list of all the works referred to in your notes, as well as other works you consulted in preparation for the assignment—or a list headed 'References' or 'Works Cited' (for the Chicago style), which is an alphabetical list of all the evidence cited in the text.

Abbreviations

This referencing style uses a different number for each source in the text. So the same source used in an assignment at a number of different points will have more than one number allocated to it. Therefore, to save you having to keep repeating the same full reference information in your footnotes or endnotes, abbreviations are used to link the references, as shown below.

- **ibid.**   (*ibidem*) Meaning: in the same book, chapter, passage etc. and in the *previous* reference. If used, you should always give the relevant page numbers.

- **op. cit.**   (*opere citato*) Meaning: in the work quoted. This is used for a further reference to a source previously cited, but *not the one immediately preceding it.* If you use it, give some means of identifying the previous reference, such as author's name and date of publication, and give a page number.

- **loc. cit.**   (*loco citato*) Meaning: in the same place in a work previously cited, i.e. a reference to the same work, the same volume or same page. Loc. cit. is used in place of ibid. when the reference is not only to the work immediately preceding, but also refers to the *same page*. Loc. cit. is also used instead of op. cit. when reference is made to a work previously cited, and to the *same page* in that work.

---

[2]Hoggart, R. The role of the teacher. Originally published in J. Rogers (Ed.), Teaching on equal terms, BBC Publications, 1969, and cited in Rogers, J. *Adults learning.* 3rd edition. Milton Keynes: Open University Press, 1989, p.81.

*Examples of these abbreviations and how they might appear
in a bibliography*

1. Ali, L. and S. Graham. *The counselling approach to careers guidance*. S. Lendrum (ed.). London: Routledge, 1996.
2. Parsloe, E. and M. Wray. *Coaching and mentoring*. London: Kogan Page, 2000.
3. ibid. p.71.
4. Ali, L. and S. Graham. op. cit. p.85.
5. Parsloe, E. and M. Wray. loc. cit.

Some source examples

With both the MHRA and Chicago styles, there are differences between the way the source is shown in the footnote or endnote and the way it is presented in the Bibliography. The following examples illustrate the differences between British Standard consecutive number, MHRA and Chicago styles (OSCOLA is treated separately with examples of referencing legal sources shown in Chapter 11).

Here follow some general comments about the styles.

British Standard

- British Standard guidelines are not prescriptive as to how citation numbers are displayed in the text—superscript, or round or square brackets, can be used, provided that you are consistent.
- The numbers in the text connect with a list of full reference information arranged in numerical order. This is usually at the end of the relevant text, which may be the assignment, report or, in the case of a longer document, at the end of each chapter or section.
- It is common practice to italicise the main source element, e.g. book title, name of journal.
- Capitalisation of titles: the British Standard is not prescriptive on this, but BS examples illustrate full references with the first letter of the title in capitals, then lower case, except for proper nouns.
- The last name of the author (or organisational name) is the first element in the reference list, followed by his or her initials; the year of publication and page numbers, if applicable, are the last items.
- Although British Standard presents examples of fully capitalised names, e.g. BROWN, F., in its guidelines for presenting full reference information, this is not a formal requirement and it is common practice now to use lower case beyond the first letter of the author or organisational name, e.g. Brown, F. (But always be guided by your institution's own advice on this.)

MHRA

- With MHRA style, the footnote or endnote form recommended is to show the full name of the author, with first name preceding the last, and to include the place, name of the publisher and year of publication in brackets, concluding with page number(s), if applicable.
- However, in the Bibliography, which can include all works consulted, as well as those cited, the order of author names is reversed, with the last name preceding the first for the first named author, but not for subsequent authors named.

- As the relevant page number was shown in the footnote/endnote, it does not need to be repeated in the bibliographic entry.
- The MHRA style also tends to favour commas to separate parts of a reference, ending with a stop in the footnote/endnote entry (although not in the Bibliography).
- For books in English, the first letters of principal words throughout the title are capitalised, plus the first letter of words after any colon in the title. For titles in other languages, follow the way the title is presented in the source, or conform to any known referencing guidelines for the language in question.

In addition:
- the main source is always italicised for MHRA
- unless page numbers are shown, the year of publication is the last item in the entry for both British Standard and MHRA styles
- the first time you cite a source, full author information is given, but for subsequent citations you can use a shortened version, with relevant page number(s), e.g. Grafton, *Footnote: A Curious History*, p.30
- if you are referring to the book generally, you do not need to include a page number or numbers, but if you want to pinpoint a particular section, add page number(s).

Chicago

- With the Chicago style you can either provide full details of a source in the footnote or enough information to help a reader to identify the source in the References or Bibliography. The first time you cite a source in a footnote/endnote you should give full information; for example:

> Anthony Grafton, 1999, *The Footnote: A Curious History*, (United States: Harvard University Press) p.35.

However, subsequent citations require less detail, e.g. Grafton, *The Footnote*, 85.

- In the References or Bibliography, sources are listed alphabetically.
- As stated earlier, a reference list contains *only* the full details of those sources cited in your text, while the Bibliography contains a list of sources cited and other sources consulted in the preparation of the assignment.
- Each source shown in the References or Bibliography should be *single-spaced*, but with a double space between sources.
- In the References, you should capitalise the first and last word of the source title, and any proper noun, major word, and the first word of any subtitle within it.
- Note how the footnotes are presented in a slightly different way to those in the References or Bibliography. Examples of these differences follow.

Differences between Chicago footnotes and bibliographic list

- Note the difference in punctuation between footnotes and bibliographic entries: commas are used in the former, while stops separate out main elements in the latter.
- Indent the first line of each footnote, but in the References or Bibliography, the second and subsequent lines are indented.

- In a footnote, the first name(s) in full, or initials, is presented first, followed by the last name; but in the References or Bibliography, the last name is shown first.
- In a footnote, the publication information is placed within brackets, and the entry is finished with a page number, if relevant; but you do not need to use brackets with the reference list or bibliography—as the page number was shown in the footnote/endnote, it does not need to be repeated in the Bibliography entry.
- Full reference entries for secondary web sources—e.g. online newspaper articles, magazines, web pages, blogs—can be omitted, as long as detail of the source is provided in the endnote/footnote.

1. Example of a book written by a single author

(a) Using British Standard (footnote and reference)

A full reference entry for the Grafton source shown earlier would look like this:

> Grafton, A. *The footnote: a curious history.* Cambridge (MA): Harvard University Press, 1997. p.71.

- The abbreviation 'MA' distinguishes Cambridge in Massachusetts, USA, from Cambridge, UK.

(b) Using MHRA

> **Footnote/endnote: 1.** Anthony Grafton, *The Footnote: A Curious History* (Cambridge, MA: Harvard University Press, 1999), pp.25–26.
>
> **Bibliography:** Grafton, Anthony, *The Footnote: A Curious History* (Cambridge, MA: Harvard University Press, 1997)

(c) Using Chicago style

> **Footnote: 1.** Anthony Grafton, *The Footnote: A Curious History* (Cambridge, MA: Harvard University Press, 1997), 71.
>
> **Bibliography:** Grafton, Anthony. *The Footnote: A Curious History.* Cambridge, MA: Harvard University Press, 1997.

2. Chapter from an edited book

- The term 'editor' can be shorted to 'ed' or 'Ed.' (except in the Chicago bibliographic entry).
- The title of the article is also emphasised with inverted commas (single for MHRA, double for Chicago).

- Note that the main source, in both examples, is the *book* in which the chapter appeared, so the book title is italicised.

(a) Using British Standard (footnote and reference)

> Collin, Audrey. 'Human resource management in context'. In *Human resource management: a contemporary perspective.* I. Beardwell and L. Holden (Eds.). London: Pitman Publishing, 1994, pp. 29–68.

(b) Using MHRA

> **Footnote/endnote: 2.** Audrey Collin, 'Human Resource Management in Context', in *Human Resource Management: A Contemporary Perspective,* ed. by Ian Beardwell and Len Holden. (London: Pitman Publishing, 1994), pp. 29–68.
>
> **Bibliography:** Collin, Audrey, 'Human Resource Management in Context', in *Human Resource Management: A Contemporary Perspective,* ed. by I. Beardwell and L. Holden. (London: Pitman Publishing, 1994)

(c) Using Chicago style

> **Footnote: 3.**   Audrey Collin, "Human Resource Management in Context", in *Human Resource Management: A Contemporary Perspective,* ed. Ian Beardwell and Len Holden. (London: Pitman Publishing, 1994), 29–68.
>
> **Bibliography**: Collin, Audrey. "Human Resource Management in Context". In *Human Resource Management: A Contemporary Perspective*, edited by Ian Beardwell and Len Holden, 29–68. London: Pitman Publishing, 1994.

3. Example of a journal article

- The journal article example that follows has multiple authors; see how each style deals with this by the use, or otherwise, of the abbreviation 'et al.', but for more detailed information on the citation and referencing of multiple authors, see 'Frequently asked questions', Chapter 12, question 7.
- Note how the title of the article is punctuated in each example, with single quotation marks for the MHRA example and double for Chicago.
- The title of the journal (italicised) is followed by details of the volume and issue number, month (if applicable) and year, followed by page numbers.

(a) Using British Standard (footnote and reference)

> Guerrero-Berroa, Elizabeth, Ravona-Springer, Ramit, Heymann, Anthony, Schmeidler, James, Levy, Andrew, Leroith, Derek and Beeri, Michal S. 'Haptoglobin genotype modulates the relationships of glycaemic control with cognitive function in elderly individuals with type 2 diabetes'. *Diabetologia*. 1 January 2015. Vol. 58, no. 4, p. 736–744.

Note: British Standard advises that, where there are more than three authors, the names of all but the first can be omitted and replaced by 'and others' or 'et al.', but this is optional.

(b) Using MHRA

> **Footnote/endnote: 3.** Elizabeth Guerrero-Berroa and others, 'Haptoglobin Genotype Modulates the Relationships of Glycaemic Control with Cognitive Function in Elderly Individuals with Type 2 Diabetes', *Diabetologia*, 58 (2015), 736–44.
>
> **Bibliography**: Guerrero-Berroa, Elizabeth, Ramit Ravona-Springer, Anthony Heymann, James Schmeidler, Andrew Levy, Derek Leroith, and others, 'Haptoglobin Genotype Modulates the Relationships of Glycaemic Control with Cognitive Function in Elderly Individuals with Type 2 Diabetes', *Diabetologia*, 58 (2015), 736–44

(c) Using Chicago style

'et al.' can be used in the Chicago footnote, but not in the full reference, where all the authors are listed.

> **Footnote/endnote:** Elizabeth Guerrero-Berroa et al. "Haptoglobin Genotype Modulates the Relationships of Glycaemic Control with Cognitive Function in Elderly Individuals with Type 2 Diabetes", *Diabetologia*, 58 (2015), 736–44.
>
> **Bibliography:** Guerrero-Berroa, Elizabeth, Ramit Ravona-Springer, Anthony Heymann, James Schmeidler, Andrew Levy, Derek Leroith, and Michal S. Beeri. 2015. "Haptoglobin Genotype Modulates the Relationships of Glycaemic Control with Cognitive Function in Elderly Individuals with Type 2 Diabetes". *Diabetologia* 58 (4) (2015): 736–44.

4. Example of a website

(a) British Standard (footnote and reference)

> Switek, Brian. 'Basilosaurus the bone-crusher'. In *National Geographic*, March 2015. Available at: http://phenomena.nationalgeographic.com/2015/03/06/basilosaurus-the-bone-crusher/ [viewed 10 March 2015].

(b) MHRA

Footnote/endnote: Brian Switek, 'Basilosaurus the Bone-Crusher', *National Geographic*, March 6, 2015 <http://phenomena.nationalgeographic.com/2015/03/06/basilosaurus-the-bone-crusher/> [accessed 10 March 2015].

Bibliography: Switek, Brian, 'Basilosaurus the Bone-Crusher', *National Geographic*, March 6, 2015 <http://phenomena.nationalgeographic.com/2015/03/06/basilosaurus-the-bone-crusher/> [accessed 10 March 2015]

(c) Chicago style

Footnote/endnote: Brian Switek, "Basilosaurus the Bone-Crusher", *National Geographic*, March 6, 2015. Accessed 16 March 2015 http://phenomena.nationalgeographic.com/2015/03/06/basilosaurus-the-bone-crusher/

Bibliography: Not required for this type of source.

For online newspaper/magazine articles, and other secondary source online sites, a full reference entry can be omitted, provided that full information is supplied in the endnote/footnote, as shown in the example.

Recurrent number styles of referencing

The recurrent number referencing styles uses a bracketed (or superscript) number in the text, which connects with the list of references at the end of the text. If brackets are used to enclose numbers, you can use either square [ ] or curved ( ) brackets, as long as you are consistent.

What makes it different from the consecutive number styles of referencing is that the same number is repeated if a source is mentioned more than once in the same text. A number in the text of your assignment will therefore connect with the same number in your final list of references. Your tutors may also require you to include a bibliography, which would list additional sources consulted but not directly referred to in the text.

The advantage of this referencing style generally is that because only one number is used per source or note there is no need to use the abbreviations ibid., op. cit. or loc. cit., as is the case with the consecutive number styles. If you want to refer to the same source on a number of occasions in the same assignment, but to different pages, you can add the relevant page numbers to the bracketed source reference numbers, e.g. (2: 47) or (2: 47–55).

The four recurrent numbering styles found within UK higher education are as follows.

1. The bracketed numbered (or numeric) referencing examples presented by **British Standard**—see the summary in British Standard BS ISO 690:2010.

2. **Vancouver** style, as outlined by the International Committee of Medical Journal Editors (ICMJE) in their guide *International Committee of Medical Journal Editors Uniform Requirements for Manuscripts Submitted to Biomedical Journals: Sample References.*

3. The **Institute of Electrical and Electronics Engineers (IEEE)** also makes recommendations on referencing using this style of referencing. These recommendations are adopted by many electrical engineering and related disciplines in the UK. The IEEE produces an information sheet for authors, *IEEE Transactions, Journals, and Letters: Information for Authors,* via its website, although many university libraries produce IEEE referencing information sheets for their students.

4. The **Council of Science Editors (CSE)** style, while more commonly applied within the USA, is used by some UK science departments. As stated earlier, this style offers the writer the choice of using either a name–date or recurrent-number style of referencing. Guidelines for CSE referencing are shown in the latest edition of *Scientific Style and Format: The CSE Manual for Authors, Editors and Publishers* (2014).

Examples

There are only small differences between the four variants of this referencing style in relation to printed material, although the differences with electronic sources are more marked. Nevertheless, students asked to adopt one of these variants need to be aware of the differences, as described in the examples below.

Note:

- the lack of italicisation in Vancouver and CSE titles.
- capitalisation—with the CSE and Vancouver styles, only the first word of titles is capitalised; in IEEE capitalise the main words in titles, while articles (a, an, the) and conjunctions (and, but, for, or) are in lower case.
- the location of the year element in all four examples.
- there are no commas between the personal name initials in the CSE and Vancouver styles.
- indentation of second and subsequent lines of the CSE style.
- where the initials or full first name of author(s) is positioned—after family name with British Standard, Vancouver and CSE.

Table 10.2 Book reference

British Standard	Pecorari, Diane. *Teaching to avoid plagiarism: how to promote good source use.* Maidenhead: Open University Press, 2013.
Vancouver	Pecorari D. Teaching to avoid plagiarism: how to promote good source use. Maidenhead: Open University Press; 2013.
IEEE	D. Pecorari, *Teaching to Avoid Plagiarism: How to Promote Good Source Use.* Maidenhead: Open University Press, 2013.
CSE	Pecorari D. Teaching to avoid plagiarism: how to promote good source use. Maidenhead: Open University Press; 2013.

Table 10.3 Journal

British Standard	Dearing, K.F. and Gotlib, I.H. (2009). 'Interpretation of ambiguous information in girls at risk for depression'. *Journal of Abnormal Child Psychology*, vol. 37, no. 1, Jan. 2009, pp: 79–91.
Vancouver	Dearing K C, Gotlib I H. Interpretation of ambiguous information in girls at risk for depression. *Journal of Abnormal Child Psychology*, 2009; 37:1; Jan, 79–91.
IEEE	K.C. Dearing and I.H. Gotlib. "Interpretation of ambiguous information in girls at risk for depression", *Journal of Abnormal Child Psychology*, vol. 37, no. 1, pp:79–91, Jan. 2009.
CSE	Dearing K C, Gotlib, I H. 2009. Interpretation of ambiguous information in girls at risk for depression. J Abnorm Child Psych. 37:1, Jan: 79–91.

Table 10.4 Website

British Standard	*IEEE Publications & Standards*, 2015. Available at: https://www.ieee.org/publications_standards/index.html [viewed 11 March 2015].
Vancouver	IEEE. Publications & Standards. [Internet]. 2015 [cited 2015 Mar 11]; [13 screens]. Available: https://www.ieee.org/publications_standards/index.html.
IEEE	*IEEE Publications & Standards*. 2015 [accessed 2015 Mar 11]. https://www.ieee.org/publications_standards/index.html
CSE	IEEE Publications & Standards. IEEE. 2015 [accessed 2015 Mar 11]. https://www.ieee.org/publications_standards/index.html

Note the double quotation marks around the title of the article in the IEEE example, and the abbreviated journal title in the CSE example. A list of abbreviations can be found in the *Web of Science, which* can be found online within the *ISI Web of Knowledge;* you can access these through the library of your institution.

Note that the Vancouver style reference includes a wider range of information compared to other styles: name of organisation, title of the screen visited, [internet], year the site was last updated/created, [cited: year, month, day], number of screens or pages in this section of the site; available at URL information.

Example of an extract from an essay

The following brief extract from a student essay demonstrates how this recurrent number referencing style works.

> Transition and change: the terms are often used interchangeably, and indeed there is a sense of both movement and alteration conveyed in both meanings: from one state of existence to another, or transition. Hopson, Scally and Stafford highlight

the movement element implicit in transition, and see it both as a 'passage' (journey) that will last a certain 'period' (of time) and within that time something happens: "one style is developing into another" **(1)**. So, common within these definitions, is an overall sense that a transition is a cognitive 'journey' of indeterminate length at the end of which change occurs.

However, Bridges **(2)** argues that 'change' refers to the context or situation itself, whereas 'transition' is aligned to the emotional processes associated with the situational or structural change. Bridges identifies three phases of transition, or emotional change: letting go; passing through 'the neutral zone' (when emotional realignments take place); and emergence into a new situation, when every ending is a beginning.

References

The references are entered at the end of the assignment in the numerical order they appeared (and not in alphabetical order). This is how they would appear in each of the four variants of this referencing style, as follows.

(a) British Standard

1. Hopson, B., M. Scally and K. Stafford. *Transitions: the Challenge of Change*. Didcot: Mercury Business Books, 1991.
2. Bridges, William. *Managing transitions: making the most of change*. London: Nicholas Brealey, 2003.

(b) Vancouver

1. Hopson B, Scally M, Stafford K. Transitions: the challenge of change. Didcot: Mercury Business Books; 1991.
2. Bridges W. Managing transitions: making the most of change. London: Nicholas Brealey, 2003.

(c) IEEE

1. D. Hopson, M. Scally, K. Stafford. *Transitions: the Challenge of Change*. Didcot: Mercury Business Books, 1991.
2. W. Bridges, *Managing Transitions: Making the Most of Change*. London: Nicholas Brealey, 2003.

(d) CSE

1. Hopson B, Scally M, Stafford K. Transitions: The challenge of change. Didcot: Mercury Business Books. 1991.
2. W. Bridges, Managing Transitions: Making the most of change. London: Nicholas Brealey, 2003.

Part 3

11 Referencing examples

Introduction

This third section of the book presents examples of how sources are presented in reference lists or bibliographies. Two referencing styles will be shown for each source: Harvard and numerical, based on British Standard guidelines, to illustrate the way the order of elements within these two styles are listed. The exception to this will be with 'legal sources', where the OSCOLA referencing style will be introduced and examples presented.

The Harvard examples contain both the in-text citation and full reference information, while the numerical examples contain just the full reference detail, as the citation would be the relevant consecutive or recurrent number in an assignment.

Subjects featured

The subjects featured, which include internet sources where applicable, are presented in alphabetical order, as follows.

1. Advertising and promotional material, including posters
2. Art works, including painting, photography, sculpture and street art
3. Audio-visual forms of entertainment, including radio, television, music, film, video games
4. Books, booklets and pamphlets, including translated and transliterated examples
5. Cartographic resources (maps)
6. Conference papers
7. Dissertations
8. Education and training material
9. Government publications
10. Graphs and charts
11. Historical research
12. Information and display boards
13. Interviews
14. Journals (academic journal articles)
15. Lectures, speeches, talks and public readings
16. Legal sources (including live screening of Supreme Court sittings)
17. Live entertainment and performances (dance, drama, music)
18. Magazines/newsletters, printed and online
19. Music scores/sheet music

20. Newspapers and online news sites
21. Parliamentary publications
22. Patents and standards
23. Personal communications, e.g. emails, telephone calls, texts
24. Postal items/postcards
25. Public memorials
26. Record sleeves and CD inserts
27. Reference information resources, e.g. encyclopaedias, dictionaries, Wikipedia
28. Reports
29. Sacred and classical texts
30. Scripts (plays/films)
31. Social and professional networking sites
32. Theatre or other printed programmes
33. Video/computer games

1. Advertising and promotional material (including posters, leaflets, and television/radio advertising)

Advertising can be of interest to students with an interest in marketing, social history, cultural studies, graphic design or contemporary communications.

1a. Advertisement in a printed newspaper or magazine

Include in the reference:

- name of advertiser
- year
- name of product
- advertising slogan or strapline (if relevant)
- state the nature of the source [advertisement]
- name of magazine or newspaper (in italics)
- issue/volume number, if a magazine
- date of advertisement
- page number.

Harvard	**Citation:** (Epilepsy Research UK, 2015) **Reference:** Epilepsy Research UK, 2015. 'You can help change the future' [advertisement] *The Oldie*, issue 318, February, p.44.
Numerical	**Reference:** Epilepsy Research UK. 'You can help change the future' [advertisement] *The Oldie*, issue 318, February, 2015, p.44.

1b. Advertisement: online

Include all the information used for printed advertisements and add the nature of the source [online advertisement], the URL and the date the source was viewed online.

Harvard	**Citation:** (British Gas, 2015) **Reference:** British Gas, 2015. *Our tariffs*. [online advertisement]. Available at http://www.britishgas.co.uk/products-and-services/gas-and-electricity/our-energy-tariffs [viewed 15 March 2015].
Numerical	**Reference:** British Gas. *Our tariffs* [online advertisement] 2015. Available at http://www.britishgas.co.uk/products-and-services/gas-and-electricity/our-energy-tariffs [viewed 15 March 2015].

1c. Digital advertising displays

These are electronic billboards or display boards, promoting a range of products, often in quick succession.

Reference detail should include:

- advertiser
- year
- product
- main caption (in italics)
- nature of the source, e.g. [digital advertisement]
- where you saw the display board
- date and time you saw the advertisement.

Harvard	**Citation:** (Scottish Widows, 2015) **Reference:** Scottish Widows, 2015. Life Insurance advertisement: *Big things have small beginnings* [digital advertisement]. London: Kings Cross Station, 16 March 2015.
Numerical	**Reference:** Scottish Widows. Life insurance advertisement: *Big things have small beginnings* [digital advertisement] 2015. London: Kings Cross Station, 16 March 2015.

1d. Leaflets

Most leaflets do not show the name of the writer, so if that is the case, start with the name of the advertiser or sponsor of the leaflet, then show the year of distribution, the main caption, state the nature of the source, e.g. [leaflet], and where the sponsor or advertiser is located, e.g. town, city or, as in this case, with a national organisation, the country of origin.

Harvard	**Citation:** (NHS, 2009) **Reference:** NHS: National Health Service, 2009. *Important information about Swine Flu.* [leaflet] United Kingdom.
Numerical	**Reference:** NHS: National Health Service. *Important information about Swine Flu.* [leaflet] United Kingdom, 2009.

1e. Posters

Include details of the poster sponsor, year of promotion, main poster headlines or title, where you saw it and when: specific date. Make the nature of the source clear, e.g. wall poster.

Harvard	**Citation:** (The National Gallery, 2015)
	Reference: The National Gallery, London, 2015. Inventing impressionism: the man who sold a thousand Monets. Wall poster seen at Harlow Town Railway Station, 16 March 2015.
Numerical	**Reference:** The National Gallery, London. Inventing impressionism: the man who sold a thousand Monets, 2015. Wall poster seen at Harlow Town Railway Station, 16 March 2015.

1f. Television/radio advertising

Start with the name of TV/radio channel, year advertisement appeared or was heard, title of advert (or description of it), state nature of source, e.g. [television advertisement], and time and date you viewed or heard it.

Harvard	**Citation:** (Channel Four Television, 2009)
	Reference: Channel Four Television, 2009. *Adopt a child* [television advertisement] 10.00am, 14 May 2009.
Numerical	**Reference:** Channel Four Television, *Adopt a child* [television advertisement] 10.00am, 14 May, 2009.

Harvard	**Citation:** (Classic FM, 2009)
	Reference: Classic FM, 2009. *Music quest* [radio advertisement]. 10.15am, 14 May 2009.
Numerical	**Reference:** Classic FM, *Music quest* [radio advertisement] 10.15am, 14 May, 2009.

2. Art works

These include painting, photography, sculpture and street art, as used here as illustrative examples.

Start with the name of the artist, year of creation of work, and add the type of work, e.g. photograph/oil painting [in brackets] and ownership of the artwork.

If the image is online, add the URL, and the date you first viewed the image online.

Copyright: Always check the conditions of copyright for the image if you want to copy it into your own work; you may need to gain permission from the organisation hosting the site, and any permission given should be acknowledged in your work.

2a. Painting (online)

Harvard	**Citation:** (Klee, 1937)
	Reference: Klee, P. 1937. *Legend of the Nile* [painting]. In: Kunstmuseum Bern. Available at WebMuseum http://www.sai.msu.su/wm/paint/auth/klee/ [viewed 16 March 2015].
Numerical	**Reference:** Klee, P. *Legend of the Nile* [painting] 1937. Kunstmuseum Bern. Available at WebMuseum http://www.sai.msu.su/wm/paint/auth/klee/ [viewed 16 March 2015].

2b. Painting (seen in a gallery)

Harvard	**Citation:** (Klimt, 1898)
	Reference: Klimt, Gustav, 1898. *Allegory of sculpture* [painting]. Salzburg: Galerie Welz.
Numerical	**Reference:** Klimt, Gustav. *Allegory of sculpture* [painting] 1898. Salzburg: Galerie Welz.

2c. Photography

If you are referring to a photograph featured in an online collection:

- give name of the photographer; if photographer's name unknown, start with the name of the site
- year it was placed on the site, if shown
- title of work (in italics) and type of illustration [photograph]
- name of collection
- URL
- date the online image was viewed.

Copyright: You do not need permission to refer to the photograph itself in your assignment, but you may need permission from the photographer or website to copy the image into your own work; check the copyright conditions on the site for the photograph concerned.

If you find a re-pinned image on a social media site, e.g. Pinterest, try to trace the photograph back to the original source, if you can, and reference the primary source, if possible. If you cannot do this, then use the secondary source location.

2c(i). Photograph: online gallery collection

Harvard	**Citation:** (Cameron, 1864)
	Reference: Cameron, J. M. 1864. *Sadness* [photograph]. In: National Media Museum. Available at http://www.nationalmediamuseum.org.uk/collection/photography/royalphotographicsociety/collectionitem.aspx?id=2003-5001/2/21477 [viewed 13 March 2015].
Numerical	**Reference:** Cameron, J. M. *Sadness* [photograph] 1864. In: National Media Museum. Available at http://www.nationalmediamuseum.org.uk/collection/photography/royalphotographicsociety/collectionitem.aspx?id=2003-5001/2/21477 [viewed 13 March 2015].

2c(ii). Photograph: from a social media collection, e.g. Flickr, Pinterest

Reminder—see 2c above: If you find a re-pinned image on a social media site, e.g. Pinterest, try to trace the photograph back to the original source and reference the primary source, if possible.

Harvard	**Citation:** (Florea, 2015)
	Reference: Florea, Constantin, 2015. *La Vita e Bella* [photograph]. Available on Flickr at https://www.flickr.com/photos/costiflorea/16792893641/in/explore-2015-03-12 [viewed 13 March 2015].
Numerical	**Reference:** Florea, Constantin *La Vita e Bella* [photograph] 2015. Available on Flickr at https://www.flickr.com/photos/costiflorea/16792893641/in/explore-2015-03-12 [viewed 13 March 2015].

2c(iii). Photograph from a private collection

- Start with the title of photograph, or description of subject.
- Year (or circa) photograph was taken.
- Nature of the source [photograph].
- State who has ownership or custody of the photograph.

Note: Ensure you have obtained permission to use the image in your work; you could acknowledge this permission in an 'Acknowledgements' section of your assignment.

Harvard	**Citation:** (Alberta Vickridge, circa 1911)
	Reference: Alberta Vickridge, circa 1911 [photograph] Photographer unknown. In the private collection of Henry Vickridge, Otley, West Yorkshire.
Numerical	**Reference:** As above.

2c(iv). Your own photographs

If you are referencing your own photographs:

- start with your own name
- year photograph was taken
- subject of photograph
- nature of the source [photograph]
- if you have made the photographs publicly accessible, e.g. Pinterest, add source details and a link to the site.

Harvard	**Citation:** (Neville, 2014)
	Reference: Neville, C. 2014. 'Tour de France' [photographs]. Available on Pinterest at https://uk.pinterest.com/pin/318277898638758987/
Numerical	**Reference:** Neville, C. 'Tour de France', 2014 [photographs]. Available on Pinterest at https://uk.pinterest.com/pin/318277898638758987/

2d. Sculpture

Reference details should include:

- name of sculptor
- year sculpture was first displayed

- title of sculpture (in italics)
- nature of exhibit [sculpture]
- where it is located.

Harvard	**Citation:** (Shendi, 2013) **Reference:** Shendi, S. 2013. *Bent nail* [iron sculpture]. Displayed: West Yorkshire: Silsden, Wesley Place.
Numerical	**Reference:** Shendi, S. *Bent nail* [iron sculpture] 2013. Displayed: West Yorkshire: Silsden, Wesley Place.

2e. Street art/graffiti

Street art and graffiti can disappear quickly, so you need to try to record it in some way if possible, e.g. by photographing it and using the photograph as an appendix item in your assignment. However, some street artists, e.g. Banksy, have websites dedicated to their work, so you could include a URL to show the reader a copy of the image concerned.

Harvard	**Citation:** (Banksy, 2002) **Reference:** Banksy, 2002. Mona Lisa with rocket launcher [street art] Displayed: London: Soho (road unknown). Image available at http://uk.complex.com/style/2013/11/banksy-greatest-works/mona-lisa-rocketlauncher [viewed 29 March 2015].
Numerical	**Reference:** Banksy. Mona Lisa with rocket launcher [street art] 2002. Displayed: London: Soho (road unknown). Image available at http://uk.complex.com/style/2013/11/banksy-greatest-works/mona-lisa-rocketlauncher [viewed 29 March 2015].

3. Audio-visual forms of entertainment and information, including film (e.g. YouTube), music, radio, television and video games

3a. Film (movie): download from the internet

Most commercial films (movies) are the result of a teamwork approach, so the film title should be cited and shown as the first element in the reference.

However, if one person is clearly the originator for a source or if your evidence focuses on a particular aspect of production, e.g. casting or direction, you can use that person's name for the citation and as the first element in the full reference entry.

Use the film/movie title (in italics) for the citation and as the main element in the full reference, followed by the year of release and then the name of the director. State the medium [motion picture], name of studio, URL and date you downloaded the film.

Harvard	**Citation:** (*Twelve angry men*, 1957) **Reference:** *Twelve angry men*, 1957. Directed by Sidney Lumet [motion picture] USA: MGM Studios. Available at http://www.movieberry.com/12_angry_men/ [downloaded 14 March 2015].
Numerical	**Reference:** *Twelve angry men*. Directed by Sidney Lumet [motion picture] USA: MGM Studios. 1957. Available at http://www.movieberry.com/12_angry_men/ [downloaded 14 March 2015].

3b. Film: DVD

Harvard	**Citation:** (*Tracker*, 2010) **Reference:** *Tracker*, 2010. Directed by Ian Sharp. [DVD] UK Film Council and New Zealand Film Commission.
Numerical	**Reference:** *Tracker*. Directed by Ian Sharp. [DVD] UK Film Council and New Zealand Film Commission, 2010.

3c. Film: director's comments (or actor's/actress's comments)

If the focus of your evidence was on a particular aspect of the film, e.g. director's comments, start with the director's name. Similarly, if you wanted to focus on the main actor's/actress's comments, then you would start with his or her name, e.g. Ray Winstone, i.e. (Winstone, 2010).

Harvard	**Citation:** (Sharp, 2010) **Reference:** Sharp, Ian, 2010. Director's comments: *Tracker* [DVD] UK Film Council and New Zealand Film Commission.
Numerical	**Reference:** Sharp, Ian. Director's comments: *Tracker* [DVD] UK Film Council and New Zealand Film Commission, 2010.

3d. Music: download (album)

The main source is the composer, then include:

- first public performance
- title (in italics)
- date of original recording, if relevant
- if relevant, name of conductor and orchestra
- date of reissue, if applicable
- available at—name of company and URL
- date you downloaded the music.

Harvard	**Citation:** (Delius, 1909) **Reference:** Delius, F. 1909. *Mass of life*. Sir Thomas Beecham, Royal Philharmonic Orchestra. Originally recorded 1952–3. Reissued 2011. Available at Pristine Classical https://www.pristineclassical.com/pasc270.html [downloaded 20 February 2015].
Numerical	**Reference:** Delius, F. *Mass of life*. 1909. Sir Thomas Beecham, Royal Philharmonic Orchestra. Originally recorded 1952–3. Reissued 2011. Available at Pristine Classical https://www.pristineclassical.com/pasc270.html [downloaded 20 February 2015].

3e. Music: download (individual/selected tracks)

Harvard	**Citation:** (Rusby, 2015). **Reference:** Rusby, Kate. 2015. *Underneath the stars* [song] Available at http://www.last.fm/music/Kate+Rusby [downloaded 13 March 2015].
Numerical	**Reference:** Rusby, Kate. *Underneath the stars* [song] 2015. Available at http://www.last.fm/music/Kate+Rusby [downloaded 13 March 2015].

3f. Music: CD

Detail to include:

- artist(s) or arranger/producer
- year produced
- title (in italics)
- state the medium [CD]
- place of production and production company.

Harvard	**Citation:** (Roberts, 2000) **Reference:** Roberts, R. 2000. *Passive music for accelerated learning* [CD]. Carmarthen: Crown House Publishing.
Numerical	**Reference:** Roberts, R. *Passive music for accelerated learning* [CD] Carmarthen: Crown House Publishing, 2000.

3g. Music: vinyl record

Harvard	**Citation:** (Delius, 1982) **Reference:** Delius, F. 1982. *Delius*. Hallé Orchestra [vinyl LP]. Hayes: Music for Pleasure, CFP 40373.
Numerical	**Reference:** Delius, F. *Delius*. Hallé Orchestra [vinyl LP]. Hayes: Music for Pleasure, CFP 40373, 1982.

3h. Podcasts

Archived sound and vision media files, e.g. with the BBC, can be downloaded, and can be referenced as follows:

- title of programme (in italics)
- year of broadcast
- state the medium [podcast]
- date of original transmission
- available via [URL]
- date you downloaded the podcast.

Harvard	**Citation:** (*The why factor: chasing riches,* 2015) **Reference:** *The why factor: chasing riches,* 2015 [podcast] BBC World Service, 21 February 2015. Available at http://www.bbc.co.uk/podcasts/series/whyfactor [downloaded 14 March 2015].
Numerical	**Reference:** *The why factor: chasing riches* [podcast] BBC World Service, 21 February 2015. Available at http://www.bbc.co.uk/podcasts/series/whyfactor [downloaded 14 March 2015].

3i. Live radio and television programmes

Radio and television programmes can be listened to or viewed live and referenced (see also 'Podcasts', 3h above, for older, archived programmes).

You would normally cite the title of the programme (in italics) and use this as the first element in the full reference entry. Other information can be included, if you feel it is relevant, e.g. name of the writer or presenter.

What to include in the reference:

- title of the programme, in italics, and name of episode, if relevant
- title of the series, if applicable
- name of the radio or television network, e.g. BBC Radio 4
- place of broadcast, if it is a regional station, e.g. Bradford: Pulse Radio
- original broadcast or transmission date.

3j. Live radio programme

Harvard	**Citation:** (*Face the facts*, 2015) **Reference:** *Face the facts: life in gangland Britain*, 2015. BBC Radio Four, 5 March 2015.
Numerical	**Reference:** *Face the facts: life in gangland Britain*. BBC Radio Four, 5 March 2015.

3k. Archived television programme

Harvard	**Citation:** (*The Somme*, 2005) **Reference:** *The Somme*, 2005. Channel Four, 14 November 2005. Available at http://www.channel4.com/programmes/the-somme [viewed 13 March 2015].
Numerical	**Reference:** *The Somme*. Channel Four, 14 November 2005. Available at http://www.channel4.com/programmes/the-somme [viewed 13 March 2015].

Note: If you viewed the programme as it was broadcast and took notes, use the format shown for 'Live radio programme', 3j above.

3l. Spoken word: audiobook download

What to include in the reference:

- name of author or editor
- year of production, as shown on the site
- book title (in italics)
- state the medium [audiobook]
- name of narrator
- URL
- date you downloaded the book.

Harvard	**Citation:** (Sowell, 2014) **Reference:** Sowell, T. 2014. *Basic Economics*, 5th edition [audiobook]. Narrated by Tom Weiner. Available at http://www.audiobooks.com/audiobook/basic-economics-fifth-edition-a-common-sense-guide-to-the-economy/224066 [downloaded 15 March 2015].
Numerical	**Reference:** Sowell, T. *Basic Economics*, 5th edition, 2014. [audiobook] Narrated by Tom Weiner. Available at http://www.audiobooks.com/audiobook/basic-economics-fifth-edition-a-common-sense-guide-to-the-economy/224066 [downloaded 15 March 2015].

3m. Spoken word: CDs (two examples)

The first source below refers to the war poetry output generally of Wilfred Owen, written between 1914 and 1918. There was no date shown for the date of production, hence 'no date' after [CD].

If you were referring to a particular poem, you would cite the specific year and, in the reference, the title of the poem, as well as the CD collection, e.g. (Owen, 1916); 'Storm' from *The pity of war: poems of Wilfred Owen.* [CD]

Harvard	**Citation:** (Owen, 1914–18) **Reference:** Owen, Wilfred, 1914–18. *The pity of war: poems of Wilfred Owen.* [CD] [no date]. Read by Samuel West. The Wilfred Owen Society.
Numerical	**Reference:** Owen, Wilfred (1914–18). *The pity of war: poems of Wilfred Owen.* [CD]. Read by Samuel West. The Wilfred Owen Society [no date].

The following source is a modern spoken-word recording, so the citation and reference year show the date of production.

Harvard	**Citation:** (Holmes, 2014) **Reference:** Holmes, David, 2014. *71—OST* [CD]. Great Harwood: Townsend Records.
Numerical	**Reference:** Holmes, David. *71—OST* [CD]. Great Harwood: Townsend Records, 2014.

3n. Screencasts

A screencast catches what is shown on a computer screen. They are often used for information, education and training purposes—for example, on how to navigate computer hardware or software.

What to include in the reference:

- title of screencast, shortened if necessary (in italics)
- year screencast was produced
- state the medium [screencast]
- available via [URL]
- date you viewed/downloaded the resource.

Harvard	**Citation:** (*Slavery and the War*, 2015) **Reference:** *Slavery and the War: Northern Politics 1861–1862*, 2015 [screencast]. Available at http://www.screencast.com/t/ulvX17F72W [viewed 20 March 2015].
Numerical	**Reference:** *Slavery and the War: Northern Politics 1861–1862* [screencast] 2015. Available at http://www.screencast.com/t/ulvX17F72W [viewed 20 March 2015].

3o. Webcasts

A webcast is a non-interactive internet transmission of information or live events. If the webcast has no date, use 'n/d' or 'no date' in the citation, but show the date you viewed the material.

Note: Make sure the information in the webcast is a credible source—for example, the webcast featured below illustrates the work of a reputable US non-government support agency to help people overcome drink addiction.

What to include in the reference:

- name of production company/organisation
- year, if shown
- title of webcast (in italics)
- state the medium [webcast]
- URL
- date you viewed the site.

Harvard	**Citation:** (KeepSober.org, no date) **Reference:** KeepSober.org [no date]. *The science of addiction and recovery* [webcast]. Available at http://keepsober.org/Education.htm [viewed 15 March 2015].
Numerical	**Reference:** KeepSober.org *The science of addiction and recovery* [webcast] [no date]. Available at http://keepsober.org/Education.htm [viewed 15 March 2015].

3p. Video cassettes

Films on video cassette: treat as for 'Film: DVD' (3b, above), but use [video cassette] in place of [DVD].

3q. YouTube film clip

What to reference:

- name of presenter
- year video was posted
- title of film clip (in italics)
- state the medium [YouTube]
- URL
- viewed—date you viewed the film clip.

Harvard	**Citation:** (James ESL, 2015) **Reference:** James ESL, 2015. *Learn English: 3 easy ways to get better at speaking English* [YouTube] Available at https://www.youtube.com/watch?v=-pPvyzXaFWJM [viewed 17 March 2015).
Numerical	**Reference:** James ESL. *Learn English: 3 easy ways to get better at speaking English* [YouTube] 2015. Available at https://www.youtube.com/watch?v=-pPvyzXaFWJM [viewed 17 March 2015).

4. Books, booklets and pamphlets

A book can be a hardback, paperback (or 'soft cover'), or electronic publication on any subject, with one or more authors and/or editors.

A booklet is a non-fiction paperback publication with a limited number of pages, usually written for information purposes.

A pamphlet is a short essay, composition or treatise on a subject, usually printed in paperback.

Academic books go through a rigorous set of filters, including the critical scrutiny by the author's peers before they are published, so are respected in education institutions as essential sources of information.

The order in which bibliographic elements appear depends on the referencing style, but the following should be included, if applicable.

- **Name(s) of author(s) or originator(s)**. If 'Anon' (anonymous) is shown specifically on the title page, then this should be stated in the full reference entry, *but only when this happens*. If no author name is given (and 'Anon' is not shown), you can start with the first proper word of the title. If the book has been written under an assumed name, this is the one that should be referenced, although the creator's real name, if known, may be included in brackets following the pseudonym.
- **The year of publication**. If no year is shown, state 'no date' or 'n.d.' and it may be appropriate to give an approximate indication of when the book was published. This can be done by stating 'circa' and the period, e.g. 'circa 1920'.
- **Main title of the book**, in italics.
- **Title of a chapter** in an edited collection. This may be contained within single or double inverted commas, depending on referencing style.
- **Name(s) of editor(s)**, if applicable, and indicated as 'ed' or 'Ed.' or 'eds' or 'Eds.'.
- **State edition**, but only if it is *not* the first edition. With Harvard and numerical styles this can be abbreviated to 'edn.' to avoid confusion with 'Ed.' for 'editor'.
- **Place of publication and publisher**. The place of publication is the town or city where the publisher is located. If the publisher is outside the UK, state the country (unless it is obvious), then the town or city.
- **Page number or other numeration**, if applicable. The abbreviation 'p.' or 'pp.' can be used.

4a. Book: single author

Harvard	**Citation:** (Kotre, 1984)
	Reference: Kotre, J. 1984. *Outliving the self: generativity and the interpretation of lives.* USA: Baltimore: Johns Hopkins University Press.
Numerical	**Reference:** Kotre, J. *Outliving the self: generativity and the interpretation of lives.* USA: Baltimore: Johns Hopkins University Press, 1984.

4b. *Book: two or more authors (see also Chapter 12, 'Frequently asked questions', question 7).*

Harvard	**Citation:** (Saunders, Lewis and Thornhill, 2003) **Reference:** Saunders, M., P. Lewis and A. Thornhill, 2003. *Research methods for business students.* Harlow: Prentice Hall.
Numerical	**Reference:** Saunders, M., P. Lewis and A. Thornhill. *Research methods for business students.* Harlow: Prentice Hall, 2003.

4c. *Edited book*

Harvard	**Citation:** (McGinty and Williams, 2001) **Reference:** McGinty, J. and T. Williams (eds.), 2001. *Regional trends 36.* London: The Stationery Office.
Numerical	**Reference:** McGinty, J. and T. Williams (eds.). *Regional trends 36.* London: The Stationery Office, 2001.

4d. *Book: chapter from an edited collection of articles/essays*

Harvard	**Citation:** (North, Leigh and Gough, 1983) Reference: North, D., R. Leigh and J. Gough, 1983. Monitoring industrial change at the local level: some comments on methods and data sources. In: M. Healey (ed.) *Urban and regional industrial research: the changing UK data base.* Norwich: Geo Books, pp.111–29.
Numerical	**Reference:** North, D., R. Leigh and J. Gough. Monitoring industrial change at the local level: some comments on methods and data sources. In: M. Healey (ed.) *Urban and regional industrial research: the changing UK data base.* Norwich: Geo Books, 1983, pp.111–29.

4e. *Book published by an agency or organisation (no specific named author)*

When there is no named author, the organisation that published the book is the originator and thus takes first position in the reference.

Harvard	**Citation:** (APA, 2009) **Reference:** APA: American Psychological Association, 2009. *Publication manual of the American Psychological Association.* 6th edn. Washington, DC: American Psychological Association.
Numerical	**Reference:** APA: American Psychological Association. *Publication manual of the American Psychological Association.* 6th edn. Washington, DC: American Psychological Association, 2009.

4f. Translated book

Include name of translator, date of publication of source and date of publication of original work. (See 'Frequently asked questions', Chapter 12, question 8, about referencing books or other sources with non-English alphabet characters.)

| Harvard | **Citation:** (Turgenev, 1972) **Reference:** Turgenev, I. 1972. *Spring Torrents*. (L. Schapiro. Trans.). London: Eyre Methuen (Original work published 1873). |
| Numerical | **Reference:** Turgenev, I. *Spring Torrents*. (L. Schapiro. Trans.). London: Eyre Methuen, 1972 (Original work published 1873). |

4g. Chapter in a book that is part of a series

A book in a series is one sharing characteristics in common with others, in terms of the subject matter. The example below shows a chapter in one of the books in a series.
The full reference detail will show:

- name of author
- year book was published
- title of chapter, in single quotation marks
- names of volume editors
- title of book in the series, italicised
- page numbers for chapter
- title of series (in brackets and italicised)
- place of publication and name of publisher.

| Harvard | **Citation:** (Pines, 1997) **Reference:** Pines, J. 1997. 'Localization of cell cycle regulators by immuno-fluorescence'. In: John N. Abelson, Melvin I. Simon, and W. D. Dunphy (vol. eds.): *Cell Cycle Control* vol. 283, pp.99–113 (*Methods in Enzymology* series). New York: Academic Press. |
| Numerical | **Reference:** Pines, J. 'Localization of cell cycle regulators by immuno-fluorescence', 1997. In: John N. Abelson, Melvin I. Simon, and W. D. Dunphy (vol. eds.): *Cell Cycle Control* vol. 283, pp.99–113 (*Methods in Enzymology* series). New York: Academic Press. |

4h. Book in a multi-volume work

These are linked books that build a detailed picture of a subject over an extended period of time. Include in your full reference:

- author
- year of publication of book in question
- title of book (in italics)
- volume and part number, if applicable
- page numbers to find evidence in question
- name of series editor (ser. ed.) and add until when (date), if applicable.

- title of multi-volume work (italicised)
- date of series (e.g. between X and X)
- place of publication and name of publisher.

Harvard	**Citation:** (Tsien, 1985) **Reference:** Tsien, T.H. 1985. *Paper and printing*. vol. 5, pt. 1, pp. 32–39. J. Needham (ser. ed. until 1995) of *Science and Civilisation in China, 1954–2008*. Cambridge (UK): Cambridge Univ. Press.
Numerical	**Reference:** Tsien, T.H. *Paper and printing*. vol. 5, pt. 1, 1985, pp. 32–39. J. Needham (ser. ed. until 1995) of *Science and Civilisation in China, 1954–2008*. Cambridge (UK): Cambridge Univ. Press.

4i. Republished book, including book club or paperback reprint

State both the year and publisher information of the republished book, and the publication year and publisher of the original version.

If the book you are looking at was originally issued under a different title, give the new title first and publication details, and then state 'Reprint of . . .', followed by the original title and original year of publication.

Harvard	**Citation:** (Masters, 1970) **Reference:** Masters, J. 1970. *Fourteen Eighteen*. London: Corgi (originally published by Michael Joseph 1965).
Numerical	**Reference:** Masters, J. *Fourteen Eighteen*. London: Corgi, 1970 (originally published by Michael Joseph 1965).

4j. e-books

If you are focusing on, or quoting, a particular section of text, give as much information as possible to pinpoint the evidence, e.g. page number, or location number, or chapter.

What to include in the reference:

- name of author
- year of publication
- book title (in italics)
- edition (if beyond first edition)
- URL
- date you downloaded the book.

Harvard	**Citation:** (Kirk, 2014) **Reference:** Kirk, T. 2014. *Physics study guide*. Ch.2 'Projectile Motion', p.13. Oxford University Press. Available at http://www.ebooks.com/1784809/physics-study-guide-2014/kirk-tim/ [downloaded 15 March 2015].
Numerical	**Reference:** Kirk, T. *Physics study guide*. Ch.2 'Projectile Motion', p.13. Oxford University Press, 2014. Available at http://www.ebooks.com/1784809/physics-study-guide-2014/kirk-tim/ [downloaded 15 March 2015].

4k. Rare books (within a museum/library)

Books within museum or national library collections can often be viewed online. Include in the reference:

- author's name
- year of publication; this can be given as 'circa' if exact date is not known, e.g. 'circa 1930–5'
- book title (in italics)
- name of museum/library
- available online at—URL
- date you viewed the site.

Harvard	**Citation:** (Carroll, 1864) **Reference:** Carroll, Lewis, 1864. *Alice's adventures under ground*. British Library. Available online at http://www.bl.uk/onlinegallery/ttp/alice/accessible/introduction.html [viewed 15 March 2015].
Numerical	**Reference:** Carroll, Lewis. *Alice's adventures under ground*, 1864. British Library. Available online at http://www.bl.uk/onlinegallery/ttp/alice/accessible/introduction.html [viewed 15 March 2015].

If you visited the British Library and saw the book for yourself, after the title you would give details of the place, and date you visited the library. For example:

> Carroll, Lewis, 1864. *Alice's Adventures Under Ground*. London: British Library, visited 29 April 2015.

4l. Booklets and pamphlets

What to include in the reference:

- name(s) of author(s) or originator(s); if no author's name is shown, either start with the name of the organisation producing the booklet or, if that is not obvious, the title of it
- year of publication, and edition if applicable
- state the medium, if not obvious, e.g. [leaflet]
- title, in italics
- editor(s), if applicable (indicated as ed./eds.)
- place of publication and publisher
- page number or other numeration, if applicable.

4l(i). Booklet

Harvard	**Citation:** (Hands, 1992) **Reference:** Hands, T. 1992. *Thomas Hardy and Stinsford Church: a brief companion for the visitor*. Dorset: Stinsford Parochial Church Council.
Numerical	**Reference:** Hands, T. *Thomas Hardy and Stinsford Church: a brief companion for the visitor.* Dorset: Stinsford Parochial Church Council, 1992.

4l(ii). Pamphlet

Harvard	**Citation:** (Steff, 1977) **Reference:** Steff, B. 1977. *My dearest acquaintance: a biographical sketch of Mary and Henry Webb.* Ludlow: The King's Bookshop.
Numerical	**Reference:** Steff, B. *My dearest acquaintance: a biographical sketch of Mary and Henry Webb.* Ludlow: The King's Bookshop, 1977.

5. Cartographic resources (maps and related information)

Copyright: If you want to copy illustrations into your own work, you may need to gain permission from the organisation hosting the site; always check the copyright conditions.

What to include in the reference:

- name of originator(s) (e.g. Ordnance Survey); if there is no named author or editor, start with the resource title (in italics)
- year of publication
- title of map (in italics)
- sheet number and scale
- series (if applicable)
- place of publication (and publisher, if different from originator).

5a. Atlas

Harvard	**Citation:** (*Atlas of the World*, 2004) **Reference:** *Atlas of the World* 12th edn. 2004. Oxford: Oxford University Press.
Numerical	**Reference:** *Atlas of the World* 12th edn. Oxford: Oxford University Press, 2004.

5b. British Geological Survey map

Harvard	**Citation:** (British Geological Survey, 1992) **Reference:** British Geological Survey, 1992. *Thirsk* (S&D) E52. 1:50 000. Nottingham: British Geological Survey.
Numerical	**Reference:** British Geological Survey. *Thirsk* (S&D) E52. 1:50 000. Nottingham: British Geological Survey, 1992.

5c. Online map

Harvard	**Citation:** (University of Texas, 1996) **Reference:** University of Texas, 1996. *Map of Guantanamo.* Available at http://www.lib.utexas.edu/maps/americas/guantanamo_1996.jpg [viewed 18 March 2015].
Numerical	**Reference:** University of Texas. *Map of Guantanamo.* 1996. Available at http://www.lib.utexas.edu/maps/americas/guantanamo_1996.jpg [viewed 18 March 2015].

5d. Old map (online, within a library or museum collection)

What to include in the reference:

- name of library/museum
- date image added to the website, if shown (put 'no date', if no year is given)
- title of the map (in italics)
- any library reference number
- URL
- date you viewed the site.

Harvard	**Citation:** (British Library, 2009) **Reference:** British Library, 2009. *Pierre Desceliers' planisphere. Arques, 1550.* British Library ref MS 24065. Available at http://www.bl.uk/onlinegallery/onlineex/mapsviews/desceliers/large17690.html [viewed 12 April 2015].
Numerical	**Reference:** British Library. *Pierre Desceliers' planisphere. Arques, 1550.* British Library, 2009, ref MS 24065. Available at http://www.bl.uk/onlinegallery/onlineex/mapsviews/desceliers/large17690.html [viewed 12 April 2015].

5e. Google Earth

Include in your reference:

- name of originator (Google Earth)
- year images made available
- title, location and coordinates (in italics)
- URL
- date you viewed the site.

Harvard	**Citation:** (Google Earth, 2015) **Reference:** Google Earth, 2015. *City of Bradford, West Yorkshire, 53° 47' 0" North, 1° 45' 0" West.* Available at http://www.google.com/earth/ [viewed 23 March 2015].
Numerical	Google Earth. *City of Bradford, West Yorkshire, 53° 47' 0" North, 1° 45' 0" West.* Available at http://www.google.com/earth/ [viewed 23 March 2015].

5f. Ordnance Survey map

Harvard	**Citation:** (Ordnance Survey, 1974) **Reference:** Ordnance Survey, 1974. *Saxmundham and Aldeburgh* 156, 1:50 000. First series. Southampton: Ordnance Survey.
Numerical	**Reference:** Ordnance Survey. *Saxmundham and Aldeburgh* 156, 1:50 000. First series. Southampton: Ordnance Survey, 1974.

5g. Satellite image map

State the nature of the image: [satellite image]

Harvard	**Citation:** (Planet Observer, 2006) **Reference:** Planet Observer, 2006. *European map* [satellite image] 1:8.000.000. USA: National Geographic Society.
Numerical	**Reference:** Planet Observer. *European map* [satellite image] 1:8.000.000. USA: National Geographic Society, 2006.

6. Conference papers

Conference proceedings are a collection of papers from a particular conference.
What to include in the reference:

- conference organisers
- year of conference
- title of conference (in italics)
- date of conference
- where conference was held
- URL
- date you viewed the online source, if applicable; for conference papers not online, omit the 'Available at' and URL information.

6a. Example of conference proceedings online

Harvard	**Citation:** (AIChE, 2014) **Reference:** AIChE: American Institute of Chemical Engineers, 2014. *2nd CCPS China conference on process safety.* 28–29 August. China: Qingdao, Gold Hotel. Available at http://www3.aiche.org/proceedings/Group.aspx?GroupID=1965 &ConfPageMessage=Y [viewed 15 May 2015].
Numerical	**Reference:** AIChE: American Institute of Chemical Engineers. *2nd CCPS China conference on process safety.* 28–29 August, 2014. China: Qingdao, Gold Hotel. Available at http://www3.aiche.org/proceedings/Group.aspx?GroupID=1965 &ConfPageMessage=Y [viewed 15 May 2015].

6b. Conference paper

An individual paper presented at a specific conference.
What to include in the reference:

- start with name of the author of the paper
- year paper was delivered to the conference
- title of paper, in single quotation marks
- state the nature of the contribution to the conference: [paper]

- title of conference (in italics)
- date of conference
- where conference was held.

6c. *Example of individual paper presented at a conference*

Harvard	**Citation:** (Zeng, 2014) **Reference:** Zeng, A. 2014. 'Improve process safety through advanced culture' [paper] AIChE: American Institute of Chemical Engineers. *2nd CCPS China conference on process safety.* 28–29 August. China: Qindao, Gold Hotel. Available at http://www3.aiche.org/proceedings/Abstract.aspx?-PaperID=394552 [viewed 15 May 2015].
Numerical	**Reference:** Zeng, A. 'Improve process safety through advanced culture' [paper] AIChE: American Institute of Chemical Engineers. *2nd CCPS China conference on process safety.* 28–29 August, 2014. China: Qindao, Gold Hotel. Available at http://www3.aiche.org/proceedings/Abstract.aspx?PaperID=394552 [viewed 15 May 2015].

7. Dissertations

Dissertations deposited within university libraries are usually password protected, although abstracts are usually more accessible.

Start your full reference with the name of the author, then state the year the dissertation was accepted, title (in italics), level of academic study, e.g. Bachelor's, Master's, Doctorate; state name of the institution, then the URL and the date you viewed the work.

7a. *Dissertation abstract (online)*

Harvard	**Citation:** (Harris, 2006) **Reference:** Harris, C.D. 2006. *Organizational change and intellectual production: the case study of Hohokam archaeology.* University of Arizona. Abstract available at http://wwwlib.umi.com/dissertations/fullcit/3206908 [viewed 4 April 2015].
Numerical	**Reference:** Harris, C.D. *Organizational change and intellectual production: the case study of Hohokam archaeology,* 2006. University of Arizona. Abstract available at http://wwwlib.umi.com/dissertations/fullcit/3206908 [viewed 4 April 2015].

7b. *Full dissertation (online)*

Note that the URL in the reference below is incomplete for password-related reasons.

Harvard	**Citation:** (Chen, 2014) **Reference:** Chen, X. 2014. *China's foreign policy choices over its territorial disputes.* Master's dissertation, University of Bradford. Available at http://brad-finder.brad.ac.uk/iii/cpro/DigitalItemViewPage . . . [viewed 13 March 2015].
Numerical	**Reference:** Chen, X. *China's foreign policy choices over its territorial disputes.* Master's dissertation, 2014, University of Bradford. Available at http://brad-finder.brad.ac.uk/iii/cpro/DigitalItemViewPage . . . [viewed 13 March 2015].

8. Education and training material

Although lecturers' notes—online or printed—can be referenced, it is wise to seek advice from your tutors on their feelings about you doing this. Most lecture notes and teaching material from seminars would be regarded as secondary sources, unless the lecturer was presenting original evidence for the first time in the session. Lectures and seminars are usually a way of highlighting key issues, or inviting you to look at a subject from a range of perspectives, so lecturers would normally expect you to follow up points made in the classroom with reading from primary sources in your own time.

8a. Tutors' notes

Include in the reference:

- tutor's name and year the source was written or updated
- title of course (in italics) and nature of the source, e.g. [course notes]
- specific page number, if relevant
- level of study, e.g. undergraduate, postgraduate
- academic year
- place of study (town, city)
- name of institution and the relevant school or department.

Harvard	**Citation:** (Sedgley, 2013) **Reference:** Sedgley, C. 2013. *Writing for academic and professional purposes* [course notes] Level 2 undergraduate module, 2011/12. Bradford: University of Bradford, School of Management.
Numerical	**Reference:** Sedgley, M. *Writing for academic and professional purposes* [course notes] Level 2 undergraduate module, 2012/13. Bradford: University of Bradford, School of Management.

8b. Online distance learning course: set reading

Include:

- author
- year source was written
- title of reading, in single quotation marks
- describe source, if necessary, e.g. 'set reading from . . .'
- course title (in italics)
- name of institution and/or organisation offering the course
- URL
- date you viewed or downloaded the source.

Harvard	**Citation:** (Burger, 2009) **Reference:** Burger, J. 2009. 'Replicating Milgram', set reading from *Social Psychology,* distance learning course, Wesleyan University, in partnership with Coursera. Available at https://www.coursera.org/course/socialpsychology [viewed 17 April 2015].

Numerical	**Reference:** Burger, J. 'Replicating Milgram', 2009, set reading from *Social Psychology,* distance learning course, Wesleyan University, in partnership with Coursera. Available at https://www.coursera.org/course/socialpsychology [viewed 17 April 2015].

8c. PowerPoint/PowerPoint sharing sites

PowerPoint presentations can be found online on a range of education and training-related subjects and are widely used at conferences by speakers.

Check the backgrounds and experience of any presenter to make sure they are authoritative and that the evidence presented is credible—for example, ensure that any evidence presented in the slides is properly referenced by the presenter(s).

Include in the reference:

- name of presenter(s)
- year
- title of presentation (in italics)
- state the communication medium [PowerPoint]
- specific date of publication (if known or shown)
- if relevant, where presentation was made, e.g. name of conference, venue
- URL
- date you viewed the site.

Harvard	**Citation:** (Pullinger and Schneider, 2014) **Reference:** Pullinger, D. and M. Schneider, 2014. 'Rationalising referencing: changing policy and practice to smooth transition and improve the student experience'. Conference presentation: *Librarians' information literacy annual conference 2014,* Sheffield Hallam University. Summary available at http://www.slideshare.net/infolit_group/pullinger-34165457. Leeds: University of Leeds (Library).
Numerical	**Reference:** Pullinger, D. and M. Schneider. 'Rationalising referencing: changing policy and practice to smooth transition and improve the student experience'. Conference presentation: *Librarians' information literacy annual conference 2014,* Sheffield Hallam University. Summary available at http://www.slideshare.net/infolit_group/pullinger-34165457. Leeds: University of Leeds (Library).

8d. Virtual learning environments (or 'spaces') (VLEs)

These are online learning resources for students; they assist in assessment, personal reflection, student collaboration, and communication between staff and students. VLEs are accessible in a public domain, albeit limited to a particular academic community or institution, so can be referenced. Some VLEs are focused on helping students build a portfolio of learning achievements, e.g. PebblePad, while others act as teaching aids, managed by teachers, e.g. Blackboard. It is important therefore to state what type of VLE you are citing and to which part of it you are referring.

To reference VLE resources:

- start with the name of the tutor/author/originator of the material
- include the year of online publication
- state title of item (in italics)
- give name of the course or module, the name of the institution and the academic year
- state the name of the VLE system and URL (only part-URLs are shown below)
- show the date you viewed or downloaded the source.

8d(i). Pebble Pad

Harvard	**Citation:** (Williams, 2014) **Reference:** Williams, C. 2009. *My CV* [PebblePad] Personal development planning module, MBA, University of Bradford, 2013/14. Available at http://www.pebblepad.co.uk/ [viewed 4 May 2009].
Numerical	**Reference:** Williams, C. *My CV* [PebblePad] Personal development planning module, MBA, University of Bradford, 2013/14. Available at http://www.pebblepad.co.uk/ [viewed 4 May 2009].

8d(ii). Blackboard

Harvard	**Citation:** (Gregory, 2012) **Reference:** Gregory, T. 2012. 'Regional trends' course notes [Blackboard], week 6, *The changing world of work*: level 2 module, University of Bradford, 2012/13. Available at http://blackboard.brad.ac.uk/ [viewed 4 May 2013].
Numerical	**Reference:** Gregory, T. 'Regional trends', course notes [Blackboard] week 6, *The changing world of work*: level 2 module, University of Bradford, 2012/13. Available at http://blackboard.brad.ac.uk/ [viewed 4 May 2013].

8e. Library and learning support resources

Libraries and learning support units at colleges and universities often produce high-quality learning resources that can be referenced.

- If there is no named author, start with the name of the support unit and institution producing the material.
- If the material is undated, give the current year for the citation and reference entry.
- Give full information about the resource, e.g. title of the learning resource (italicised), and detail of the particular unit of learning, as shown in the example that follows.

Harvard	**Citation:** (Academic Skills Unit, University of Bradford, 2015) **Reference:** Academic Skills Unit, University of Bradford, 2015. *Maths skills for university*, lesson 6: *Differentiation*. Available at http://www.bradford.ac.uk/wimba-files/msu-course/page_23.htm [viewed 18 March 2015].
Numerical	**Reference:** Academic Skills Unit, University of Bradford. *Maths skills for university*, lesson 6: *Differentiation,* 2015. Available at http://www.bradford.ac.uk/wimba-files/msu-course/page_23.htm [viewed 18 March 2015].

9. Government publications

The publisher for many UK government publications is The Stationery Office (TSO), although documents published before 1996 are usually shown as published by HMSO (Her Majesty's Stationery Office). The Stationery Office was privatised from the HMSO (now the Office of Public Sector Information) in 1996. However, other government departments and agencies also produce their own publications—for example, the Department for Transport (DfT) and the Health and Safety Executive (HSE). Government-sponsored research may also be published by other bodies or organisations.

Include the following information in the full reference:

- name of author(s) or name of government department or agency; you may also need to mention the country of origin if it is not obvious from the place of publication
- year of publication
- title of article or title of publication, in italics
- place of publication and name of official publisher
- volume or edition date number, table or page number, if applicable.
  If an internet source, add:
- URL
- date you viewed the site.

9a. Single country: report with a named author

Harvard	**Citation:** (Sudlow, 2003) **Reference:** Sudlow, D. 2003. *Scoping study on motorcycle training.* Great Britain: Department for Transport, Road Safety Research Report no. 36. Wetherby: DfT Publications.
Numerical	**Reference:** Sudlow, D. *Scoping study on motorcycle training.* Great Britain: Department for Transport: Road Safety Research Report no. 36. Wetherby: DfT Publications, 2003.

9b. Single country: online report

Abbreviations can be used in the citation, but explain them in the full reference; see also 9e, below.

Harvard	**Citation:** (ONS, 2015) **Reference:** ONS: Office for National Statistics, 2015. *Economic Review, March 2015.* Available at http://www.ons.gov.uk/ons/rel/elmr/economic-review/march-2015/art.html [viewed 20 April 2015].
Numerical	**Reference:** ONS: Office for National Statistics. *Economic Review, March 2015.* Available at http://www.ons.gov.uk/ons/rel/elmr/economic-review/march-2015/art.html [viewed 20 April 2015].

9c. Regional (e.g. EU) report (online)

Harvard	**Citation:** (European Union, 2014) **Reference:** European Union, 2014. *Total Population (EU)*. Available at http://europa.eu/publications/statistics/index_en.htm [viewed 19 March 2015].
Numerical	**Reference:** European Union *Total Population (EU)* 2014. Available at http://europa.eu/publications/statistics/index_en.htm [viewed 19 March 2015].

9d. International report (online)

If referring to a specific part of the report, include the detail, as shown in the example below, i.e. 'Table 6'.

Harvard	**Citation:** (United Nations, 2015, Table 6) **Reference:** United Nations, 2015. *Demographic Yearbook, 2013*, Table 6. Available at http://unstats.un.org/unsd/demographic/products/dyb/dybsets/2013.pdf [viewed 12 April 2015].
Numerical	**Reference:** United Nations *Demographic Yearbook, 2013*, Table 6, 2015. Available at http://unstats.un.org/unsd/demographic/products/dyb/dybsets/2013.pdf [viewed 12 April 2015].

9e. Government-sponsored publications

Government-sponsored reports often have long titles, but usually become commonly known by the name of the Chairperson of the committee responsible. You should always give the full official title of the report in a reference (italicised), but you can also give the popular title, too, if you wish. An abbreviated title can be shown in citations in the text, but the full title must be explained in the reference, as shown in the example that follows.

Harvard	**Citation:** (UNWCED, 1987) **Reference:** UNWCED: United Nations World Commission on Environment and Development, 1987. *Our common future* (Brundtland Report). Oxford: Oxford University Press.
Numerical	**Reference:** UNWCED: United Nations World Commission on Environment and Development, *Our common future* (Brundtland Report). Oxford: Oxford University Press, 1987.

10. Graphs and charts

It is important to cite and reference all sources used to construct graphs, tables and charts in your assignments. For example, Table 11(10)a was constructed by collating information from the source shown: the Canadian Cooperation Office. You would normally make it clear in the text that the chart was your own collation, using the source(s) cited.

You should try to construct your own graphs and charts, using external data, wherever possible, rather than copying and pasting published graphs, charts or tables into your work. Check with your tutor whether or not copying and pasting in this way is permitted. If you did copy a table/chart into your work (see Table 11(10)b) you would need to make that clear in the text of your work, as well as citing and fully referencing the source.

Table 11(10)a Example of a collated chart

Population of children in Tanzania (2002)			
Age	Both sexes	Male	Female
Total Population	18,837,206	9,399,477	9,433,920
0–4 (% of total)	16.45	16.82	16.09
5–9 (% of total)	14.9	15.29	14.51
10–14 (% of total)	12.9	13.27	12.55
15–19 (% of total)	10.44	10.47	10.41

(Source: Canadian Cooperation Office, 2003, p.6)

Table 11(10)a would be referenced as follows:

Harvard	**Citation:** (Canadian Cooperation Office, 2003) **Reference:** Canadian Cooperation Office, 2003. *Canadian government support to the education sector in Tanzania*. Table: 'Population of children in Tanzania, 2002'. Dar es Salaam, Tanzania: as author.
Numerical	**Reference:** Canadian Cooperation Office. *Canadian government support to the education sector in Tanzania*. Table: 'Population of children in Tanzania, 2002'. Dar es Salaam, Tanzania: as author, 2003.

Table 11(10)b copied into your work

Remember, if it is permitted by your tutors, and you do copy graphs, charts or tables into your work, you *must* always give full information on the source, including page number if originally from a printed source. For example, if you pasted in the following table, you would need to cite the source immediately below it, e.g. Transit Project, 2012.

Table 11(10)b Full-time undergraduate UK students by science subject

Subject area	2009/10	2010/11
Medicine & dentistry	65,800	66,840
Subjects allied to medicine	305,220	299,800

Table 11(10)b (*continued*)

Subject area	2009/10	2010/11
Biological sciences	183,035	190,035
Veterinary science	5,360	5,540
Agriculture & related subjects	18,920	20,790
Physical sciences	91,030	93,580
Mathematical sciences	39,125	41,110
Computer science	100,785	99,025
Engineering & technology	156,985	160,885
Architecture, building & planning	65,990	62,780
Total science	**1032245**	**1040375**

(Transit Project, 2012, unit 1, p.10)

The full reference entry for this source would look like this:

Harvard	**Citation:** (Transit Project, 2012) **Reference:** Transit Project, 2012. *Transit Science: student workbook*, Table: 'Full-time undergraduate UK students by science subject', Bradford: University of Bradford. Available at http://www.brad.ac.uk/transit/students/8-science/ [viewed 24 April 2015].
Numerical	**Reference:** Transit Project. *Transit Science: student workbook*, Table: 'Full-time undergraduate UK students by science subject', in unit 1, p.10, 2012. Bradford: University of Bradford. Available at http://www.brad.ac.uk/transit/students/8-science/ [viewed 24 April 2015].

11. Historical research

Detail to include in your reference:

- if referring to a specific named person start with this; if not, use a source descriptive name, e.g. UK Census (date)
- name of country, if not obvious
- record or source
- title of specific document or list (in italics)
- reference number, if applicable
- locality information (if applicable)
- other identifying source features.

If using an online source:

- include the name of any database or person hosting the information, and the date the information was posted or updated on the site

- URL address
- date the information was viewed or retrieved.

11a. Census record (online)

Harvard	**Citation:** (UK Census, 1881) **Reference:** UK Census, 1881. *Residents of Bolton Union Workhouse, Fishpool, Farnworth, Lancashire.* Available at http://www.workhouses.org.uk/Bolton/Bolton1881.shtml [viewed 19 March 2015].
Numerical	**Reference:** As above.

11b. Birth certificate

Harvard	**Citation:** (Mansbridge, 1947) **Reference**: Mansbridge, E. *Birth Certificate*: 28 July 1947. Certificate GA976389, Romford Registration District Office, Essex.
Numerical	**Reference:** As above.

11c. Military record (online)

Include in the reference:

- name of person featured on the record
- date document in question was published online
- title or description of document (in italics)
- name of organisation publishing the information online
- any identifying numbers
- URL
- date you viewed the site.

Harvard	**Citation:** (*Frederick Birks*, 2015) **Reference:** *Frederick Birks*, 2015. Summary of war record. Available at the AIF Project at http://www.aif.adfa.edu.au:8080/showPerson?pid=23232 [viewed 19 March 2015].
Numerical	**Reference:** As above.

11d. Document in an archive, library or museum collection

Details to include:

- name of originator of document
- year
- title of manuscript/document, in italics
- specific date of document, if shown
- reference number
- location of archive/library/museum
- name of archive/library/museum.

Harvard	**Citation:** (Christie, 1918) **Reference:** Christie, Agatha, 1918. *Letter to Alberta Vickridge*, dated 1 Jun 1918. Ref. BCMS20C Vickridge. Leeds: University of Leeds Library, Special Collection.
Numerical	**Reference:** Christie, Agatha. *Letter to Alberta Vickridge*, dated 1 Jun 1918. Ref. BCMS20C Vickridge, Box 2. Leeds: University of Leeds Library, Special Collection.

11e. Online document in an archive, library or museum collection

Harvard	**Citation:** (Thomas of York, 1105) **Reference:** Thomas of York, 1105. *Letter from Thomas of York to Lanfranc.* In: British Library, Collection of Letters. Available at http://www.bl.uk/onlinegallery/onlineex/illmanus/cottmanucoll/a/011cotvese00006u00205v00.html [viewed 15 April 2015].
Numerical	**Reference:** Thomas of York. *Letter from Thomas of York to Lanfranc,* 1105. In: British Library, Collection of Letters. Available at http://www.bl.uk/onlinegallery/onlineex/illmanus/cottmanucoll/a/011cotvese00006u00205v00.html [viewed 15 April 2015].

12. Information and display boards

Display and information boards, in museums, galleries and elsewhere, can be useful sources of information and so can be referenced.

- It is unlikely that the writer will be named, but if so start the full reference with his or her name.
- If the author is not identified, give the name of the **originator** of the information, e.g. the name of the gallery/museum/local authority etc.
- If the panel is dated, show the year; if not, give the year you looked at the information.
- State the title (italicised), either taken directly from the panel, or one that is your summation of the information shown, and indicate the nature of the source, e.g. [display board]. State the date you looked at the information, and its location.

12a. Display panel

Harvard	**Citation:** (Bradford Museums Service, 2009) **Reference:** Bradford Museums Service, 2009. *The Busby Family History* [display board] 21 January, 2009. Bradford: Industrial Museum.
Numerical	**Reference:** Bradford Industrial Museum. *The Busby Family History* [display board] 21 January, 2009. Bradford: Industrial Museum.

13. Interviews

13a. Interview printed in a newspaper

Include:
- interviewer's name
- year of interview
- title of interview (or newspaper heading) in single quotation marks

- interviewee's name, if not shown in the title
- title of publication (in italics)
- publication details, including full date and page number.

Harvard	**Citation:** (Flanagan, 2005) **Reference:** Flanagan, B. 2005. 'Turner's secret: the short haul factor. Interview with Nigel Turner, BMI's new CEO'. *Observer* (Business Section), 22 May 2005, p.18.
Numerical	**Reference:** Flanagan, B. 'Turner's secret: the short haul factor. Interview with Nigel Turner, BMI's new CEO'. *Observer* (Business Section), 22 May 2005, p.18.

13b. Television interview

Similar to newspaper interview, but include the name of the TV station (in italics).

Harvard	**Citation:** (Winfrey, 2013) **Reference:** Winfrey, O. 2013. 'Lance Armstrong interview with Oprah Winfrey', *CBS* 15 January 2013.
Numerical	**Reference:** Winfrey, O. 'Lance Armstrong interview with Oprah Winfrey', *CBS* 15 January 2013.

13c. Personal interviews

Interviews you conduct for any dissertation would normally be described in the 'Methodology' section or chapter of your project, rather than referenced. The Methodology chapter would normally include the numbers and general characteristics of the interviewees; details of the way information was collected and collated, how interviewees were selected, questions asked etc. Detailed statistics of the characteristics of interviewees would normally feature in the appendices to the dissertation.

Note: Interviewees *must* always be given reassurance about confidentiality and told who will see the data obtained; this is particularly important if the subject is a sensitive one and you plan to make the data public, e.g. in an article or dissertation open to others to view. The interviewees should be assured that their views will be anonymous and generalised in the final report, unless the interviewees wish or agree otherwise. Your tutor may need you to supply a transcript or audio recording of the interview.

14. Journals

Academic journals are important sources of primary source evidence for students, as they often contain new research findings or challenges to conventional wisdom.

In the full reference include details of:

- name of author/writer
- title of article, in single quotation marks
- name of journal (in italics)
- volume, issue or part numbers (see note below); if it is a special edition or supplement to a journal, you need to indicate this, e.g. (Suppl.)
- the page numbers in the journal featuring the article, e.g. (pp.36–40)

If online:

* URL or digital object identifier (DOI)
* date viewed (unless using a DOI).

When referring to volume, issue or part numbers, this can be done either using words, e.g. volume 69, part 3; or by abbreviations, e.g. vol. 69, pt. 3; or by using numbers, e.g. **69**(3), with the volume number in bold. Be consistent whichever approach you adopt; a range of examples are given below for illustrative purposes.

References to journal articles do not usually include the name of the publisher or place of publication, unless there is more than one journal with the same title, e.g. *Banking Weekly* (New York) and *Banking Weekly* (London).

14a. Printed journal article

Harvard	**Citation:** (Yang, 2005) **Reference:** Yang, D. 2005. 'Culture matters to multinationals' intellectual property business'. *Journal of World Business,* vol. 40, pp.281–301.
Numerical	**Reference:** Yang, D. 'Culture matters to multinationals' intellectual property business'. *Journal of World Business,* 2005, vol. 40, pp.281–301.

14b. Printed journal article (multiple authors)

For more detail about citing and referencing multiple authors, see 'Frequently asked questions', Chapter 12, question 7.

If you wanted to identify a page number to highlight a particular point or quote, you could include this in the citation; see the example below.

Harvard	**Citation:** (Takaichi et al., 2003, p.233) **Reference:** Takaichi, S., V. Mizuhira, H. Hasegawa, T. Suzaki, M. Notoya, S. Ejiri, H. Ozawa, and J.H. Van Wyk, 2003. 'Ultrastructure and early embryonic shell formation in the terrestrial pulmonate snail: *Euhada Hickonis.*' *Journal of Molluscan Studies,* **69**(3), pp.229–244.
Numerical	**Reference:** Takaichi, S., V. Mizuhira, H. Hasegawa, T. Suzaki, M. Notoya, S. Ejiri, H. Ozawa, and J.H. Van Wyk. 'Ultrastructure and early embryonic shell formation in the terrestrial pulmonate snail: *Euhada Hickonis.*' *Journal of Molluscan Studies,* 2003, **69**(3), pp.229–244.

14c. Special issue of a journal (printed version)

Harvard	**Citation:** (Trendafilova, 2006) **Reference:** Trendafilova, I. 2006. 'Vibration-based damage detection in structures using time series analysis'. *Journal of Mechanical Engineering Science* (Special Issue on 'Chaos in Science and Engineering'), **220**(C3) pp.361–272.
Numerical	**Reference:** Trendafilova, I. 'Vibration-based damage detection in structures using time series analysis'. *Journal of Mechanical Engineering Science* (Special Issue on Chaos in Science and Engineering), 2006, **220**(C3) pp.361–272.

14d. Online journal (URL link)

Harvard	**Citation:** (Howard and Davies, 2009)
	Reference: Howard, R.M. and L.J. Davies, 2009. 'Plagiarism in the Internet Age'. *Educational Leadership*, volume 66, part 6, pp.64–67. Available at: http://stats.lib.pdx.edu/proxy.php?url=http://search.ebscohost.com/login.aspx?direct=true&db=a9h&AN=36666628&site=ehost-live&scope=cite [viewed 20 March 2015].
Numerical	**Reference:** Howard, R.M. & L.J. Davies. 'Plagiarism in the Internet Age'. *Educational Leadership*, 2006, volume 66, part 6, pp.64–67. Available at: http://stats.lib.pdx.edu/proxy.php?url=http://search.ebscohost.com/login.aspx?direct=true&db=a9h&AN=36666628&site=ehost-live&scope=cite [viewed 20 March 2015].

14e. Online journal (with DOI link)

A digital object identifier (DOI) is a unique number that is a permanent identifier offering a consistent way to find an online source, including academic journals. Because it will always connect you to the source—unlike URLs, which can easily disappear—you do not need to include the [viewed . . . date] part of the full reference.

Harvard	**Citation:** (Christensen, 2011)
	Reference: Christensen, G.J. 2011. 'Plagiarism: can it be stopped?' *Business Communication Quarterly*, **74**(2), pp.201–204. Available at DOI: 10.1177/1080569911404403
Numerical	**Reference:** Christensen, G.J. 'Plagiarism: can it be stopped?' *Business Communication Quarterly*, 2011, **74**(2), pp.201–204. Available at DOI: 10.1177/1080569911404403

14f. Pre-print and post-print journal articles online

A pre-print is a draft, or work in progress, of a paper that has not yet been published in a peer-reviewed journal. These are contained and maintained within online repositories, and digital copies are made accessible to others. This gives authors early feedback from their peers to help them revise their work; students can benefit from access to these papers to find out what research is in progress.

Post-print articles have been peer reviewed and are awaiting publication in a journal.

14f(i). Pre-print example

Harvard	**Citation:** (Fedele, 2015)
	Reference: Fedele, F. 2015. 'On Oceanic rogue waves' [pre-print] Submitted 14 January 2015 to *AMS Journal of Physical Oceanography*. Available at http://arxiv.org/abs/1501.03370 [viewed 24 March 2015].
Numerical	**Reference:** Fedele, F. 'On Oceanic rogue waves' [pre-print] Submitted 14 January 2015 to *AMS Journal of Physical Oceanography*. Available at http://arxiv.org/abs/1501.03370 [viewed 24 March 2015].

14f(ii). Post-print example

Harvard	**Citation:** (Sierra, 2012) **Reference:** Sierra, J.C. 2012. [post-print] 'A remark on Zak's theorem on tangencies'. *Mathematical Research Letters*. 2012. Available at http://arxiv.org/abs/1203.0208 [viewed 24 March 2015].
Numerical	**Reference:** Sierra, J.C. [post-print] 'A remark on Zak's theorem on tangencies'. *Mathematical Research Letters*. 2012. Available at http://arxiv.org/abs/1203.0208 [viewed 24 March 2015].

15. Lectures, speeches, talks and public readings

As these are delivered in the public domain, they can be referenced, although if it is an academic lecture, check with the lecturer first, as he or she may prefer you to reference the primary sources from your reading list, rather than the secondary source of a lecture.

15a. Course lecture

What to include:

- start with the name of the lecturer/speaker and year
- title of the lecture/talk/speech/reading (in italics)
- state nature of the event, e.g. [lecture]
- venue detail
- if an education lecture, state name of the institution, including school or department, and title of the course
- date of the event.

Harvard	**Citation:** (Sedgley, 2014) **Reference:** Sedgley, M. 2014. *Why all this referencing in UK higher education?* [lecture] University of Bradford, School of Management, MBA programme, 12 September 2014.
Numerical	**Reference:** Sedgley, M. *Why all this referencing in UK higher education?* [lecture] University of Bradford, School of Management, MBA programme, 12 September 2014.

15b. Speech

A speech is usually a formal and one-directional address to an audience. They are often associated with social and political causes and gatherings.

Harvard	**Citation:** (Benn, 2006) **Reference:** Benn, Tony, 2006. [political speech] Tolpuddle Martyrs' Festival. Dorset: Tolpuddle, 16 July 2006.
Numerical	**Reference:** Benn, Tony. [political speech] Tolpuddle Martyrs' Festival. Dorset: Tolpuddle, 16 July 2006.

15c. Talks

'Talks' and 'lectures' are both formal presentations of ideas. However, a 'lecture' is often (but not always) delivered in an academic setting, whereas a 'talk' can be given in less formal surroundings, e.g. a library or village hall. Both lectures and talks can involve interaction with an audience, although a talk is more likely to do this—and it may be expected by the audience.

Harvard	**Citation:** (Qureshi, 2014)
	Reference: Qureshi, I. 2014. *Bollywood in Britain* [talk] Bradford: City Park Library, 24 April 2014.
Numerical	**Reference:** Qureshi, I. *Bollywood in Britain* [talk] Bradford: City Park Library, 24 April 2014.

15d. Reading (e.g. poetry, book extract)

Harvard	**Citation:** (Duffy, 2006)
	Reference: Duffy, Carol Ann, 2006. *Timekeeping* [poetry reading] West Sussex: Chichester Festival, 22 July 2006.
Numerical	**Reference:** Duffy, Carol Ann. *Timekeeping* [poetry reading] West Sussex: Chichester Festival, 22 July 2006.

16. Legal sources

Students on law degree or related courses will learn a referencing style that is particular to this subject, which in the UK is usually the Oxford Standard for Citation of Legal Authorities (OSCOLA). This is the style used by the *Oxford University Commonwealth Law Journal*, which contributed to its development. However, students on other courses, who occasionally have to cite legal cases, may also find this section helpful.

An example of referencing a live screening of UK Supreme Court proceedings is shown as example 16d in both the OSCOLA and Harvard styles—the latter for the benefit of non-law students.

OSCOLA style of referencing

More detailed information on the OSCOLA style of referencing can be obtained from the website of the Faculty of Law, University of Oxford; most institutions of higher education that offer law degrees will offer students summary versions of the OSCOLA guide. Briefly, the OSCOLA referencing style links with the consecutive numbering style of referencing in that it uses raised, or superscript, numbers in the text combined with footnotes (not endnotes). OSCOLA style is, however, different to the four main referencing styles in the way it is presented. A free pdf guide to using OSCOLA can be downloaded from http://www.law.ox.ac.uk/published/OSCOLA_4th_edn.pdf.

16a. Legal journals

Use abbreviations for the titles of journals. Journals will often have their abbreviations on the front page; if so, use these without punctuation between the letters.

Alternatively use the Cardiff Index to Legal Abbreviations, which can be found at http://www.legalabbrevs.cardiff.ac.uk/.

Include in the reference:

- name of author (as shown on title page)
- title of article in inverted commas
- year
- volume number
- abbreviated journal name
- first page number of the article
- if you wanted to specify a particular page, put a comma after the first page number and add the particular page number in question (as shown below).

There should be no full stop at the end of the reference.

Example:

Beverley Clough, 'Vulnerability and capacity to consent to sex—asking the right questions' (2014) 26 CFLQ 371, 373

16b. Case citation

Case citation is a frequent occurrence in law course assignments. You need to include:

- names of the parties
- year, in square brackets
- volume number
- abbreviated name of the law report series
- first page of the reference.

Case names should be italicised in assignments. For example:

Murphy v Brentwood District Council [1990] 2 All ER 908

When referring to a case for the first time, give its full name exactly as it appears in the report. In subsequent references a case can be referred to by a shortened name, e.g. *Murphy v Brentwood District Council,* and can be referred to as 'the *Murphy* case'.

16c. Judges' names

When a judge's name is being quoted or referred to in a particular passage, the name should be given in the text. If the judge is a peer, use their full title. For example:

Lord Mackay in *Pepper v Hart* [1993] 1 All ER 42 at 47 argued that . . .

If the judge were not a peer, you would use the letter 'J' for judge, or if a Lord or Lady Justice, 'LJ'.

Example:

Brown LJ commented . . .

Harris J was of the opinion that . . .

16d. Live screening: UK Supreme Court

In 2015, the UK Supreme Court introduced live screening of its sittings. This is likely to be of interest to law students, and others interested in the workings of the British Judiciary.

The OSCOLA guidance on referencing websites would apply:

- start with the originator's name
- title of proceedings
- date of proceedings
- URL (within angle brackets)
- date you viewed the site.

Both OSCOLA and Harvard style examples (the latter for non-law students) are shown, as follows:

OSCOLA	**Reference:** Supreme Court, 'Secretary of State for Work and Pensions (Appellant) v Tolley' [live screening] (5 May 2015) <https://www.supremecourt.uk/live/court-02.html> accessed 5 May 2015.
Harvard	**Citation:** (Supreme Court, 2015) **Reference:** Supreme Court, 2015. 'Secretary of State for Work and Pensions (Appellant) v Tolley' [live screening] 5 May 2015. Available at https://www.supremecourt.uk/live/court-02.html [viewed 5 May 2015].

17. Live entertainment and performances

To determine the order of elements in citations and full referencing entries, the key question to ask is, 'Who is the main *originator* for the performance?' With a dance performance, it is the choreographer; with music, it is the composer; and with theatre, it is the playwright, followed closely by the director. Others can be mentioned in the text of your work, if relevant to the evidence you are presenting.

17a. Dance (including ballet)

Include:

- choreographer; state specifically: [choreographer]
- year of production
- title of production (in italics)
- details of medium (e.g. contemporary dance; ballet) unless obvious from the name of company)
- name of dance troupe or company
- date of performance
- place of performance.

Harvard	**Citation:** (Nixon, 2003) **Reference:** Nixon, D. [choreographer] 2003. *Wuthering Heights*. Northern Ballet, Saturday 20 May 2003. Leeds: Grand Theatre.
Numerical	**Reference:** Nixon, D. [choreographer] *Wuthering Heights*. Northern Ballet, Saturday 20 May 2003, Leeds: Grand Theatre.

17b. Live music

To reference a live music performance, you would normally start with the name of the music composer, year the work was written or distributed, title of work (in italics), name of artist, performers or orchestra, date of performance and place of performance.

Other details can be included, if relevant, including name of conductor or leader, and names of musicians, as shown in the first example that follows. It may occasionally be necessary to clarify that it is a music performance, if this is not obvious from other details supplied.

Three examples:

Harvard	**Citation:** (Mozart, 1775–7)
	Reference: Mozart, W. 1775–7. *Piano Concerto No. 10*. London Mozart Players. Pianists: G. and S. Pekinel. Leeds: Town Hall, 14 October 2006.
Numerical	**Reference:** Mozart, W. *Piano Concerto No. 10*, 1775–7. London Mozart Players. Pianists: G. and S. Pekinel, Leeds: Town Hall, 14 October 2006.
Harvard	**Citation:** (Thomas and Lee, 2001)
	Reference: Thomas, R. and S. Lee, 2001. *Jerry Springer—the opera*. Bradford: Alhambra Theatre, 22–27 May, 2006.
Numerical	**Reference:** Thomas, R. and S. Lee. *Jerry Springer—the opera*, 2001. Bradford: Alhambra Theatre, 22–27 May, 2006.
Harvard	**Citation:** (Rusby, 2007)
	Reference: Rusby, Kate, 2007. *The Lark* [folk song] performed 15 April 2015. Gateshead: The Sage.
Numerical	**Reference:** Rusby, Kate. *The Lark* [folk song] 2007, performed 15 April 2015. Gateshead: The Sage.

17c. Theatre and theatrical productions

You are likely to encounter two types of theatrical production: a devised production and an authored play (see also 'Scripts', item 30 below).

- A devised production is where there is no writer, and often no director, where the actors create an improvisatory performance—for example, on the street and responding intuitively to their audience.
- An authored play is one that is written and scripted by a named playwright or group of people.

17c(i). Devised production

What to include in the reference:

- name of producer or company
- year of production
- title of production (in italics)

- name of director, if there is one
- date of performance
- location of performance.

Harvard	**Citation:** (TangledFeet, 2015) **Reference:** TangledFeet, 2015. *Kicking and screaming*, 22 March 2015, Saltburn Community Theatre.
Numerical	**Reference:** TangledFeet. *Kicking and screaming*, 22 March 2015, Saltburn Community Theatre.

17c(ii). Authored play (live production)

The originator for an authored play is the playwright, but the way it is interpreted is usually of importance, too, as is the place and date of the production in question.

What to include in the reference:

- start with the name of the playwright; for plays that originate with no written script, but develop by improvisation into a set production—for example, *Abigail's Party*—cite the director, e.g. Mike Leigh, and start the reference with the director's name
- year you saw the play
- title of play (in italics)
- director
- date of performance in question
- place of production.

Harvard	**Citation:** (Kempinski, 2014) **Reference:** Kempinski, T. 2014. *Duet for one* [play] Directed by Elizabeth Newman, Saturday 10 May 2014 at Bolton: Octagon Theatre.
Numerical	**Reference:** Kempinski, T. *Duet for one* [play] Directed by Elizabeth Newman, Saturday 10 May 2014 at Bolton: Octagon Theatre.

17c(iii). Shakespeare play

Harvard	**Citation:** (Shakespeare, performed 2015) **Reference:** Shakespeare, W. 2015. *Love's labour's lost*. Directed by Christopher Luscombe, 12 March 2015 at Stratford: Royal Shakespeare Company.
Numerical	**Reference:** Shakespeare, W. *Love's labour's lost*. Directed by Christopher Luscombe, 12 March 2015 at Stratford: Royal Shakespeare Company.

18. Magazines/newsletters

What to include in the reference:

- name of writer; if there is no named writer, start with the title (italicised) of the magazine

- year
- title of article
- name of magazine (in italics)
- date, and edition, if applicable
- page numbers.

If online:

- URL
- date you viewed the site.

18a. Magazine

Harvard	**Citation:** (Harper, D. et al. 2015) **Reference:** Harper, D., J. Kellow, H. Bond and P. Mundy, 2015. 'Expert advice Q & A'. *Healthy Food Guide*, March 2015, p.34.
Numerical	**Reference:** Harper, D., J. Kellow, H. Bond and P. Mundy. 'Expert advice Q & A'. *Healthy Food Guide*, March 2015, p.34.

18b. Online magazine

Harvard	**Citation:** (Sanguinetti, 2015) **Reference:** Sanguinetti, G. 2015. 'Teach English abroad'. *Jaquo.com* Spring edition, p.19. Available at http://issuu.com/jaquo/docs/jaquomagazine-spring2015/1?e=16456599/12033731 [viewed 24 March 2015].
Numerical	**Reference:** Sanguinetti, G. 'Teach English abroad'. *Jaquo.com* Spring edition, 2015, p.19. Available at http://issuu.com/jaquo/docs/jaquomagazine-spring2015/1?e=16456599/12033731 [viewed 24 March 2015].

18c. Newsletter

Harvard	**Citation:** (Street, 2014) **Reference:** Street, F. 2014. 'A mug's game'. *Moorcroft Collectors' Club Newsletter*, November 2014, number 81, pp.29–31.
Numerical	**Reference:** Street, F. 'A mug's game'. *Moorcroft Collectors' Club Newsletter*, November 2014, number 81, pp.29–31.

19. Music scores/sheet music

To reference music scores:

- start with the name of the composer
- year(s) of composition
- title of work (italics)
- place of publication
- name of publisher.

If there is no year of publication shown for the score, put 'no date'. Two examples are shown below.

| Harvard | **Citation:** (Bruch, 1867)
 Reference: Bruch, Max. 1867. *Concerto in G Minor, Op.26.* New York: G. Schirmer (no date). |
| Numerical | **Reference:** Bruch, Max. *Concerto in G Minor, Op.26.* 1867. New York: G. Schirmer (no date). |

| Harvard | **Citation:** (Lennon and McCartney, 1962)
 Reference: Lennon, J. and P. McCartney, 1962. *Please, please me.* London: Dick James Music. |
| Numerical | **Reference:** Lennon, J. and P. McCartney. *Please, please me,* 1962. London: Dick James Music. |

20. Newspapers and online news sites

Include the following information:

- name of writer, if shown; if no writer name is shown, start with the title of the newspaper
- year of publication
- title of article
- name of the newspaper (in italics)
- day, month and year of publication
- details of any special identifying feature, e.g. late edition, review sections, supplements; if a particular edition is involved, e.g. late edition, this can be shown next to the date, e.g. 4 June 2006 (late edn.)
- page number(s).

If it is a local paper, it is helpful to include the city of origin, e.g. (Bradford *Telegraph and Argus*, 21 June, 2004, p.4). If the item is in a supplement, give information on this after the name of the newspaper, e.g. *Financial Times: FTfm (Fund Management)* 12 Dec. 2005 p.3; or *Financial Times (FT Companies and Markets supplement)* 12 Dec. 2005, p.24.

20a. Printed newspaper (writer's name shown)

| Harvard | **Citation:** (Thorpe, 2015)
 Reference: Thorpe, V. 2015. 'Call for museums and art galleries to appoint more women to top jobs.' *Observer* 22 March 2015, p.11. |
| Numerical | **Reference:** Thorpe, V. 'Call for museums and art galleries to appoint more women to top jobs.' *Observer* 22 March 2015, p.11. |

20b. Printed newspaper (no writer's name given)

Cite the name of the newspaper in italics.

Harvard	**Citation:** (*Observer*, 2015)
	Reference: *Observer,* 2015. 'Democracy has taken root in Tunisia. Let's ensure it thrives'. 22 March, p.44.
Numerical	**Reference:** *The Observer.* 'Democracy has taken root in Tunisia. Let's ensure it thrives'. 22 March 2015, p.44.

20c. Online article (named writer)

Harvard	**Citation:** (Whipple, 2015)
	Reference: Whipple, T. 2015. 'Scientists find why animals run days before an earthquake'. *The Times Online,* 25 March 2015. Available at http://www.thetimes.co.uk/tto/science/article4392133.ece [viewed 25 March 2015].
Numerical	**Reference:** Whipple, T. 'Scientists find why animals run days before an earthquake'. *The Times Online,* 25 March 2015. Available at http://www.thetimes.co.uk/tto/science/article4392133.ece [viewed 25 March 2015].

20d. Online article (no named writer)

Cite the name of the online site in italics.

Harvard	**Citation:** (*Guardian*, 2015)
	Reference: *Guardian,* 2015. 'Consuming three alcoholic drinks a day may cause liver cancer—study.' Available at http://www.theguardian.com/society/2015/mar/25/three-alcoholic-drinks-a-day-liver-cancer-study [viewed 25 March 2015].
Numerical	**Reference:** *Guardian.* 'Consuming three alcoholic drinks a day may cause liver cancer—study.' Available at http://www.theguardian.com/society/2015/mar/25/three-alcoholic-drinks-a-day-liver-cancer-study [viewed 25 March 2015].

21. Parliamentary publications

There are differences in the way UK Acts of Parliament post- and pre-1963 are referenced.

21a. Acts of Parliament (after 1963)

For Acts of Parliament published *after 1963* include the following information:

* title of the act and year (in italics)
* chapter number—'c' and sub-section number, if applicable
* place of publication
* publisher.

If from the internet:

- URL
- date you viewed the site.

21a(i). Acts of Parliament (after 1963)

Harvard	**Citation:** (*Serious Crime Act 2015*) **Reference:** *Serious Crime Act 2015*. c.1(10) London: The Stationery Office.
Numerical	**Reference:** As above.

21a(ii). Online version of above

Harvard	**Citation:** (*Serious Crime Act 2015*) **Reference:** *Serious Crime Act 2015*. c.1(10). Available at http://www.legislation.gov.uk/ukpga/2015/9/contents/enacted [viewed 25 March 2015].
Numerical	**Reference:** As above.

21b. Acts of Parliament published before 1963

Additional information needs to be included for acts published *before 1963*, as follows:

- title of act and year
- regnal year (year of the reign of the sovereign at the time) and abbreviated name of the sovereign
- chapter number of the act—'c'
- place of publication and publisher (but see the note below regarding online documents).

Harvard	**Citation:** (*The Education Act 1944*) **Reference:** *The Education Act 1944*. (8 & 9 Geo.6, c. 2). London: HMSO.
Numerical	**Reference:** As above.

To reference an online version of the above, omit 'London: HMSO' and replace with the URL and date viewed, i.e. http://www.legislation.gov.uk/ukpga/Geo6/7-8/31/contents/enacted [viewed . . . date].

21c. Command Paper

Command Papers are those 'commanded' by the sovereign to be presented to Parliament, including White or Green Papers, reports of committees of inquiry, responses to Select Committee reports, and other important departmental reviews or reports.

References to Command Papers should include:

- name of the originating department or departments
- year

- title of paper (in italics)
- command paper number (in brackets)
- place of publication/publisher (but see the note below the following example regarding online documents).

Harvard	**Citation:** (LPC & DBIS, 2015)
	Reference: LPC & DBIS: Low Pay Commission and Department for Business, Innovation & Skills, 2015. *National Minimum Wage: Low Pay Commission Report 2015* (Cm 9017). London: The Stationery Office.
Numerical	**Reference:** LPC & DBIS: Low Pay Commission and Department for Business, Innovation & Skills *National Minimum Wage: Low Pay Commission Report 2015* (Cm 9017). London: The Stationery Office.

If referencing this information as an online document, omit 'London: The Stationery Office', and replace with the URL and date you viewed the site, i.e. Available at https://www.gov.uk/government/publications/national-minimum-wage-low-pay-commission-report-2015 [viewed . . . date].

21d. House of Commons/Lords Parliamentary Bills

- title and year of bill (in italics)
- house, i.e. HC (Commons) or HL (Lords)
- bill number
- parliamentary session
- place of publication
- publisher.

Harvard	**Citation:** (*Assisted Dying Bill*, 2014–15)
	Reference: *Assisted Dying Bill 2014–15* (HL Bill 6, 2014–15). London: The Stationery Office.
Numerical	**Reference:** As above.

If referencing this information as an online document, see the note after example 21c, above.

21e. Hansard

Hansard is the collective name of the independent record of debates and speeches in the Chamber of the House of Commons, sub-chamber in Westminster Hall, and in Standing Committees of the House of Lords. In Select Committees there is no Hansard record published, but instead 'minutes of evidence' are published by the Committee and form part of its report. House of Commons debates, statements, petitions, oral and written questions and answers, from November 1988 onwards, are now searchable online (from 1995 for the House of Lords).

A guide to Hansard, including citation style, is available at the House of Commons Information Office: http://www.parliament.uk/about/how/guides/factsheets/general/g17/.

The Hansard guide advises that the following abbreviations should be used:

- HC Deb—House of Commons Debate
- W—Written Answers (Common)
- WA—Lords
- WH—Westminster Hall
- WS—Written Statements
- SC—Standing Committee
- c—column numbers.

21e(i). Hansard: printed

Harvard	**Citation:** (*Hansard*, 1977) **Reference:** *Hansard* HC Deb 3 February 1977, vol. 389 c.973
Numerical	**Reference:** As above.

21e(ii). Hansard: online

Harvard	**Citation:** (*Hansard*, 2014) **Reference:** *Hansard* HL 16 June 2014, c.WA19. Available at http://www.publications.parliament.uk/pa/ld201415/ldhansrd/text/140616w0001.htm#1406171000229 [viewed 23 March 2015].
Numerical	**Reference:** As above.

21f. Select Committee reports

Select Committees examine particular and selected subjects of wide public interest or concern. In the House of Commons they review the running of each of the main government departments and associated public bodies, and have the power to take evidence and issue reports.

In the House of Lords, Select Committees examine broader issues, such as the European Union, and Science and Technology.

You should include the name of the Select Committee, title of the report, and HC or HL to indicate House of Commons or House of Lords respectively, the serial number of the report, date published, and the place of publication/publisher.

Harvard	**Citation:** (Health Committee, 2015) **Reference:** Health Committee, 2015. *End of Life Care*, 5th Report (HC 805) published 15 March 2015. London: The Stationery Office.
Numerical	**Reference:** Health Committee *End of Life Care*, 5th Report (HC 805) published 15 March 2015. London: The Stationery Office.

21g. Acts of the Scottish Parliament

- title of the act (in italics)
- asp (Act of the Scottish Parliament) and the number (brackets)

- URL
- date you viewed the site.

Harvard	**Citation:** (*Children and Young People (Scotland) Act 2014*)
	Reference: *Children and Young People (Scotland) Act 2014* (asp 8). Available at http://www.legislation.gov.uk/asp/2014/8/contents [viewed 25 March 2015].
Numerical	**Reference:** As above.

If your source is a printed version of the above, replace the URL and date of access with place and name of publisher.

21h. Acts of the Northern Ireland Assembly

Harvard	**Citation:** (*Work and Families Act (Northern Ireland) 2015*)
	Reference: *Work and Families Act (Northern Ireland) 2015*. Available at http://www.legislation.gov.uk/nia/2015/1/contents [viewed 26 March 2015].
Numerical	**Reference:** As above.

If your source is a printed version of the above, replace the URL and date of access with place and name of publisher.

21i. Wales: Assembly Measures

- title of legislation and year (in italics)
- act of the National Assembly of Wales (anaw) number
- URL
- date you viewed the site.

Harvard	**Citation:** (*Higher Education (Wales) Act 2015*)
	Reference: *Higher Education (Wales) Act 2015*. (anaw 1). Available at http://www.legislation.gov.uk/anaw/2015/1/contents/ enacted [viewed 25 March 2015].
Numerical	**Reference:** As above.

PDF Downloads

It is often possible to download pdf files from government-sponsored sites, and elsewhere. If you wanted to quote or pinpoint information from these, you could extend your reference to include this information, including the chapter/part/section numbers and title of the relevant section. Example:

Higher Education (Wales) Act 2015. (anaw 1) pdf download, part 2, section10 'Limits on student fees'. Available at http://www.legislation.gov.uk/anaw/2015/1/contents/enacted [viewed 25 March 2015].

22. Patents and standards

22a. Patents

The full reference should include:

- name(s) of inventor(s) or patentee(s)
- year of publication
- title of patent (in italics)
- country of origin and serial number
- date of application and date of acceptance.

Harvard	**Citation:** (Lund-Anderson, 2001) **Reference:** Lund-Anderson, B. 2001. *Device for the damping of vibrators between objects.* US Patent 6296238. Appl. 24 June 1999. Acc. 2 Oct. 2001.
Numerical	**Reference:** Lund-Anderson, B. *Device for the damping of vibrators between objects.* US Patent 6296238. Appl. 24 June 1999. Acc. 2 Oct. 2001.

22b. Standards

The full reference should include:

- the number and year of the standard, e.g. BS 5605:1990
- year of publication and if applicable, republication
- title of standard (in italics)
- place of publication and name of publisher.

22b(i). British Standards

This example shows year of original publication (1990), followed by a republished date: 1999.

Harvard	**Citation:** (BS: 5605:1990) **Reference:** BS 5605:1990, 1999. *Citing and referencing published material.* London: British Standard Institution.
Numerical	**Reference:** BS 5605:1990. *Citing and referencing published material.* London: British Standard Institution, 1999.

22b(ii). International Organization for Standardization (ISO)

Harvard	**Citation:** (ISO 14001, 2004) **Reference:** ISO 14001:2004. *Environmental management systems.* Geneva: International Organization for Standardization.
Numerical	**Reference:** As above.

23. Personal communications (emails, faxes, telephone calls, interviews and other conversations)

Significant personal email messages can be referenced—but be cautious. Wherever possible, you should obtain permission from the sender to use personal email correspondence, particularly if the correspondence will appear in the public domain. You may also need to save a copy of the correspondence to enable a tutor to read it (consult with your tutor on this).

If the message is included as a reference, do not give the email address of the sender as this would be a breach of confidentiality and might lead to unwarranted correspondence being sent to the sender (see also 'Tweets' below, in section 30: 'Social and professional networking').

23a. Emails, letters, faxes, telephone conversations

These can all be referenced in the same way (using the appropriate medium: Email to . . .; Letter to . . .; Fax to . . .; Text message to . . .; Telephone conversation with . . .).

Harvard	**Citation:** (Davis, 2015) **Reference:** Davis, J. 2015. Email to Charles Harris re oral history project, 12 January 2015.
Numerical	**Reference:** Davis, J. Email to Charles Harris re oral history project, 12 January 2015.

24. Postal items/postcards

24a. First day issues

First day issues (also known as first day covers) are envelopes bearing the cancellation dates of the first day of issues of stamps; they can be of interest as historical or postal design sources. They are usually mailed from the place where the stamp first came into circulation.

In the reference you should include country of origin, year, nature or type of first day cover, number (if it is a limited edition), design features of stamp, if relevant, and any significant markings or postal franking on envelope.

Harvard	**Citation:** (Postal Services, Canada, 1928) **Reference:** Postal Services, Canada, 1928. *First flight cover via Amos to Siscoe.* 28 October, bearing 'Amos', 'Quebec', 'New York', 'Siscoe' and other postmarks on illustrated envelope.
Numerical	**Reference:** Postal Services, Canada. *First flight cover via Amos to Siscoe.* 28 October 1928, bearing 'Amos', 'Quebec', 'New York', 'Siscoe' and other postmarks on illustrated envelope.

24b. Postmarks

The study of postmarks is called marcophily; postmarks can be of interest to philatelists and postal historians.

| Harvard | **Citation:** (Stamps of the World, 2014)
Reference: Stamps of the World, 2014. *Russian postmarks*. Available at http://www.stampsoftheworld.co.uk/wiki/Category:Russia_Postmarks [viewed 27 March 2015). |
| Numerical | **Reference:** Stamps of the World *Russian postmarks*, 2014. Available at http://www.stampsoftheworld.co.uk/wiki/Category:Russia_Postmarks [viewed 27 March 2015). |

24c. Postcards

Postcards can be of interest as primary or secondary social history sources.

You would normally describe the features of the relevant postcard in the text of your assignment, so the full reference would just contain enough information to help the reader identify the location of the postcard, e.g. gallery, private collection, plus other relevant identifying features, i.e. reference number or title. These can include the name of the artist, or photographer, if known, and date, or estimated date, of first printing.

Unless there is a specific title, you do not need to italicise or underline the general description of the item (see the first example below).

24c(i). Postcard (known artist)

| Harvard | **Citation:** (McGill, 1927)
Reference: McGill, D. 1927. Seaside cartoon postcard. Ref.115 at Holmfirth: Postcard Museum. |
| Numerical | **Reference:** McGill, D. Seaside cartoon postcard, 1927. Ref.115 at Holmfirth: Postcard Museum. |

24c(ii). Postcard (artist unknown)

| Harvard | **Citation:** (*John Knox's House*, circa 1890s)
Reference: *John Knox's House*, circa 1894 [postcard]. Photographer unknown. National Library of Scotland. Available at http://www.nls.uk/collections/rare-books/collections/postcards [viewed 2 May 2015]. |
| Numerical | **Reference:** *John Knox's House* [postcard]. Photographer unknown, circa 1894. National Library of Scotland. Available at http://www.nls.uk/collections/rare-books/collections/postcards [viewed 2 May 2015]. |

25. Public memorials

The names and inscriptions on public memorials can be helpful for historians and these can be referenced, although it is advisable to take a photograph of the monument to include in an assignment—for example, as an appendix item.

25a. Inscription (general interest)

The full reference would normally include:

- name of the memorial

- type of memorial
- year erected
- type of inscription
- location
- date you visited, or viewed online, the memorial in question.

The text of your assignment is likely to feature the inscription in full, as shown in the example that follows. Include the original spelling of words.

Harvard	. . . *What dangers do surround poor miners everywhere/And they that labour underground/Thay should be men of prayer* **Citation:** (Bramhope Tunnel Memorial Stone, 1849) **Reference:** Bramhope Tunnel Memorial Stone, 1849. Poem inscribed to miners killed in construction of Bramhope railway tunnel. West Yorkshire: Otley Churchyard. Visited 11 May 2015.
Numerical	**Reference:** As above.

25b. Named individual

You would normally include the inscription in the text of your assignment, so the reference would include details of its source:

- the name of the memorial
- year memorial erected
- type of memorial
- location
- if any internet images are available, add the URL and date you viewed them.

Harvard	'Percy Lambert 'Killed 11th April 1918, aged 19'. **Citation:** (Silsden War Memorial, 1923) **Reference:** Silsden War Memorial, 1923. West Yorkshire: Silsden, Wesley Place. Images available at http://www.ww1-yorkshires.org.uk/html-files/silsden.htm [viewed 26 March 2015].
Numerical	**Reference:** As above.

26. Record sleeves and CD inserts

Include in the full reference:

- name of the writer
- year
- title of notes (or nature of the notes, e.g. 'introduction')
- title of recording (in italics)
- source of text, e.g. [CD accompanying notes]; [vinyl record sleeve notes]
- name of record company/publisher.

Harvard	**Citation:** (Clarke, 2012)
	Reference: Clarke, N. 2012. Introduction notes to *Military Wives: Stronger Together* [CD: accompanying notes] Decca Records.
Numerical	**Reference:** Clarke, N. Introduction notes to *Military Wives: Stronger Together* [CD: accompanying notes] Decca Records, 2012.

27. Reference information resources

See Chapter 3 for information about when to use secondary sources.

Reference books and online sites rarely feature the names of individual writers, but if a writer's name (not the editor's) is shown, then start the reference entry with this. However, if no writer's name is shown, start with the originator: the name of the reference book or site (in italics).

If no online date is given for the entry in question, put 'no date'. State the title of the subject consulted, and page numbers if relevant.

For printed works, the editor and publisher of a well-known reference work can be omitted, but the page numbers for the entry in question can be included in the citation.

27a. Encyclopaedias: online

Harvard	**Citation:** (*Encyclopaedia Britannica*, no date)
	Reference: *Encyclopaedia Britannica* [no date]. 'Bismarck'. Available at http://www.britannica.com/EBchecked/topic/66986/Bismarck [viewed 26 March 2015].
Numerical	**Reference:** *Encyclopaedia Britannica*. 'Bismarck'. Available at http://www.britannica.com/EBchecked/topic/66986/Bismarck [no date]. [viewed 26 March 2015].

27b. Encyclopaedia: printed

Harvard	**Citation:** (Reader's Encyclopaedia, 1965, p.197)
	Reference: *The readers encyclopedia*, 2nd edn. 1965. 'Manuel Chrysoloras'. London: A&C Black.
Numerical	**Reference:** *The readers encyclopedia*, 2nd edn. 'Manuel Chrysoloras'. London: A&C Black, 1965.

27c. Directories/yearbooks (printed)

Harvard	**Citation:** (*Writers' and Artists' Yearbook*, 2012, p.707)
	Reference: *Writers' and Artists' Yearbook* 105th edn. 2012. 'The Copyright Licensing Agency', pp.707–8. London: Bloomsbury Publishing.
Numerical	**Reference:** *Writers' and Artists' Yearbook* 105th edn. 'The Copyright Licensing Agency', pp.707–8. London: Bloomsbury Publishing, 2012.

27d. Dictionaries (online)

Harvard	**Citation:** (*Oxford Dictionaries*, 2015) **Reference:** *Oxford Dictionaries*, 2015. 'Definition of plagiarism'. Available at http://www.oxforddictionaries.com/definition/english/plagiarism [viewed 28 March 2015].
Numerical	**Reference:** *Oxford Dictionaries*. 'Definition of plagiarism'. Available at http://www.oxforddictionaries.com/definition/english/plagiarism [viewed 28 March 2015].

27e. Wikipedia and other online reference sites

Wikipedia tries to ensure accuracy of information by using external editors, who supervise initial entries and check that evidence is properly referenced before an article is first published. These can often provide succinct overviews of many subjects, and useful links to other related sources.

However, some Wikipedia entries have been criticised for incomplete or biased information—see 'Criticism of Wikipedia' (on Wikipedia!) at http://en.wikipedia.org/wiki/Criticism_of_Wikipedia.

Students should therefore use Wikipedia (and similar sites) with caution. It is also predominantly a secondary source for the subjects presented, although the external links can lead to useful primary source material.

If you do use Wikipedia as a source in your work (perhaps in the absence of other relevant material), then Wiki entries can be referenced as follows:

- originator—name of website
- year article published (with Wikipedia, look at the 'View History' section for the article to trace when it was first published)
- title of article
- URL
- date you viewed the site.

Harvard	**Citation:** (*Wikipedia*, 2014) **Reference:** *Wikipedia*, 2014. 'W.R. Mitchell'. Available at http://en.wikipedia.org/wiki/W_R_Mitchell [viewed 26 March 2015].
Numerical	**Reference:** *Wikipedia* 'W.R. Mitchell', 2014. Available at http://en.wikipedia.org/wiki/W_R_Mitchell [viewed 26 March 2015].

28. Reports (and discussion, occasional or working papers)

For all reports, discussion, occasional or working papers, you should include in the full reference the following information, if shown:

- author's name (if given)
- if no name of author is shown, start with the name of the organisation sponsoring the report; if you use abbreviations in the citation, you need to start with these in the full reference and explain their meaning (as shown in example 28a, below)

- year of publication
- full title of report (in italics)
- sub-section or sub-title information and edition number
- place of publication
- name of publisher or originating organisation
- volume, sections, page number(s) if not cited in the text.

28a. Annual report (no named author)

Harvard	**Citation:** (ODI, 2003) **Reference:** ODI: Overseas Development Institute, 2003. *Annual Report 2002/3*: 'finance: balance sheet summary', pp.30–33. London: ODI.
Numerical	**Reference:** ODI: Overseas Development Institute *Annual Report 2002/3*: 'finance: balance sheet summary', pp.30–33. London: ODI, 2003.

28b. Annual report (online, with a named writer)

What to reference:

- start with the named writer
- year
- state what position the writer holds within the organisation, if not obvious
- title of section or chapter concerned
- title of main report (in italics)
- URL
- date you viewed the site.

Harvard	**Citation:** (Khan, 2014) **Reference:** Khan, J. 2014. 'Chief Executive's Introduction', Barnardo's Annual Review and Accounts, 2014, p.5. Available at http://www.barnardos.org.uk/what_we_do/who_we_are/corporate_information.htm [viewed 27 March 2015].
Numerical	**Reference:** Khan, J. 'Chief Executive's Introduction', Barnardo's Annual Review and Accounts, 2014, p.5. Available at http://www.barnardos.org.uk/what_we_do/who_we_are/corporate_information.htm [viewed 27 March 2015].

28c. Other reports

Give as much information as possible to identify the relevant section and sub-sections of the report in question.

Harvard	**Citation:** (Business Ratio Reports, 2004) **Reference:** Business Ratio Reports, 2004. *Security Industry*, edn. 26, section 4: 'Performance League Tables': Sales: 4-2. Hampton: Keynote.
Numerical	**Reference:** Business Ratio Reports *Security Industry*, edn. 26, section 4: 'Performance League Tables': Sales: 4-2. Hampton: Keynote, 2004.

28d. Discussion paper (named authors)

Discussion papers are circulated by their authors for the purposes of stimulating information and discussion on any topic. They are often presented in the form of a question, as seen in one of the examples that follow. The title of the paper is shown in italics.

Harvard	**Citation:** (Anand and Sen, 1996) **Reference:** Anand, S. and A.K. Sen. 1996. *Sustainable human development: concepts and priorities.* United Nations Development Programme (UNDP), Discussion Paper Series. New York: UNDP: Office of Development Studies, p.23.
Numerical	**Reference:** Anand, S. and A.K. Sen. *Sustainable Human Development: Concepts and Priorities.* United Nations Development Programme (UNDP), Discussion Paper Series. New York: UNDP: Office of Development Studies, 1996. p.23.

28e. Discussion paper, online (named authors)

Harvard	**Citation:** (Kanbur and Wagstaff, 2015) **Reference:** Kanbur, R. and A. Wagstaff, 2015. *How useful is inequality of opportunity as a policy construct?* Ref. DP10508, Centre for Economic Policy Research. Available at http://www.cepr.org/active/publications/discussion_papers/dp.php?dpno=10508 [viewed 27 March 2015].
Numerical	**Reference:** Kanbur, R. and Wagstaff, A. *How useful is inequality of opportunity as a policy construct?* Ref. DP10508, Centre for Economic Policy Research, 2015. Available at http://www.cepr.org/active/publications/discussion_papers/dp.php?dpno=10508 [viewed 27 March 2015].

28f. Working paper

Working papers are circulated to share ideas to gain critical feedback before submitting the paper to, usually, an academic journal or edited book for publication.

Harvard	**Citation:** (Baldwin, 2014, p.3) **Reference:** Baldwin, A. 2014. 'Putting the philosophy into PhD', *Working Papers in the Health Sciences*, 1:10, Winter 2014, pp.1–4. Southampton: University of Southampton. Available at http://www.southampton.ac.uk/wphs/current_issue.page? [viewed 30 March 2015].
Numerical	**Reference:** Baldwin, A. 'Putting the philosophy into PhD', *Working Papers in the Health Sciences*, 1:10, Winter 2014, pp.1–4. Southampton: University of Southampton. Available at http://www.southampton.ac.uk/wphs/current_issue.page? [viewed 30 March 2015].

28g. Occasional paper

Occasional papers are usually short publications, often based on talks or lectures given, with a view to making the ideas accessible to a wider group of people. The main source is italicised—in the example below it is the title of the occasional paper series.

Harvard	**Citation:** (Balaklytskyi, 2015) **Reference:** Balaklytskyi, M. 2015. 'Religious issues in the Ukrainian media after Euromaidan', *Occasional Papers on Religion in Eastern Europe:* vol. 35, iss.1. Available at http://digitalcommons.georgefox.edu/ree/vol35/iss1/1 [viewed 28 March 2015].
Numerical	**Reference:** Balaklytskyi, M. 'Religious issues in the Ukrainian media after Euromaidan', *Occasional Papers on Religion in Eastern Europe,* 2015, vol. 35, iss.1. Available at http://digitalcommons.georgefox.edu/ree/vol35/iss1/1 [viewed 28 March 2015].

29. Sacred and classical texts

29a. Sacred texts

Sacred texts include the Bible, Talmud, Qur'an and Upanishads. If you are simply quoting a verse or extract from any sacred text, you do not need to give full reference entries. Instead, you should include the detail in the text of your assignment. For example:

> The film script at this point echoes the Bible: 'And God looked upon the earth, and, behold, it was corrupt; for all flesh had corrupted his way upon the earth'
> (Gen. 6:12).

> 'And seek help in patience and prayer'
> (al-Baqarah 2:45).

> 'Remain in awe of God, serve Him, cling to Him.'
> (Deuteronomy, 10:20).

Abbreviations can be used in citations, e.g. Gen. for Genesis; Ezek. for Ezekiel. An online guide to bible abbreviations can be found at www.aresearchguide.com/bibleabb.html.

However, if you are referring to a particular edition of a sacred text for a significant reason, e.g. extended discussion on a particular extract, it could be listed in full in the main references. For example:

Good News Bible (2004). Rainbow Edition. New York: HarperCollins.

Ali, A.Y. (2003) *The Holy Qur'an: Texts and Translations*. Selangor, Malaysia: Islamic Book Trust Kuala Lumpur.

29b. Classical texts

The format for citing classical text sources is normally as follows:

- name of author
- title (in italics)
- details of book/poem
- line number.

For example, Homer, *Iliad* 18.141–143.

If an author wrote only one work, e.g. Herodotus, you may omit the name of the work, i.e. *Histories*.

Page numbers should be from the translation or edition cited. However, citations to Plato and Plutarch should be included in the text using the Stephanus pagination, whenever possible. This is a system of reference based on the 1578 edition of Plato's complete works, published by Henricus Stephanus, and still used today in modern translations of Plato and Plutarch. This shows the works divided into numbers, and each number will be divided into equal sections: a, b, c, d and e. The numbers, however, must be used in conjunction with a title to make sense of them, e.g. *Republic*, 344a2.

The works of Aristotle are usually cited using the Bekker system of numbers. These numbers take the format of up to four digits, a letter for column 'a' or 'b', then the line number(s). These should be shown against the title of the particular work of Aristotle, e.g. *Politics*: 1252a1–4.

Abbreviating authors and titles is acceptable, but these need to be consistent: the *Oxford Classical Dictionary* has a list of abbreviations that can be used.

The full details of the book used should be included in the References, Bibliography or 'Works Cited' section (see the section above on referencing 'books'). However, it is important to distinguish editor from author. If your primary focus is on the author, this will be the starting point for both the citation and full reference entry, although you would need to include the editor in the full reference. For example:

> Aristotle (1934) *Nicomachean Ethics*. Edited by H. Rackham. Loeb Classical Library, no.73. Cambridge (MA): Harvard University Press.

30. Scripts (plays/films)

Scripts are usually available in printed form, so you should be able to give details of the playwright and the publisher. To reference scripts, start with the name of the playwright, then state year of publication followed by title of play (in italics). You also need to state the medium, e.g. [theatre script]; [radio script]; [film script], unless it is obvious, and include, if relevant to the evidence you are presenting, details of the act, scene and/or page number. Finally, include the publisher information.

Harvard	**Citation:** (Kempinski, 1983) **Reference:** Kempinski, Tom. (1983). *Duet for one*. [theatre script] Act 1, p.21. London: Samuel French.
Numerical	**Reference:** Kempinski, Tom. *Duet for one*. [theatre script] Act 1, p.21. London: Samuel French, 1983.

31. Social and professional networking sites

31a. Social networking sites

There are thousands of social networking sites offering a chance for people to communicate news and opinion. These sites offer interesting cultural snapshots of our times and, as such, are of increasing interest to scholars, particularly those in the arts and social science fields of study.

However, the information on these sites should be treated with caution in terms of their credibility and reliability. They are also predominantly secondary sources, unless the author is clearly presenting original information, backed up with cited evidence.

If your tutor does not have access to any of these sites (some are password protected), it may be necessary to copy information to use as an appendix item, as well as referencing the source.

A few illustrative examples are shown here to give you a framework for referencing the many others not featured.

31b. Blogs

- start with the name of the blog, and year it was created, if shown
- state the medium [blogpost]
- title of blogpost (in italics)
- specific date of blogpost
- URL
- date you viewed the site.

Harvard	**Citation:** (Woodbine Books, 2014) **Reference:** Woodbine Books, 2014. [blogpost] *Designer Bookbindings*, 19 July 2014. Available at http://woodbinebooks.blogspot.co.uk/ [viewed 20 March 2015].
Numerical	**Reference:** Woodbine Books. [blogpost] *Designer Bookbindings*, 19 July 2014. Available at http://woodbinebooks.blogspot.co.uk/ [viewed 20 March 2015].

31c. BuzzFeed

This is a popular site for sharing short items of news, gossip, lifestyle etc.

Start your reference with the name or pseudonym of the writer, then:

- year of post
- title of post (italicised)
- name of site, e.g. [BuzzFeed]
- specific date of post onto the site
- URL
- date you viewed the site.

Harvard	**Citation:** (Umer, 2015) **Reference:** Umer, N. 2015. *Can you pass an eighth-grade science test from 1912?* [BuzzFeed] 16 March. Available at http://www.buzzfeed.com/natashaumer/can-you-pass-an-eighth-grade-science-test-from-1912#.wwAm1x2rG [viewed 17 March 2015].
Numerical	**Reference:** Umer, N. *Can you pass an eighth-grade science test from 1912?* [BuzzFeed] 16 March 2015. Available at http://www.buzzfeed.com/natashaumer/can-you-pass-an-eighth-grade-science-test-from-1912#.wwAm1x2rG [viewed 17 March 2015].

31d. Facebook

Start with the author's name, as shown, which can be a pseudonym or name of a group, company or organisation. Then state year of post, title of post (in italics) and the medium: [Facebook]. Include the URL and date you viewed the information.

Harvard	**Citation:** (Stanza Stones Community, 2015)
	Reference: Stanza Stones Community, 2015. *Poetry Trail Guide*. [Facebook] Available at https://www.facebook.com/stanzastones?fref=ts [viewed 17 March 2015].
Numerical	**Reference:** Stanza Stones Community. *Poetry Trail Guide*. [Facebook] Available at https://www.facebook.com/stanzastones?fref=ts [viewed 17 March 2015].

31e. Pinterest

For referencing images from Pinterest, see 'Photograph from a social media collection' (art related, number c(iv), above).

31f. Revenue sharing sites, e.g. HubPages

These sites encourage users to post articles and earn money from the advertisement revenue generated by their pages; *HubPages* is one of the largest of these sites.

Note: Information presented on these sites should be treated with great caution, as there may be inaccuracy and bias present. Check any 'facts' presented by the writers.

The source would be referenced in this order:

* name of writer (which may be a pseudonym)
* year of posting
* title of post (in italics)
* name of site, e.g. [HubPages]
* URL
* date you viewed the site.

Harvard	**Citation:** (Vercillo, 2012)
	Reference: Vercillo, K. 2012. *Why it is important for teachers to understand child development stages* [HubPages] Available at http://hubpages.com/hub/WhyTeachersMustUnderstandChildDevelopment [viewed 17 April 2015].
Numerical	**Reference:** Vercillo, K. *Why it is important for teachers to understand child development stages*, 2012. [HubPages] Available at http://hubpages.com/hub/WhyTeachersMustUnderstandChildDevelopment [viewed 17 April 2015).

31g. Twitter

Reference detail:

* personal or organisational name

- year
- give the full text of the tweet (italicised)
- state the medium: [Twitter]
- day and month posted
- URL
- date you viewed the site.

31h. Personal tweet

See also 'Organisation tweet', below.

Harvard	**Citation:** (Fry, 2015) **Reference:** Fry, S. 2015. *My friend Ayse is raising £2K for a short film in support of #MentalHealth. Your help will make it happen. http://kck.st/1vt4HFO* [Twitter] Posted 15 February. Available at https://twitter.com/stephenfry/ [viewed 17 March 2015].
Numerical	**Reference:** Fry, S. *My friend Ayse is raising £2K for a short film in support of #MentalHealth. Your help will make it happen. http://kck.st/1vt4HFO* [Twitter] Posted 15 February. Available at https://twitter.com/stephenfry/ [viewed 17 March 2015].

31i. Professional networking

Access to professional networking sites is often password protected, so unless your tutor can gain access to the non-public parts of the site, you may need to copy the source for use as an appendix item in your assignment (check with your tutor).

Start the reference with the name of the author of the item in question; use the name shown, including pseudonyms. If there is no named author, cite and start with the organisational name.

If you use the initials of the organisation in the citation, start with these in the full reference, but give the full organisational name immediately after, as shown below. Give the title of the item (italicised), the nature or location of the item, e.g. [blog] and the date it was posted on the site.

Two examples follow.

Harvard	**Citation:** (NFP, 2015) **Reference:** NFP: Networking for Professionals, 2015. Charles Bernard: criteria for success [video], 18 March 2015. Available at http://www.networkingforprofessionals.com/ [viewed 18 March 2015].
Numerical	**Reference:** NFP: Networking for Professionals. Charles Bernard: criteria for success [video], 18 March 2015. Available on Home Page at http://www.networkingforprofessionals.com/ [viewed 18 March 2015].

Harvard	**Citation:** (Labroots.com, 2015) **Reference:** Labroots.com, 2015. *Living bacteria captured by X-ray* [blogpost] 26 February 2015. Available at http://blog.labroots.com/ [viewed 20 March 2015].
Numerical	**Reference:** Labroots.com. *Living bacteria captured by X-ray* [blogpost] 26 February 2015. Available at http://blog.labroots.com/ [viewed 20 March 2015].

31j. Organisational tweet

See also sections 31g and 31h, above.

Harvard	**Citation:** (BBC Scotland, 2015) **Reference:** BBC Scotland, 2015. *Tagged Atlantic bluefin tuna tracked in effort to understand appearance in Scottish waters http://bbc.in/1EYO4EY* [Twitter] Posted 17 March. Available at https://twitter.com/bbcnews [viewed 17 March 2015].
Numerical	**Reference:** BBC Scotland *Tagged Atlantic bluefin tuna tracked in effort to understand appearance in Scottish waters http://bbc.in/1EYO4EY* [Twitter] Posted 17 March 2015. Available at https://twitter.com/bbcnews [viewed 17 March 2015].

32. Theatre or other printed programmes

You can reference theatrical or other programmes as these often contain useful information on the historical background to the production, details of performers, music details etc.

- If the name of the writer is shown, start with this and then give the year of the production.
- If no writer's name is shown, start with the name of the production.
- State the title of the item in the programme, the nature of the source, e.g. [theatre programme] and give page numbers, if shown.
- Next, give the title of the production (in italics).
- Finally, give details of place, name of theatre and the dates of the performance.

Harvard	**Citation:** (Ludlow, 1980) **Reference:** Ludlow, P. 1980. 'There is nothing like a dame', [theatre programme] pp.8–9. *Jack and the Beanstalk*, Bradford: Alhambra Theatre: 23 December–21 February, 1980–81.
Numerical	**Reference:** Ludlow, P. 'There is nothing like a dame' [theatre programme] pp.8–9. *Jack and the Beanstalk*. Bradford: Alhambra Theatre: 23 December–21 February, 1980–81.

33. Video/computer games

The reference should include:

- name of originator/producer

- date of production or release, if shown
- title of game (in italics)
- state the medium [video game]
- distributor and place of production, if shown.

Also include, if applicable:

- URL
- date downloaded.

Harvard	**Citation:** (Ubisoft, 2014) **Reference:** Ubisoft, 2014. *Assassin's Creed Unity—PlayStation 4* [video game]. Newcastle: Ubisoft UK.
Numerical	**Reference:** Ubisoft. *Assassin's Creed Unity—PlayStation 4* [video game], Newcastle: Ubisoft UK, 2014.

12 Frequently asked questions

This chapter presents a range of questions that students most frequently ask about referencing. These are as follows.

1. What is the difference between a list of 'References' and a 'Bibliography'?
2. Is it worth spending time learning how to use referencing management software?
3. When should I use page numbers in my in-text citations?
4. The author of the book I read mentions another author. I want to refer to this other author. How do I reference this?
5. How do I cite and reference books or other sources from an author that has published more than once in the same year?
6. How do I cite in my assignment where an author has written different books, but has made similar points in each?
7. Referencing multiple authors: how do I cite and reference works written and edited by more than one author?
8. I read a book in my own (non-English) language. Do I give you an English translation of the title in the full reference?
9. What punctuation and capitalisation style should I use in referencing?
10. The source has no date. How can I reference this?
11. Can I use abbreviations in references?
12. I have noticed that some writers cite more than one author occasionally in support of a particular argument or point of view. When and why should I do this?
13. Are quotations and all the name–date or page citations in the text counted in the assignment word count?
14. How do I cite sources where no author name is shown?
15. How do I cite sources that are recorded on microfiche/microfilm/microform?
16. I have noticed that both brackets ( ) and square brackets [ ] are sometimes used in full references. Why is this?
17. How do I reference foreign author names?
18. When I am writing an assignment, I sometimes want to respond to a writer's point of view from what I have learned in the past—but I cannot always remember the source of my inspiration. What can I do in this situation?
19. How can I present and distinguish my own ideas and opinions in an assignment from those in published sources?

1. What is the difference between a list of 'References' and a 'Bibliography'?

This issue was raised in Chapter 6, but here is a summary of the differences.

References (or 'Works Cited' in the MLA style) are the items you have read and specifically referred to (or cited) in your assignment. A **Bibliography** (or 'Works Consulted' in the MLA style) is a list of everything you consulted in preparation for writing an assignment, whether or not you referred specifically to it in the assignment. A Bibliography will, therefore, normally contain sources that you have cited in the assignment *and* those you found to be influential but decided not to cite. The Bibliography can give a tutor an overview of which authors have influenced your ideas and arguments, even if you do not specifically refer to them. You would normally only have either a 'References' (Works Cited) *or* 'Bibliography' (Works Consulted) section, unless your tutor has asked you to provide both.

2. Is it worth spending time learning how to use referencing management software?

Chapter 7 looks at this issue in more detail, but on balance the answer is 'yes'. Referencing management software has become very easy to use and there are excellent free or subscription versions you can download for use at home, as well as free versions you can use with the support of your institution. The software offered by your institution is likely to produce referencing lists that conform to the referencing styles required on your course.

Referencing management software will help you to locate sources, and prepare in-text citations and full reference lists in a chosen reference style, all of which will save you time and relieve you of a chore many students find the worst aspect of referencing.

What referencing software cannot do is to help you to understand the how and why of referencing; it cannot help you discriminate between sources and it may produce a reference entry that does not connect exactly to the referencing style required: the accuracy of the formatting details of your reference list may still need to be checked before you submit your assignment.

3. When should I use page numbers in my in-text citations?

Only the MLA style of referencing shows page numbers as an integral part of the citation. With the other referencing systems, the following comments apply.

Single-topic books

Many single-subject books often have a main or dominant message, perspective or argument that forms the essential core or essence of the book. Authors build their arguments around these cores by presenting evidence and examples to back up their perspectives, or by challenging counter-arguments. If you wish to offer evidence in your assignment that summarises these essential core perspectives, then a page number is not necessary. You could, though, include a chapter number if you wanted to isolate a particular feature of the core perspective.

However, if you use and include a quotation from the book you will need to include a page number in the citation, as shown here using the Harvard style:

> Ron Todd of the Transport and General Workers' Union commented, 'we've got three million on the dole and another 23 million scared to death'
>
> (quoted by Bratton, 1992, p.70).

You can also include a page number in the citation, if you are referring to some specific detail that is secondary or incidental to the book's core point or perspective, and that would be hard to find without a page number. This might include, for example:

- statistics
- illustrative examples
- author comments not directly related to the main topic
- definitions.

You would also give a page number if you were using the book as a **secondary source** (see question number 4 in this chapter).

Other books and sources

The same comments for books on a single topic apply for other sources. If the reader will struggle to find precisely what you looked at without the benefit of page numbers in the citation, then include them.

If it is an electronic-online source, your full reference will include the digital object identifier (DOI) or uniform/universal resource locator (URL) to enable the reader to go straight to the text that you looked at, or will include search terms to lead the reader from an opening page to the source. You may need, however, to include in the reference a section or paragraph subheading if the section that encompasses the evidence is a lengthy one.

4. The author of the book I read mentions another author. I want to refer to this other author. How do I reference this?

This is called secondary referencing. Read Chapters 3 and 6 for more information on referencing secondary sources. But, briefly, you need to make clear in the main text of your assignment what you have actually read. For example:

> Illich (1981) has coined the term 'shadow work', meaning the tasks in society that were once the responsibility of extended families and close communities
>
> (in Sherman and Judkins, 1995, p.121).

The citation—(in Sherman and Judkins, 1995, p.121)—makes it clear that this is the source you have looked at. If anyone wanted to track down the Illich book, they can look at the Bibliography in the Sherman and Judkins book and find the full Illich source detail listed there.

With the **MLA style**, you can use the term 'qtd. in' (for 'quoted in'), followed by the author or originator name of the source you looked at, e.g. (qtd. in Raimes 78). But, as with the **Harvard** and **APA** styles, you would reference only the source you looked at in your list of works cited.

However, with numerical styles of referencing, including **MHRA,** the expectation is that you will present full information about both sources, as footnotes and endnotes are useful for containing this additional information. Your footnote should be worded in such a way as to make it clear which text you have read (see the example below). For example, with the British Standard consecutive number referencing style, your footnote on a secondary source, as shown in Chapter 6, could look like this:

Hoggart, R. 'The role of the teacher'. Originally published in J. Rogers (ed.), *Teaching on equal terms*, BBC Publications, 1969, and cited in J. Rogers, *Adults learning.* 3rd edition. Milton Keynes: Open University Press, 1989, p.81.

The last part of the reference implicitly suggests that the Rogers source is the one you read.

The specific advice to students following the **Vancouver** numeric referencing style is also to cite the author whose work you wish to use (even if you have not read it) and to give details of the secondary source in the reference list. For example:

Illich I. Shadow-work. Cape Town: University of Cape Town Press (ZA); 1980. In: Sherman B, Judkins P. Licensed to work. London: Continuum International Publishing Group; 1995.

5. How do I cite and reference books or other sources from an author that has published more than once in the same year?

Within the name–date **Harvard** and **APA** styles (see Chapter 9) you use letters a, b, c and onwards in your citations to differentiate between the different sources. For example:

The term 'communication apprehension' was coined by James McCroskey (1976**a**) and is defined as . . .

Later in the assignment you might want to refer to the same author, writing in a different source published in the same year. For example:

Studies suggest that high CA can impact on a person's behaviour, relationships, the perceptions of others, occupational choice and employment opportunities and education (McCroskey, 1976**b**; McCroskey and Richmond, 1979 . . .

In the References/Bibliography, you would then link the two different sources to the citation (as shown here in the Harvard style):

McCroskey, J.C. 1976**a**. The effects of communication apprehension on nonverbal behavior. *Communication quarterly,* vol. 24, pp.39–44.

McCroskey, J.C. 1976**b**. The problems of communication apprehension in the class-room. *Speech communication journal,* vol. 4, pp.1–12.

Within the author–page **MLA** style, you can either (a) make it clear in your text which book or other source you are referring to, or (b) give a shortened version of the title in a citation. For example:

(a)   McCroskey, in his book 'Problems of Communication Apprehension in the Classroom', argued that . . . (45)
       or
(b)   (McCroskey, Problems 45)

With numerical styles of referencing (see Chapter 10) there is less of a problem.

- With the **consecutive number** referencing styles, you allocate a different number to each source cited, and link these with footnotes or endnotes.
- With the **recurrent number** styles of referencing, you allocate a number to the source in question, repeat this number in the text each time you refer to the source, and link the number with the full reference list at the end of the assignment.

6. How do I cite in my assignment where an author has written different books, but has made similar points in each?

With the name–date **Harvard** and **APA** styles you might on occasion want to refer to two or more books that an author has written in a single citation—as the author may have presented the same argument on more than one occasion. You can cite the author with the earlier works listed first, e.g. (Handy, 1984; 1994; 1997). These are then listed in chronological order in your full list of references.

With the author–page **MLA** style, if the points made by the author are at the core of the book, i.e. a central recurring theme, it might be easier to refer to the author and years in the text. For example:

Handy has argued over nearly 20 years that . . .

You could then list the sources you have in mind, along with the sources you specif-ically cite, in a list at the end labelled 'Works Consulted', which, like 'Bibliography', indicates that the list of sources is not confined to just those specifically cited in the text. If you did need to refer to specific page numbers, these could be linked to a title or shortened version of book titles concerned. For example:

Handy has argued for over nearly 20 years that . . .
                    (see 'Future of Work': 34; 'Empty Raincoat': 45; 'Hungry Spirit': 55).

With the numerical styles of referencing, a specific number can be allocated to each of the sources. Here are some examples.

(a) Consecutive number referencing styles

Handy has argued for over nearly 20 years 13, 14, 15, that . . .

The footnotes would show the respective sources:

Footnotes

13. Handy, C. *The future of work*. Oxford: Blackwell, 1984.

14. ibid. *The empty raincoat: making sense of the future*. London: Hutchinson. 1994.

15. ibid. *The hungry spirit: beyond capitalism; a quest for purpose in the modern world*. London: Hutchinson, 1997.

A list of references or a bibliography, at the end of the assignment, would also list all sources referred to/consulted, including the sources shown in the footnotes.

(b) Recurrent number styles

Handy has argued for over nearly 20 years (1, 2, 3) that . . .

These sources would be shown in your 'References' list at the end of the assignment in numerical order, as follows:

1. Handy, C. *The future of work*. Oxford: Blackwell, 1984.
2. Handy, C. *The empty raincoat: making sense of the future*. London: Hutchinson. 1994.
3. Handy, C. *The hungry spirit: beyond capitalism; a quest for purpose in the modern world*. London: Hutchinson, 1997.

7. Referencing multiple authors: how do I cite and reference works written and edited by more than one author?

This depends on the style of referencing. A distinction also needs to be made about what happens in the in-text citation with the name and date styles, and in the full reference entries for these styles.

Note: The abbreviation 'et al.' is mentioned in this Q&A. It is Latin for 'and others'. As 'al.' is an abbreviation, it has a full stop after it.

(a) APA style

In the APA citations:

- when a work has two authors, both names should be cited each time the source is mentioned in the text.
- when a work has three to five authors, all of them should be cited the first time the source is mentioned; in subsequent citations only the last name of the first (lead) author is mentioned, followed by et al., plus the year of publication, e.g. Saunders et al. (2003)
- if the same source is used again in the same assignment, the year can be omitted in the citation, e.g. Saunders et al.
- if you have two or more different sources, but with the same lead author, cite the last names of as many of the subsequent authors as necessary to distinguish the sources from one another, followed by a comma and et al.
- if a work has six or more authors, you should cite only the last name of the first author followed by et al. and the year.

In the full APA reference:

- the full name information of the first five authors should be given; with six or more authors, start the full reference with the first named author and substitute et al. for the remaining names.

(b) Harvard, British Standard numerical styles and CSE styles

British Standard offers advice on this for the Harvard and both numerical styles, as follows.

In the citation

If a document has one to three authors, their names should be given in the citation. If there are more than three, the name of the first should always be given, but the names of the others may be omitted and replaced by et al. For example: (Burchell et al., 1999). You need to be consistent in which method you adopt and you need to follow your institutional guidelines, as some may vary from this general advice.

In the full reference

When there are four or more authors, the names of all may be given *or* the name of the first author only, followed by et al. (or by writing 'and others'). But, as with citations, you need to be consistent in which method you adopt. Again, you need to follow your institutional guidelines, as some may vary from this.

(c) Chicago referencing style

In the Chicago citation:

- for a source with up to three authors, include all the names in the in-text citation; for a source with four or more authors, use only the first author's name followed by et al.

In the full Chicago reference:

- list all the authors' names—do *not* use et al.
- put the last name first for the first named author only, e.g. Brown, Jim, Mary Clarke, Alice Edwards, Thomas Evans.

(d) IEEE referencing style

The guidelines are to use et al. when three or more names are given in the full reference list.

(e) MHRA referencing style

In the reference list the names of up to three authors should be given in full. For works by four or more authors, the name of only the first should be given, followed by 'and others', *not* et al.

(f) MLA referencing style

In the MLA citation:

- for a work with up to three authors, include all the names in the in-text citation; for a work with four or more authors, give the first author's name followed by et al.

In the full MLA reference:

- give names of the three authors in the order in which they appear on the title page, but put the last name first for the first named author only, e.g. Brown, Jim, Timothy Edwards and Mary Lacy
- when the work has more than three authors, you can use et al. (not italicised) to replace all the author names, except the first.

(g) Vancouver

In the full reference the first six authors are always listed; you can add et al. *after* the sixth author.

8. I read a book in my own (non-English) language. Do I give you an English translation of the title in the full reference?

When the foreign-language source is written in an English alphabet, reference it as it appears on the source; a translation is not necessary. For example:

Webb, P. 1996. *Un Oiseau sur la branche.* Paris: Presses De La Cité.

However, when referencing a source in another alphabet, such as Chinese, you should transliterate the details into the English alphabet and present this in the full reference, as follows.

Original source: 王晓 2013 在为时太晚之前 山西人民出版社

This would be presented in your reference list (Harvard style), as follows:

Wang, X. 2013. *Before it's too late*. Shanxi Peoples' Publishing House.

If the book has been translated from the original language, the name of the translator should be shown. British Standard (1989: 6.2) gives an example of this:

Gorki, Maxim. *Delo Artamonovykh* [The Artamonovs]. Translated from the Russian by Alec Brown. London: Folio Society, 1955.

9. What punctuation and capitalisation style should I use in referencing?

Punctuation

In relation to APA and the British Standard (BS), Harvard and both numerical styles of referencing, the APA and BS recommendations present examples that show sentence stops or commas after each distinct part of the reference. For example:

- **Harvard:** Handy, C. 1994. *The empty raincoat: making sense of the future*. London: Hutchinson.
- **APA:** Handy, C. (1994). *The empty raincoat: Making sense of the future*. London: Hutchinson.

In other referencing styles—for example, Vancouver, OSCOLA and IEEE—punctuation is more sparing; see the examples in Chapter 10 and/or consult your institution's referencing guides to these styles.

Capitalisation

You are likely to find institutional variations, so it is important that you adhere to the referencing style guidelines issued by your college or university. The examples in Chapters 9 and 10 illustrate capitalisation of titles, but here are some summarised guidelines.

- **APA:** Capitalise first word of book and article titles and subtitle, and any proper nouns. The titles of journals are capitalised.
- **British Standard Harvard and numeric styles:** British Standard is not prescriptive on this, but BS examples illustrate full references with the first letter of title in capitals, then lower case, except for proper nouns. The titles of journals are capitalised.
- **Chicago:** Capitalise the first and last letter of the first word, any proper noun, major word, and the first letter of the first word of any subtitle.
- **CSE:** Only the first word of titles is capitalised. The title is not italicised. Journal articles are capitalised, but shown in an abbreviated form.
- **IEEE:** Capitalise the principal words of titles. Articles (a, an, the) and conjunctions (and, but, for, or) should be in lower case.

- **MHRA:** Capitalise the first word, then all principal words, including the first word in a subtitle or after a colon.
- **MLA:** as MHRA.
- **Vancouver:** as CSE.

10. The source has no date. How can I reference this?

Older books may not show a date of publication. In this event, state 'no date' in your citation and in the reference, or use the abbreviation 'n.d.' You may find other sources, e.g. videos, without apparent production dates, so 'no date' or 'n.d.' can be used with other undated sources.

11. Can I use abbreviations in references?

Abbreviations in the text of assignments are not generally encouraged by tutors, except in scientific and technical writing, in tables, graphs and charts, and in relation to the terms 'ibid.', 'op. cit.' and 'loc. cit.', discussed in Chapter 10. However, in footnotes and in lists of references or bibliographies they can be used, although clarity should always take precedence over brevity in references—use a full word if the abbreviation might confuse readers.

British Standard guidelines, the MLA Handbook for Writers of Research Papers (2009) and APA style guide (2009) all give advice on abbreviations commonly found and acceptable within full references. However, Table 12.1 presents a common list of abbreviations found in most styles of referencing; MLA referencing style exceptions are shown.

Table 12.1 Abbreviations found in most styles of referencing

Term	Abbreviation
abbreviated/abbreviation	abbr.
abstract	abs.
adapted	adapt.
bibliography	bibliogr. (MLA: bibliog.)
compact disc read-only	CD-ROM
cassette	cas.
chapter	ch. or chap.
circa	c. or ca.
Department of –	Dept. of –
diagram	diagr.
disk	dk.
edition	edn.
(Revised edition)	Rev. edn.
Second edition etc.	2nd edn.
Editor(s)	ed/s. or Ed/s

Table 12.1 (*continued*)

Term	Abbreviation
figure	fig.
folio	fol.
from	fr.
index	ind.
Number/number	No./no.
no date	n.d.
opus (work)	op.
page	p.
pages	pp.
paragraph	par.
part	pt. or part (in music)
plate (as in photographic) or plural	pl.
record(ed)	rec.
series	ser.
summary	sum.
supplement	suppl. (MLA: supp.)
table	tab.
Technical Report	Tech. Rep.
track	tr.
tome	t.
variant	var.
volume	vol.

12. I have noticed that some writers cite more than one author occasionally in support of a particular argument or point of view. When and why should I do this?

A number of authors can be cited in support of particularly key or important points that you want to make, or to support contentious statements or arguments presented by others. The following example was given earlier, in Chapter 4, to illustrate this:

As the behavioural response of communication apprehension (CA) is to avoid or discourage interaction with others, it is not surprising that CA has been linked to feelings of loneliness, isolation, low self esteem and the inability to discuss personal problems with managers or others (McCroskey, Daly, Richmond and Falcione, 1977; Daly and Stafford, 1984; Richmond, 1984; McCroskey and Richmond, 1987; Scott and Rockwell, 1997).

Multiple sources can add emphasis to a specific point—particularly if it is a central one for your assignment or is the subject of ongoing debate. If you use multiple sources in this way, you can list them chronologically, as shown in the example above, to illustrate the time progression to the idea in question.

But, as stated earlier (also in Chapter 4), you should be careful not to take this practice to ludicrous proportions, and citing five or six authors, or groups of authors, is a suggested maximum for this practice; see also question 13, below, for word count-related reasons that discourage the overuse of multiple citations.

13. Are quotations and all the name–date or page citations in the text counted in the assignment word count?

Normally, yes, although check with your institution on this, as some course leaders may have decided differently. The general view is that, if you include quotations in your assignment you take 'ownership' of them. You have decided to include quotations for emphasis or to make a particular point, so normally you must include them in your word count, unless your tutor indicates otherwise.

In addition, name–date or author–page citations in the text are also usually included in the word count on most courses, so '(Handy, 1994)' would count as two words. However, footnotes, endnotes and the References, Bibliography or Works Cited lists are normally excluded from the word count. (But, again, there can be institutional variations on this point!)

14. How do I cite sources where no author name is shown?

(a) Books

If a book has no author or editor name shown on the title page, you can cite and reference by starting with the title and listing the source alphabetically, but ignore any prefix article words: 'The', 'An', 'A'. However, if the book shows 'Anonymous' or 'Anon' on the title page, against the author, this can be cited and referenced as such, but only in these circumstances.

(b) Magazine/journals/newspapers

If no author's name is shown, British Standard recommends citing and starting the reference within the Harvard and British Standard numerical styles with the 'originator's' name, e.g. the name of the newspaper, magazine or journal. You can omit the word 'The' from the reference, e.g. the *Observer* can be referenced as *Observer*.

With the Chicago, MHRA, MLA and APA styles, cite the title, and start the full References or Bibliography by letter of alphabet of first significant starting word in the title, again ignoring any article word, e.g. 'The', 'An', 'A'.

(c) Internet sources

- Do not put a www address as a citation in the text, unless there is no other way of identifying the originator of the site/source.
- Do not put the name of a search tool or engine, e.g. 'Google'.

If no author's name is shown, look for the name of the organisation that produced the source or, failing that, the name of the host site, e.g. (Business World, 2006) to cite, and this title will connect with your full reference entry.

The **MLA** style, however, is to cite and begin the Works Cited entry with the **title** of the document if the author's name is absent. This could be shortened if it is lengthy.

15. How do I cite sources that are recorded on microfiche/microfilm/microform?

Sources that have been photographed and stored on microfilm are referenced as for the original item, e.g. book, journal, map etc. (see the examples in Chapter 11).

16. I have noticed that both brackets ( ) and square brackets [ ] are sometimes used in full references. Why is this?

The use of square brackets [ ] in a full reference entry is reserved for elements that do not feature in the title of the source but are needed for clarification or identification purposes. So they would be used, for example, to indicate the type of source, e.g. [CD]; [Facebook]; [vinyl record]; [Braille]; [map] or to add an informative dimension to a URL or DOI, e.g. [Available at DOI . . .] or [viewed on . . .].

Round brackets ( ) are normally used in references to add an important clarifying detail to the source. For example, British Standard guide, BS ISO 690:2010, p.11, illustrates how they are used to highlight the location of a town or building where there is more than one with the same name, e.g. Trinity College (Cambridge) and Trinity College (Dublin); or to distinguish source titles from one another, e.g. *Natura* (Amsterdam) and *Natura* (Bucharest); or to identify the status of a person named in the reference, e.g. P. Ellis (ed.).

Although the year a source was published is usually an integral and clearly stated part of it, rather than a clarifying detail, the APA style features full reference entries with the year enclosed in round brackets. For example:

Murray, R. (2005). *Writing for academic journals.* Maidenhead: Open University Press.

And many, if not most, versions of Harvard style, including those presented by referencing management software, copy this APA practice of enclosing the publication year in round brackets in the full reference entry. This is probably because the Harvard and APA styles are very similar—almost identical—in the way many sources are formatted, so that the more advisory British Standard Harvard style version has tended gradually over the years to hybridise with the more prescriptive APA version.

The British Standard guideline version of Harvard shows the year of source publication, in full referencing entries, without brackets, for the reasons stated above; this interpretation has been the benchmark for the Harvard examples in this edition of this book. However, as stated throughout this book, students need to follow their own institutional guidelines on the way Harvard style is presented in their assignments.

17. How do I reference foreign author names?

When alphabetising names for citations and reference lists in languages other than English, you should treat the last name in accordance with the conventions that apply in the country of origin. For instance, when the name of an author consists of several words, the choice of first word to use in the full reference entry is determined, as far as possible, by agreed usage in the country concerned.

In parts of Asia, for example, a father's personal name is commonly combined with the son's name, so that in two-worded names the *second* is the father's personal name and not the family name. You may need, therefore, if you are unfamiliar with these conventions, to seek advice from the librarian at your institution, or the help of a fellow student from the country in question. Fortunately, most journal articles will present a reference for you to copy, and referencing management software should iron out these difficulties for you—another good reason to use it.

However, here are some recommendations for some specific countries or global regions.

European names

- **French:** The 'de' following a first name is not normally used with the last name for referencing purposes. However, there are some exceptions, as follows: when De is normally used or associated with the name, e.g. De Quincy, or when the last name has only one syllable, e.g. de Gaulle, or when the name begins with a vowel, e.g. d'Arcy, or when the prefixes Du and Des are applied.
- **German:** the prefix 'von' is usually not used with the last name in references, unless it has become associated by tradition and convention with a particular person.
- **Italian:** Renaissance or pre-Renaissance names are cited and alphabetised by first name, e.g. Leonardo da Vinci. Post-Renaissance and modern Italian family names are often prefixed with da, de, del, della, di or d', which should be included in the reference, although the alphabetisation should be with the last name, e.g. De Sica, placed in the alphabet under 'S'.
- **Spanish:** last names should be shown in full, e.g. García Márquez; García Lorca. The prefix Del is capitalised and used with the last name for referencing purposes.

Arabic names

The family name is usually preceded by a first or given name. Arabic last (family) names that begin with al- or el- should be alphabetised against the name that follows. For example, al-Hakim would be listed under H. Arabic names that begin with Abu, Abd and Ibn are similar to Scottish names beginning with Mac, so they should be alphabetised accordingly, e.g. Abd would precede Abu.

Asian names

In some countries, e.g. China, Korea and Japan, the family name is followed by a given or personal name. So the male Chinese name Mao Zedong consists of the family name, Mao, and his given or personal name, Zedong. This would be referenced in the Harvard style as Mao, Z.

Some full names often consist of three parts, e.g. Kim Yong-il. In this example, Kim would be treated as the surname, while Yong indicates the generation of the person, and il the personal name (Akhtar, 2007). In a reference entry under the Harvard style this would appear as Kim, Yong-il.

However, some people who live or work frequently outside their home countries adopt a Westernised name by simply reversing the order of their names, and/or by adopting a Westernised personal name, e.g. Deli Yang. You need, therefore, to establish the **family name**, because some referencing styles, e.g. Harvard, require you to use this as the citation in your text and to start the main reference entry with this name.

If an author has adopted a Christian-European name, which they place first in their full name, this should be reversed in the reference, so that, with the example James Kim Jun-Orr, the citation would present the full Korean name, i.e. (Kim Jun-Onn) and the full reference entry would start Kim Jun-Onn, J.

If, however, you are unable to establish the family name/last name, then it is reasonable, and culturally respectful, to give the name in full in the citation, which is repeated in the same order in the full reference.

18. When I am writing an assignment, I sometimes want to respond to a writer's point of view from what I have learned in the past—but I cannot always remember the source of my inspiration. What can I do in this situation?

What is behind a question like this is often a worry or concern about plagiarism. You may be concerned that you will be accused of plagiarism if you advance your own interpretation or response to a topic—and find that someone has published an identical or similar response.

For your peace of mind, it is a good idea to get into the habit of always recording in note or electronic forms the sources of all of your reading for academic purposes (see Chapter 7 on using referencing management software).

However, we are influenced by ideas all the time—this is how we learn—and it can sometimes be difficult, if not impossible, to remember the sources that have influenced us. A student in my 2009 survey made this point well:

> As a mature student, I have been reading around my subject for the past 30 years. I can't always remember where I read a particular fact—just that I 'know' it. How much research do I need to do to find a 'source' for something I've absorbed over the years? (Postgraduate, Italian cinema)

If you find yourself in this situation, you can present a personal interpretation—but *make it clear it is your own view* (see question 19). In an otherwise well-referenced essay, most tutors will appreciate that such an unreferenced statement is a genuine attempt by a student to express his or her own ideas, or to interpret events in their own ways, drawn from their past experiences, and will not accuse them of plagiarism. Most experienced tutors can easily spot plagiarists and plagiarism (see Chapter 5). Now read the next FAQ!

19. How can I present and distinguish my own ideas and opinions in an assignment from those in published sources?

Students often want to include their own view on an assignment topic, but are not sure how to do this, particularly in essays where their tutors have advised them to write in the third person and avoid using the first-person term 'I'. Tutors often have mixed views about students using 'I', and this can depend on the subject, the tutor's own academic background and their views on academic writing. However, if you have been advised to avoid using the term 'I' in assignments, it is important to be aware of conventions in academic writing on how to distinguish the ideas of others from your own. Table 12.2 presents some phrases that could be used to introduce evidence.

Table 12.2 Phrases to introduce evidence

When citing the work of others	When implying the perspective is your own
• It has been argued . . . (state by whom, e.g. Devlin, 2005; and Hague, 2007) • XYZ has argued/asserted/implied • XYZ has suggested/stated/claimed • Recent evidence suggests . . . (state who has suggested it) • It has been shown by (state by whom) that . . . • Strong evidence was found by (state by whom) that . . . • A positive correlation was found by (state by whom) between . . . • The relationship between X and Y has been explored by (state by whom)	• It may be argued that . . . • It can be argued that . . . • Arguably, . . . • The problem with this perspective is, however, that . . . • Another perspective on this topic is that . . . • It may/might/could be that . . . • A question that needs to be asked, is this . . . • However, a contradiction to this argument could/might/may be/is that . . .

The phrases in the right-hand column, if presented unreferenced, would suggest to the tutor that the perspectives presented were your own (albeit based on a wide reading of the topic). These personal comments could also be linked with evidence from sources that connect with, and reinforce, your own perspective.

So you could, for example, start a sentence *with your own view*, and then use supporting evidence to back this up, e.g. 'It can be argued that . . .' and (later) 'The work of Smith (2008) supports this (perception/view/argument) to a large extent, as her work suggests . . .'.

References

Aggarwal, R., I. Bates, J.G. Davies and I. Khan, 2002. 'A study of academic dishonesty among students at two pharmacy schools'. *Pharmaceutical Journal*, 269, 12 October.

Anderson, E. 2014. 'New app means students can create essay footnotes and references in seconds'. *Telegraph*, 2 December 2014.

Angélil-Carter, S. 2000. *Stolen language? Plagiarism in writing*. Harlow: Pearson Education.

APA: American Psychological Association, 2009. *Publication manual of the American Psychological Association*. 6th edn. Washington, DC: American Psychological Association.

Bailey, C. and R. Challen, 2015. 'Student perceptions of the value of Turnitin text-matching software as a learning tool' [post-print] *Practitioner Research in Higher Education*. Available at http://wlv.openrepository.com/wlv/handle/2436/344418 [viewed 13 April 2015].

Bailey, C. and J. Pieterick, 2008. 'Finding a new voice: challenges facing international (and home!) students writing university assignments in the UK'. Conference presentation: *Third annual European first year experience conference*, 7–9 May 2008, Wolverhampton: University of Wolverhampton. Available at http://wlv.openrepository.com/wlv/bitstream/2436/98516/1/cb-jp_final_edit.pdf [viewed 13 April 2015].

Barrett, R. and J. Malcolm, 2006. 'Embedding plagiarism in the assessment process'. *International Journal for Educational Integrity*, **2**(1).

Becker, H.S. 1986. *Writing for social scientists*. Chicago: University of Chicago Press.

Bennett, R. 2005. 'Factors associated with student plagiarism in a post-1992 university'. *Assessment and Evaluation in Higher Education*, **30**(2), pp.137–162.

Biggs, J. and D. Watkins, 1996. The Chinese learner in retrospect. In: D. Watkins and J. Biggs (eds.) *The Chinese learner: cultural, psychological, and contextual influences*. Melbourne: Australian Council for Educational Research.

Bowers, W.J. 1964. *Student dishonesty and its control in a college*. New York: Bureau of Applied Social Research, Columbia University.

British Council, 2015. *IELTS band scores and descriptions*. Available at http://www.ielts.org/institutions/test_format_and_results/ielts_band_scores.aspx [accessed 28 April 2015].

BSI: British Standard Institution, 1983. *Recommendations for citation of unpublished documents*. BS 6371:1983. London: BSI.

BSI: British Standard Institution, 1989. *Recommendation for references to published materials*. BS 1629:1989. London: BSI.

BSI: British Standard Institution, 1990. *Recommendations for citing and referencing published material*. BS 5605:1990. London: BSI.

BSI: British Standard Institution, 1997. *Information and documentation – Bibliographic references. Part 2: Electronic documents or parts thereof*. BS ISO 690-2:1997. London: BSI.

BSI: British Standard Institution, 2000. *Copy preparation and proof correction – part 1: Design and layout of documents*. BS 5261-1:2000. London: BSI.

BSI: British Standard Institution, 2009. *Information and documentation – Guidelines for bibliographic references and citations to information resources*. BS ISO-690-3. London: BSI.

BSI: British Standard Institution, 2010. *Information and documentation – Guidelines for bibliographic references and citations to information resources*. BS ISO 690:2010. London: BSI.

Carroll, J. 2007. *A handbook for deterring plagiarism in higher education*. 2nd edn. Oxford: Oxford Centre for Staff and Learning Development.

Chernin, E. 1988. 'The "Harvard system": a mystery dispelled'. *British Medical Journal*, 297, pp.1062–1063.

Cohen, J. 2007. *Using Turnitin as a formative writing tool*. Report presented at CETL Research Symposium: 'Opening the gateway: Keys to understanding student learning and writing'. Liverpool Hope University, 26 June 2007.

Culwin, F. 2002. *Source code plagiarism in UK HE computing schools: issues, attitudes and tools*. London: South Bank University, SCISM Technical Report 2000–2001.

Dachis, A. 2010. *Plagiarism? And is it always bad?* [blogpost] Available at http://lifehacker.com/5686165/what-is-plagiarism-and-is-it-always-bad [viewed 5 April 2015].

Davis, M. and J. Carroll, 2009. 'Formative feedback within plagiarism education: Is there a role for text-matching software?' *International Journal for Educational Integrity*, **5**(2).

Dennis, L.A. 2005. *Student attitudes to plagiarism and collusion within computer science*. University of Nottingham. Available at http://eprints.nottingham.ac.uk/archive/00000319/ [viewed 15/04/2015].

Dordoy, A. 2002. *Cheating and plagiarism: staff and student perceptions at Northumbria*. Working paper presented at Northumbrian Conference: 'Educating for the future', Newcastle, 22 October 2003.

Eisenstein, E.L. 1983. *The printing revolution in early modern Europe*. New York: Cambridge University Press.

Gibaldi, J. 2003. *The MLA handbook for writers of research papers*. 6th edn. New York: Modern Language Association of America.

gov.uk, 2014. *Government digital inclusion strategy*. London: UK Government Digital Service. Available at https://www.gov.uk/government/publications/government-digital-inclusion-strategy/government-digital-inclusion-strategy [viewed 30 March 2015].

Grafton, A. 1997. *The footnote: a curious history*. London: Faber & Faber.

Hart, M. and T. Friesner, 2004. 'Plagiarism and poor academic practice – a threat to the extension of e-learning in higher education?' Academic Conferences Limited. Available at pubs.mch-net.info/papers/ppap.pdfhttps://www.google.co.uk/?gws_rd=ssl [viewed 13 Mar. 2015].

Hopkins, J.D. 2005. Common knowledge in academic writing. Guidance to students, University of Tampere, FAST Area Studies Program, Department of Translation Studies, Finland. Available at http://www.uta.fi/FAST/PK6/REF/commknow.html [viewed 26 Feb. 2015].

Hounsel, D. 1984. 'Essay writing and the quality of feedback'. In: T.E. Richardson, M.W. Eysenck and D.W. Piper (eds.) *Student learning: research in education and cognitive psychology*, pp.109–119. Milton Keynes: Open University Press.

Howard, R.M. 1995. 'Plagiarisms, authorships, and the academic death penalty'. *College English*, 57, pp.788–806.

Hutchings, C. 2013. 'Referencing and identity, voice and agency: adult learners' transformations within literary practices'. *Higher Education Research & Development*, **33**(2), pp.312–324. Published online 18 Oct. 2013. Available at http://dx.DOI.org/10.1080/07294360.2013.832159.

Introna, L., N. Hayes, L. Blair and E. Wood, 2003. *Cultural attitudes towards plagiarism*. Report. Lancaster: Lancaster University (Dept. of Organisation, Work and Technology).

Jones, K.O., J.M.V. Reid and R. Bartlett, 2005. *Student plagiarism and cheating in an IT age*. [paper] International conference on computer systems and technologies – CompSysTech 2005, 16–17 June 2005.

Learnhigher, 2015. 'Academic writing'. Available at http://www.learnhigher.ac.uk/writing-for-university/academic-writing/ [viewed 15 April 2015].

Lensmire, T.J. and D.E. Beals, 1994. 'Appropriating others' words: traces of literature and peer culture in a third-grader's writing'. *Language in Society*, 23, pp.411–425.

Maxwell, A.J., G. Curtis and L. Vardanega, 2008. 'Plagiarism among local and Asian students in Australia'. *Guidance and Counselling*, **21**, pp.210–215.

McCourt Larres, P. 2012. 'Perceptions of authorial identity in academic writing among undergraduate accounting students: implications for unintentional plagiarism'. *Accounting Education*, **21**(3), pp.1–18.

McKie, A. 2014. 'Experiencing that eureka moment! Using Turnitin as a formative learning tool to enhance students' academic literacies'. [paper] 2014 International Plagiarism Conference, Newcastle. Available at http://plagiarismadvice.org/research-papers/item/experiencing-that-eureka-moment-using-turnitin-as-a-formative-learning-tool-to-enhance-students-academic-literacies [viewed 10 April 2015].

MLA: Modern Language Association of America, 2009. *MLA handbook for writers of research papers*. 7th edn. New York: MLA.

Modern Humanities Research Association, 2013. *MHRA style guide: a handbook for authors, editors and writers of theses*. 3rd edn. Cambridge: MHRA.

Moore, S., C. Neville, M. Murphy and C. Connolly, 2010. *The ultimate study skills handbook*. Maidenhead: Open University Press.

Munger, D. and S. Campbell, 2011. *Researching online*. 5th edn. New York: Pearson Education.

Neville, C. 2007. *The complete guide to referencing and avoiding plagiarism*. Maidenhead: Open University Press.

Neville, C. 2009. 'Student perceptions of referencing'. [paper] Referencing and Writing Symposium, University of Bradford, 8 June 2009. Available at https://brad.academia.edu/ColinNeville.

Neville, C. 2010. 'International students, writing and referencing'. [paper] International Students, Writing and Referencing Symposium, University of Bradford, 9 June 2010. Available at https://brad.academia.edu/ColinNeville.

Neville, C. 2012. 'Referencing: principles, practice and problems'. *RGUHS Journal of Pharmaceutical Sciences*, **2**(2). Available at DOI:10.5530/rjps.2012.2.1.

Norton, L.S. 1990. 'Essay-writing: what really counts?' *Higher Education*, 20, pp.411–442.

Pecorari, D. 2013. *Teaching to avoid plagiarism. How to promote good source use*. Maidenhead: Open University Press/McGraw-Hill.

Pennycook, A. 1996. 'Borrowing others' words: text, ownership, memory and plagiarism'. *TESOL Quarterly*, **30**(2), Summer 1996, pp.210–223.

Potts, M. 2012. 'Who writes your essays?' *Guardian*. Available at http://www.theguardian.com/education/mortarboard/2012/feb/06/essay-writing-for-students [viewed 22 April 2015].

Power, L.G. 2009. 'University students, perception of plagiarism'. *Journal of Higher Education*, **80**(6), pp.643–662.

Pullinger, D. and M. Schneider, 2014. 'Rationalising referencing: changing policy and practice to smooth transition and improve the student experience'. Conference presentation: Librarians' information literacy annual conference 2014, Sheffield Hallam University. Summary available at http://www.slideshare.net/infolit_group/pullinger-34165457. Leeds: University of Leeds (Library).

Rumsey, S. 2008. *How to find information: a guide for researchers*. 2nd edn. Maidenhead: Open University Press.

Sanders, J. 2009. 'Hooray for Harvard? Reverential referencing and the fetish of footnotes'. [paper] Open University 'Making connections: exploring scholarship for the digital age' conference, Milton Keynes, 2–3 June 2009.

Sherman, J. 1992. *ELT Journal*, **46**(2), pp.190–198. Available at DOI:10.1093/elt/46.2.190.

Srivastava, A. 2014. *2 billion smartphone users by 2015: 83% of internet usage from mobiles*. Available at http://dazeinfo.com/2014/01/23/smartphone-users-growth-mobile-Internet-2014-2017/ [viewed 28 February 2015].

Style Manual Committee Council of Science Editors, 2014. *Scientific style and format: the CSE manual for authors, editors, and publishers*. 8th edn. USA: University of Chicago Press.

Taylor, G. 1989. *The student's writing guide for the arts and social sciences*. Cambridge: Cambridge University Press.

Times Higher Education, 2013. 'Working students clock up 20 hours a week.' Available at http://www.timeshighereducation.co.uk/news/working-students-clock-up-20-hours-a-week/148965.article [viewed 11 April 2015].

University of Chicago, 2010. *The Chicago manual of style: the essential guide for writers, editors, and publishers.* 16th edn. USA: University of Chicago Press.

University of Sheffield, 2013. *Plagiarism and collusion.* Department of Physics and Astronomy. Available at https://www.sheffield.ac.uk/physics/teaching/plagiarism-collusion [viewed 7 April 2015].

Write Now, 2007. 'Write Now CETL self evaluation: selected writing mentors feedback'. Available at http://www.writenow.ac.uk/oldsite/cetl_evaluation/4.%20Selected%20Feedback%20from%20Student%20Writing%20Mentors%20at%20London%20Metropolitan%20.pdf [viewed 15 April 2015].

Zeegers, P. and L. Giles, 1996. 'Essay writing in biology: an example of effective student learning?' *Research in Science Education*, **26**(4), pp.437–459.

Index

Doing Your Research Project
A Guide for First-time Researchers
6th Edition

Judith Bell and Stephen Waters

ISBN: 978-0-335-26446-9 (Paperback)
eBook: 978-0-335-26447-6
2014

Step-by-step advice on completing an outstanding research project. This is **the** market-leading book for anyone doing a research project for the first time. Clear, concise and extremely readable, this bestselling resource provides a practical, step-by-step guide from initial concept through to completion of your final written research report.

Key features:

- A brand new chapter describing the benefits of using social media in research
- Tips on using online tools such as Delicious, Mendeley, Dropbox, EndNote and RefWorks
- Guidance on searching efficiently and effectively online

www.openup.co.uk

The Good Research Guide
For Small-Scale Social Research Projects
5th Edition

Martyn Denscombe

ISBN: 978-0-335-26470-4 (Paperback)
eBook: 978-0-335-26471-1
2014

The Good Research Guide by bestselling author Martyn Denscombe has established itself as THE introductory book on the basics of social research. It provides practical and straightforward guidance for those who need to conduct small-scale research projects as part of their undergraduate, postgraduate or professional studies.

Key features include:

- The use of social media in research, including guidelines on the use of social networking sites
- More on internet research and how to run online surveys
- How to conduct systematic literature reviews

www.openup.co.uk

OPEN UNIVERSITY PRESS
McGraw - Hill Education

Studying at a Distance
A guide for students
Fourth Edition

Talbot

ISBN: 9780335262540 (Paperback)
eBook: 9780335262557
2016

This essential guide provides practical help and support for anyone who is embarking on a distance learning course. Ideal for those who have not previously studied at a distance or for students returning to study after a break, it covers fundamental issues such as motivation, goal-setting, time management and coping strategies.

Key features include:

- How to understand the distance learning experience and what your institution expects of its distance learners
- The practicalities of learning at a distance, including how to get support when you need it
- Updated information on the use of new technologies in distance learning, including mobile learning
- Tips and advice on doing a research project at a distance
- Coverage of key study skills including reading and note-making, completing written assignments, developing critical analysis skills and avoiding plagiarism
- Support for international students in understanding how to make the most of studying remotely at a UK Higher Education institution

www.mheducation.co.uk

OPEN UNIVERSITY PRESS
McGraw - Hill Education

Printed in Great Britain
by Amazon